PREVIOUS TITLES BY STEFAN KANFER

The Last Empire
A Summer World
A Journal of the Plague Year
The Eighth Sin
Fear Itself
The International Garage Sale

SERIOUS BUSINESS

The Art and Commerce
of Animation in America
from Betty Boop to Toy Story

STEFAN KANFER

SCRIBNER

SCRIBNER
1230 Avenue of the Americas
New York, NY 10020

Copyright © 1997 by Stefan Kanfer

SCRIBNER and design are trademarks of Simon & Schuster Inc.

DESIGNED BY ERICH HOBBING

Set in Bembo

Manufactured in the United States of America

10 9 8 7 6 5 4 3 2 1

Library of Congress Cataloging-in-Publication Data.
Kanfer, Stefan.
Serious business : the art and commerce of animation in
America from Betty Boop to Toy Story / Stefan Kanfer.
p. cm.
Includes index.
(alk. paper)
1. Animated films—United States. I. Title.
NC1766.U5K36   1997
741.5—dc21   96-37819
                            CIP
ISBN 0-684-80079-9

ILLUSTRATION AND PHOTO CREDITS—Page 5: Courtesy of Chuck Jones: Roadrunner is a registered trademark of Warner Bros., a Time Warner Entertainment Company. AM and © 1996. All rights reserved; 13: Courtesy of John Canemaker; 14: Courtesy of Donald Crafton; 16, 18, 22, 25, 26, 29, 32, and 34: Courtesy of John Canemaker; 39: Courtesy of Donald Crafton; 42–3: Courtesy of Richard Fleischer; 46: Courtesy of Donald Crafton; 51: Courtesy of Richard Fleischer; 62–63: Courtesy of John Canemaker; 66 and 73: Courtesy of Richard Fleischer; 85: Courtesy of the Associated Press; 97: Courtesy of MCA/Universal Walter Lantz; 110: Courtesy of MCA/Universal Walter Lantz; 121: Courtesy of Warner Brothers; 131: Courtesy of Sody Clampett and Warner Brothers; 142: Courtesy of MGM/Turner Entertainment; 145: Courtesy of Richard Fleischer; 154: Courtesy of MGM; 158: Courtesy of Warner Brothers; 160: Courtesy of Warner Brothers; 161: Courtesy of Warner Brothers; 180: Courtesy of Jay Ward; 189: Courtesy of Charles Schulz productions; 198: Courtesy of United Artists; 209: Courtesy of Warner Brothers
COLOR INSERT—1: Courtesy of John Canemaker; 2: Courtesy of John Canemaker; 3: Courtesy of Warner Brothers; 4: Courtesy of Walter Lantz; 5: "Anchors Away" © 1945 Turner Entertainment Co. All Rights Reserved.; 6: Courtesy of Warner Brothers; 7: Courtesy of Turner Entertainment; 8: Courtesy of Faith Hubley and John Canemaker; 9: Courtesy of United Artists; 10: Courtesy of Ralph Bakshi; 11: Courtesy of Charles Schulz; 12: Courtesy of 20th Century Fox

For Alyssa, for the first time,
and for Lea again

CONTENTS

	FOREWORD	11
	PREFACE	15
1.	"IT'S ALL IN DREAMLAND, YOU KNOW"	17
2.	WHAT WE CALL "PERSONALITY"	33
3.	FIGHTING THE MOUSE	55
4.	THE WILDER SHORES OF COMEDY	77
5.	MORE HELLS THAN SWEDENBORG	101
6.	LAUGHING AT THE ENEMY	125
7.	WHO'S DIRECTING THIS PICTURE?	149
8.	WE COULD GET AWAY WITH LESS	173
9.	AKIN TO STATUTORY RAPE	193
10.	THE ANIMATED MIRROR	213
	NOTES	237
	ACKNOWLEDGMENTS	243
	INDEX	245

Among animals, *one* has a sense of humor.
Humor saves a few steps, it saves years.

MARIANNE MOORE,
The Pangolin

FOREWORD

In *Serious Business* Stefan Kanfer again clearly establishes the obscure and often neglected truth that no facet of human failure or human accomplishment can exist in a vacuum. Whether writing of diamond merchants (*The Last Empire*), merchants of marriage (*A Summer World*), or the merchants of death (*The International Garage Sale*), he clearly defines the time and circumstances attendant to the birth, life, and decline or triumph of his subject. He does not fail us in this new volume concerning the life, neglect, and current rebirth of the animated cartoon and its merchants of laughter.

One of my earliest encounters with Stefan Kanfer was high in the imposing offices of the Time/Life Building in Manhattan, where the senior book editor was to be found playing on a saw. Not playing *with* a saw, a natural enough pastime for the inquisitive mind, but *on* the saw, in the following manner: The handle was gripped firmly between the knees, the blade curled dramatically, roughly north by northwest/half west, the tip was held gracefully in the off hand adjusting the curve of the blade to the needs of the music. The right, or bow, hand holds the bow and draws the taut hair of a failed Secretariat across the obscure or unnotched side of the blade. The ensuing melody of that bygone day, if melody memory serves, was either "Throw Him Down McClosky," a ditty made famous in the twentieth century by Michigan J. Frog, or "Return My Love," music by Richard Wagner, lyrics by Mike Maltese. Kanfer was accompanied by several members of Time/Life cultural venue—on the block flute, the kazoo, the tin flute, crooningly assisted by a vocal chorus.

As I do on every occasion in a long and surprising series of encounters with this accomplished musician, I thanked the assembled company and suggested a footnote to the program notes: "Wagner's music is better than it sounds"—Mark Twain.

Yes *that* Mark Twain, who long ago founded my personal scout troop: a highly select group of trustworthy companions including Stefan Kanfer, Herb Block, my good dog Teddy, my good wife Marian, my good daughter Linda, and a few others.

Gustav Flaubert earned his merit badge by writing, "Human speech is like a cracked kettle upon which we beat tunes for bears to dance to, when all the while we wish to stir the stars to pity." What then, of *Serious Business,* which stirs us to pity with tunes for pigs to dance to? In the same sense that the song "Brother Can You Spare a Dime?" demonstrated a reluctant awareness by motion picture studios that there was indeed a great economic depression in the world circa 1929–1939 (although not in the motion picture business itself, which flourished in the self-same circa), Kanfer shows that "Who's Afraid of the Big Bad Wolf," the theme to Disney's *The Three Little Pigs,* reached the top of the charts when people were indeed afraid of that self-same wolf, lurking uncomfortably at the door. Later, we find that foolish bravado, in animation or any place else, can only exist in wartime. A song such as "You're a Sap, Mr. Jap" (1944) becomes an embarrassment in 1964 or 1994, and among those embarrassed—by producing animated cartoons such as *Tokio Jokio or Bugs Bunny Nips the Nips*—were animators. Kanfer defines with sad yet incisive logic that animators behaved very much like human beings under the pressure of the social doings around them. These two broad strokes merely hint at the skill of Kanfer's creative research in *Serious Business.*

All artistry, all drama, and of course, all comedy is serious indeed and, we find, controlled by two prime factors: the love you have for what you hope to accomplish and your willingness to invest the maximum effort to achieve that purpose—and in the end, only the love should show. To further compound the matter, Jackie Gleason insists that comedy is the most demanding of all drama because there is an immediate critic: laughter. It seems to me that Stefan Kanfer, through his love of animation and animators, is, as they say, eminently qualified to write seriously, without sacrificing laughter, the true biography of animation as a craft and about the craftsmen who fashioned it into an art form.

I give you, then, Stefan Kanfer, a happy cross between Thomas

Babington Macaulay (*History of England*) and Terrence Hanbury White (*The Sword in the Stone*), a whimsical historian if I've ever met one. I urge you to read this very *Serious Business* and never trust an author who cannot play a saw.

CHUCK JONES

PREFACE

Animators have always been fond of quoting the dictionary definition of their art. Actually, as far as cartoons are concerned, Webster's may be spiritually correct but it is technically wrong. Animation, it says, means "to give life, to bring to life." In fact, film—all film—is an illusion in which life lies behind the screen, not on it. Slowed down, animated movies can be seen as a series of static drawings: In the felicitous phrase of theater historian Harold Clurman, they are "lies like truth." But those little deceptions—twenty-four of them per second sliding past the projector gate—have created their own world, a place where natural law has no authority, where ducks may have tantrums and rabbits may be witty, where a cat can break into a hundred little cats and merge into one again, where mice and men fly without wings and dogs explode and birds run faster than jets. It is no wonder that Americans took them to heart from the beginning.

Amusement is the first thing that comes to mind when we think of cartoons made in the United States. They seem to be bright, brittle entertainments without much substance or importance. It is the purpose of this book to show that the assumption is very often wrong. To be sure, a lot of animated films are no more than a series of chases, outrageous puns, and spectacular pratfalls. Yet many more defy the studio labels of Silly Symphonies and Looney Tunes. In their own eccentric way, they provide an extraordinary reflection of the society and politics of their time. They also reveal a great deal about the psychology of the people who made them.

It is a commonplace that many a truth is told in jest. In classic plays, the jesters' perceptions are no accident; despite their extravagant costumes, the fools are deliberately set up to be the wisest of personae. In cartoons, particularly those made before this self-conscious era, no such attempt was made to give the creatures "importance." They were simply produced to beguile the moments between full-length features. Nevertheless, the animated clowns blithely transmitted information about the people who made the shorts and the society that watched them. They do so today. It is the aim of *Serious Business* to decipher that encoded information without any agenda except the truth. En route, we will see the development of an art and a science unlike any other. Some splendid books have traced this arc, most notably Leonard Maltin's *Of Mice and Magic,* Giannalberto Bendazzi's *Cartoons,* and Charles Solomon's delightful coffee table volume *Enchanted Drawings,* now, happily, back in print. Many biographies, histories, and magazines have been dedicated to animators, to animation studios, and even to animated characters. And recently, a great deal of research has been devoted to the Jurassic era of animation, led by Donald Crafton's *Before Mickey.* Of course, of the making of books about Walt Disney there is no end. They are all accounted for in the following pages. *Serious Business* is not an attempt to replace the work that has gone before but an attempt to augment it.

CHAPTER ONE

"IT'S ALL IN DREAMLAND, YOU KNOW"

The attempt to make drawings appear to move is almost as old as language. The drawings on ancient Roman vase portray an acrobat in various postures. If photographed in succession, they would show the man performing a somersault. Artisans of the ancient world, the medieval era, and the quattrocento portrayed motion with a series of progressive drawings. But it was not until the invention of the Zoetrope ("life-wheel") that pictures became active. The device, invented in 1834 by the Englishman W. G. Horner, used a drum-shaped object with slits in its side. A strip of sketches, usually of a clown capering or an animal running, was placed inside the cylinder. When viewers spun the Zoetrope on its spindle and peered through the slits, they saw a figure appear to move in repeated cycles. Another contraption, the Praxinoscope ("action-look"), was invented later in the century by a Belgian professor, Emile Reynaud. This one used much the same principle—the retina retains the image of something it has seen a split second before—but its subject matter was quite different. Viewers were to see much of this kind of humor in the coming decades: It showed a black boy juggling with his own head.

Reynaud might have seemed ahead of his time, but actually he was behind it. As he worked with his crude renderings, the Lumière brothers, Louis and Auguste, busied themselves with something called cinema, and Thomas Edison improved his newfangled motion picture projector. From here on, animation would involve photography, and the Belgian knew it. In 1910, he threw his apparatus into the Seine. The inventor died in a sanatorium eight years later, in poverty and obscurity. By that time,

James Stuart Blackton, a vaude-ville chalk-talk artist who billed himself as The Komikal Kartoon-ist, had produced America's first truly animated motion picture. Today, *Humorous Phases of a Funny Face* seems as elemental as a child's scrawl. Blackton's hand outlines a face on a blackboard; his hand withdraws and the face changes expression; a couple flirt with each other, then vanish, line by line. The art of filmmaking was as prim-itive as its subject matter. The movie camera shot a still picture, Blackton erased part of his artwork, then redrew the face in a slightly different pose. The process was repeated hundreds of times until the artist grew weary and called a halt. For all its crudity, however, *Phases* was a breakthrough piece, and a revealing view of popular culture. The short film concludes with a visual trick: The words *Coon* and *Cohen* become caricatures of an African American and a Jew.

Over the next few years, a number of filmmakers experimented with animation. The second best, a Frenchman named Emile Cohl, mixed live action and cartoons to create a series of piquant comedies. But those that survive display more in the way of gimmickry than ingenuity. Winsor McCay needed no such contrivances. In a business where "genius" is applied to anyone whose picture is nominated for a Golden Globe Award, he is the exception: There has never been a filmmaker more deserving of the title.

McCay was born in Michigan shortly after the Civil War. As soon as he could hold a pencil, the boy began drawing what he saw. Winsor's father remembered that the child "used to get whipped in school for drawing sketches on the leaves of his books until I told the teachers it was of no use; nothing could stop him." With minimal instruction, Winsor became a master of perspective and detail. At nineteen, he was hired to render the scenes of crimes, trials, and social events for the *Cincinnati Commercial Tribune*. By the age of twenty-six, in 1903, he was on the staff of two New York newspapers—the *Herald* and the *Telegram*—and a regular contributor to a humor magazine called *Life*. Three years later, he began to experiment with one of journalism's most glamorous features: the comic strip. Humorous drawings and caricatures had long been a staple of American journalism; back in the mid-century, Boss Tweed had railed against cartoonist Thomas Nast for his lampoons of Tammany Hall. "Stop them damn pictures," the Boss demanded. "I don't care so much what the papers write about me. My constituents can't read. But damn it, they can see pictures!" Still, comic art never achieved widespread popularity until the four-color press was invented in the mid-nineties. Then newspaper comics abruptly changed from gargoyles to ornaments, and publishers boomed the Sunday Funnies. William Randolph Hearst topped them all; he advertised the comics in his *American* as "eight pages of iridescent polychromous effulgence that makes the rainbow look like a piece of lead pipe." He treated his artists accordingly, and there would come a time when McCay could no longer resist the temptation of Hearst's larger paycheck and promises of better conditions.

Meanwhile, he stayed at the *Herald,* working on "Little Sammy Sneeze." The strip recorded the misadventures of a boy whose explosive sneezes could bring down buildings and destroy circuses. It was a one-joke affair, and not a very good joke. But it paraphrased one of the most celebrated sneezes of the period: Thomas Edison's historic film of an assistant, Thomas Ott, his face hilariously writhing and grimacing before the sudden unheard "kerchoo." Little Sammy served to introduce the artist's uniquely decorative and energetic line to a wider public. Then, in 1904, he stumbled on a new and strangely profound theme. On the surface, "Dreams of the Rarebit Fiend" was as simple as Sammy. An individual finds himself in bizarre situations: a dentist climbs inside a patient's mouth to repair a tooth; a baby's toy blocks fall down and ultimately topple a city; a man out for a stroll encounters fourteen multiple images of himself, all of them distortions, like the figures in a funhouse mirror. In the last panel, the victim in these varied episodes wakes up and comments on the vivid dream he has just experienced.

Ostensibly, McCay was presenting a situation farce with all the customary objects of derision: mothers-in-law, overweight businessmen, pompous doctors, meek clergymen. Actually, he was using the strip as a kind of exorcism. Winsor's younger brother Arthur had been insane since adolescence and was permanently institutionalized in 1898. McCay's discerning biographer, John Canemaker, notes that Winsor never mentioned his brother in public. "But in his art he remembered

Arthur and the terrible thing that had happened to him. 'The Dream of the Rarebit Fiend' comic strip often dealt with paranoid behavior, delusions of persecution, hallucinations, irrationality, and insanity." The artist, he concludes, "feared and hated the horrible possibility that he would suffer Arthur's unfortunate fate. His drawing ability saved him from that, and so he kept on drawing for escape, for survival, and for salvation."

McCay grew restive when intellectuals approached. He thought of himself as a practical newspaperman concerned with deadlines and expenses; analyses of his work made him uncomfortable. But there was no getting away from them. To speak of a Winsor McCay strip is to join the ancient, unending discussion about the relation of fantasy and reality. In ancient China, Chuang-tzu put it succinctly: "I do not know whether I was then a man dreaming I was a butterfly, or whether I am now a butterfly dreaming I am a man." For thousands of years, artists had used their nightly fantasies as inspiration, but the references were usually muted and oblique. They erupted on the canvases of Hieronymus Bosch and Peter Breughel, then lay quiescent until the nineteenth century, when painters began to meet their dreams head-on. William Blake maintained that he had been given art lessons by a person he met in a dream. Blake's friend Henry Fuseli offered canvases of disturbing nightmare visions that refused to disperse in daylight. Odilon Redon and Gustave Moreau experimented with fabulous images breaking through the skin of everyday experience. What was the meaning of these strange visions, their patrons inquired. The artists could only reply that it was a mystery and go on with their canvases. Sigmund Freud would not settle for evasions: mysteries were there to be cracked. He announced the solution: "[T]he dream is a compromise between and the defense against the unconscious emotions; in it the unconscious wish is represented as being fulfilled."

Freud's findings were very much in the air by 1905, and discussed and illustrated in literary salons, galleries, professional journals, and, ultimately, in magazines and newspapers. It would only be a question of time before the topic seeped into the images of popular art. Consciously or unconsciously, McCay began his most Freudian strip, "Little Nemo in Slumberland," in October of that year. Unlike "Dreams of a Rarebit Fiend," this was a richly layered and continuous narrative. The fresh-faced Nemo, modeled after McCay's seven-year-old son

Robert, strode, rode, or flew through the illogical world of Slumberland, flanked by two companions. According to one of McCay's friends, Flip the clown was based on "a rotund black man with a greenish cast to his face." The artist had seen him smoking a cigar on a Brooklyn street. Flip was trailed by Impie, a grass-skirted black child of nature from the exotic Candy Islands. Slumberland had strong links to Oz and Alice's Wonderland. Nothing in Nemo's dream universe was stable. Time and mass became meaningless. Familiar objects could be

cooperative or treasonous. Animals that never walked upon the earth—a blue camel, a green dragon, a hundred-foot-high turkey—went galumphing over the ground or hurtling through a celestial backdrop. The ground could open up and swallow the walker, and free fall, one of humanity's elemental terrors, was a constant occurrence. McCay insisted that he was only creating "clean humor" well drawn. But something must have occurred to him, at least occasionally, as it did to his more acute readers. Nemo had tapped into his creator's unconscious, disguising its desires and terrors with sumptuous visual comedy. The episode of Queen Crystalette is typical. Nemo rises from his bed to get a glass of water and finds himself in a world peopled by men and women made entirely of glass. The little boy is taken before the Queen, a woman so finely made that she can barely return his bow. "Blind and deaf with infatuation," Nemo embraces the royal figure and bends her backward in a kiss far too passionate for his years. The Queen shatters like a tumbler dropped on stone; so does her retinue. Nemo, "heartsick and frightened," awakens with "the groans of the dying guardsmen still ringing in his cars."

Slumberland flourished in the golden era of Sunday supplements, when strips attained their greatest authority. H. L. Mencken, always quick to note changes in the way his contemporaries thought and felt, observed that the comics' "influence upon the general American vocabulary must be very potent and no doubt they also have some influence upon American ways of thinking." Many strips entered the folklore of the nation. Among them were the "Katzenjammer Kids" and "Mutt and Jeff," which were to enjoy sixty-year runs; "Krazy Kat"; the bizarre, complicated Rube Goldberg inventions; "Bringing Up Father"; the "Yellow Kid," for whom Yellow Journalism was named; "Buster Brown"; and "Alfonse and Gaston." But McCay's work was in another category entirely. It belonged less to the annals of newspaper art than to the aesthetic current leading from Breughel and Bosch to the Surrealists. Even in that day of cutthroat Hearst versus Pulitzer competition, McCay turned his rivals into admirers. Indeed, they were the first to recognize Nemo as the most brilliantly designed strip of their time. The publishers and the public were not far behind, and after them came the moral authorities.

At a 1909 dinner of the Associated Press and the American Newspaper publishers, the Reverend R. J. Burdette, who had no use for

Freud, thundered against the Sunday Funnies. "The morality of the comic supplement," he stated, "is damnable when it is not puerile, and out of all those I have seen I can find only one that pleases me as being sweet, and clean and beautiful and that is Little Nemo." Victor Herbert was even more enthusiastic. He decided to base his next Broadway operetta on the strip. "The idea appeals to me tremendously," he told a reporter. "It gives opportunities for fanciful incidents and for 'color.' It's all in Dreamland, you know, and that gives great scope for effects." Carefully scrubbed of any sexual content, Little Nemo opened at the Victoria Theater on October 20, 1908, played for fifteen weeks and went on tour for two years. By then, McCay had become something of a theatrical attraction himself, touring the vaudeville circuit as a chalk-talker, entertaining audiences with anecdotes and quick sketches. As the highlight of his act, the artist presented "The Seven Ages of Man." He began by drawing a pair of babies. For the next twenty minutes—a new and intricate picture every thirty seconds—he moved them in stages from infancy through adolescence and childhood to maturity and old age. As remarkable as this act was, it proved to be a mere prelude to the most important part of McCay's creative life. The maker of rarebit fantasies and Slumberland was about to show the world the most enduring and provocative dream of all.

Until the cannons went off in 1914, most Americans suffered from a common delusion: Technology was about to turn the earth into Eden. Who could blame them? All the ancient fantasies were coming true. The railroad and the automobile had changed the traditional meaning of distance. Voices and music were carried invisibly over the ether; spirits could do no more. The concept of human flight, a yearning as old as the race itself, was now within reach—indeed, Little Nemo would spend many happy weeks touring Slumberland in a magical airship like the ones being used by grown-up pilots. Pictures no longer had to stay frozen in time; D. W. Griffith's epics were magically unreeling at nickelodeons. In this age of miracles, why shouldn't drawings move as well as photographs? The thought had occurred to McCay innumerable times; his strips were so full of motion that characters would frequently burst through the margin to enter the next panel. In 1909, he decided to animate his work. His son had brought home several "flip books"—collections of consecutive photographs that the reader riffles through to produce the sense of motion pictures. "From this germ," McCay later wrote, "I evolved the modern cartoon movies."

The genesis was somewhat more complicated. A colleague remembered that a group of cartoonists "kidded McCay because he was such a rapid worker. . . . Jokingly, they suggested that [Winsor] make several thousand drawings, and photograph the result in theaters. . . . On a dare from his friends McCay claimed he would produce enough line drawings to sustain a four- or five-minute animated cartoon showing his Little Nemo characters and would use the film as a special feature of his already popular vaudeville act." McCay wanted to achieve on film what he had done for the mind's eye: to make his characters go from place to place with articulated motion, to make them truly leap and run and laugh and grieve as they only *appeared* to do in newspapers. This would require an entirely new kind of cartoon, far different from anything by Blackton or Cohl. To accomplish this, he would have to reinvent animation. At the time, silent movies flashed sixteen frames per second onto the screen. McCay, said his assistant John Fitzsimmons, "timed everything with split-second watches. That's how he got nice smooth action. For every second that was on the screen, McCay would draw 16 pictures. . . . He had nothing to follow, he had to work everything out himself." Some four thousand separate pen-and-ink drawings went into the film, each rendered by the artist himself. Integrity of movement and fluency of action was vital, so "after each drawing was completed, and a serial number assigned to it, marks for keeping it in register with the other drawings were placed on the upper right and left corners. . . . [T]he purpose of being so critical regarding this phase of the operation was the urgency of eliminating all unnecessary vibration in the picture on the screen. If this explanation on the first part of the operation sounds technical, that's because it was, and handling each unit of the entire process many times was a long, tedious piece of work for McCay."

Vitagraph, Blackton's old studio, had the inside track on animation, and became McCay's distributor. On April 8, 1911, the film was released to motion picture theaters. Three days later, McCay used it as the lodestar of his vaudeville act at the Colonial Theater in Manhattan. The footage is preserved, and holds up remarkably well after the passage of almost nine decades. We see exactly what audiences viewed that

spring: The movie begins with a live-action sequence. In a restaging of the actual event, McCay accepts the bet from his fellow cartoonists and gets to work. Amid the bustle and confusion of the one-man operation there are glimpses of the "checking machine" and close-ups of some rice paper sketches. The rest of the process is undisclosed. One month later, according to a title card, the bettors gather around a projector and the cartoon starts.

Flip makes the first appearance, smoking a cigar and waving the smoke away. Impie comes onscreen in sections and gathers himself together. The two figures bounce and tumble like circus performers, moving toward and away from the viewer, swelling and shrinking to indicate perspective. Little Nemo makes his entrance as a series of fine lines. They cohere into the boy dreamer, caparisoned Lord Fauntleroy style in tights, cape, and plumed hat. He stands between Flip and Impie, raising and lowering his arms. With each gesture, the clowns elongate or diminish, an encore of the funhouse mirror images in Rarebit Fiend. Without warning, Nemo becomes an artist—in effect, McCay himself—outlining a beautiful, fully animated Princess. A rose springs up and blooms. He gives her the blossom. Incongruously, the dragon from the comic strip enters the frame and opens its maw. In it are two thrones. The boy and his lady climb into the creature's mouth, seat themselves, and wave to the audience. The dragon backs away and slithers into the distance. Flip and Impie try to make their own exit in a broken-down jalopy. But before it can pick up speed the machine explodes and they fall down slowly, settling on yet another person from Slumberland, a Dr. Pill. Live footage follows the cartoon, showing McCay collecting his bet.

Nemo puzzled as much as it dazzled. Ticket holders were not sure whether the film was a trick or an accomplishment. "Little Nemo was pronounced very lifelike," McCay remembered, "but my audiences declared that it was not a drawing but that the pictures were photographs of real children." Cartoonists were not so skeptical; they knew they were witnessing a historical event. One cartoonist, Claud Brandon, particularly cherished the moment with the rose, when "a young man turns and plucks it and hands it to the girl beside him. That's all there was to it, but it excited me greatly, and no wonder! I had witnessed the birth of a new art." Altogether, McCay made ten animated films, ranging from "Bug Vaudeville," featuring a butterfly corps de ballet; "Flip's Circus," a centaurs' pastorale; and the highly symbolic "Story of a Mosquito," in which an immense, formally dressed insect named Steve settles down on a drunk and drills him with his long proboscis, swelling with each new penetration. In a few moments, the mosquito is too wobbly to fly straight, and too gluttonous to survive. He explodes in a wash of blood.

"Mosquito" increased McCay's reputation as an enchanter. "Mankind's greatest disease is laziness," he told his colleagues, and if that was true, the artist deserved to be called the healthiest man in New York. In addition to drawing comic strips and editorial cartoons and touring the vaudeville circuit, he announced plans for a new animated movie based on "the great monsters that used to inhabit the earth." "There are skeletons on exhibition," he told a reporter for *Motograph,* a trade weekly, "and I expect to draw pictures of these animals as they appeared in real life thousands of years ago." It took two years to bring "Gertie the Dinosaur" to fruition, and what McCay produced was more cartoon than re-creation of the Jurassic era. Even so, it offered the first instance of personality animation. His Gertie could demonstrate petulance and docility, and she could interact with another performer—in this case McCay himself, who showed the film in his new vaudeville act. As he stood to the right of a screen, the head and long neck of a diplodocus shyly slithered into view. Cracking his whip in the manner of a ringmaster, McCay coaxed the dinosaur to come all the way in. Gertie moved with the regular steps of a large reptile, her legs fully articulated, her body suggesting bulk and authority. The artist then put her through her paces, occasionally irritating her so severely that she nipped at him. He ducked out of the way and admonished her, and tears formed in her eyes and brimmed over. He offered her a real apple and palmed it, just as a cartoon apple popped onscreen. Gertie struck funny poses, threw a rock at a mastodon, drank from a lake, and even executed a few dance steps. As the pièce de résistance, McCay walked offstage—and appeared a second later on the screen as a cartoon version of himself. Stepping into her mouth, he allowed himself to be borne away, bowing.

"Gertie" was another box-office success. This time, however, the popularity came at a price. McCay had signed on with Hearst and set up shop at the *American.* At first, things went well, then Hearst, absolute ruler of his domain, set down the law. McCay was to cease

such trivial entertainments as comic strips and vaudeville. There would be no loss of income, the boss would compensate his employee for moneys lost. But Little Nemo would no longer dream, and there would be no more chalk talks. Deprived of these creative outlets, McCay determined to make the kind of animated film that would stand on its own, without the need of an interlocutor. There would be no tricks, no stagy asides, just animated drawings in their purest form. It was to be called "The Sinking of the *Lusitania,*" and it would depict the 1915 disaster no newsreel had recorded—the torpedoing of the British luxury liner off the coast of Ireland by a German U-boat. Hearst, then in his most Anglophobic phase, ordered his papers to blame the victim. "Whether the *Lusitania* was armed or not," said an editorial in the *American,* "it was properly a spoil of war, subject to attack and destruction under the accepted rules of war." McCay was of the opposite opinion. To him, King George V's Britain was the victim and Kaiser Wilhelm's Germany the aggressor. Whether the *Lusitania* had been outfitted for eventual military service, whether the British Admiralty had failed to give her proper protection, whether she was secretly carrying arms and explosives was quite beside the point. Some 1,200 innocent civilians had been killed, among them 128 U.S. citizens. The Boss must be defied; attention must he paid.

McCay and two assistants began preliminary work on his most ambitious film in 1916, using "cels" for the first time. These celluloid sheets carried the action drawings; a stationary horizon showed through. McCay devised a cycle of waves, sixteen drawings for every second the ship was shown. Altogether, 25,000 separate cels went into the final film; it took twenty-two months to complete the picture, widely advertised as "The Only Record of the Crime That Shocked Humanity!" Released on July 20, 1918, "The Sinking of the *Lusitania*" met with virtually unanimous approval in the United States. By then, the original Little Nemo had become Sergeant Robert McCay of the 27th Army Division, and the animator's political opinions had been ratified by the public at large. It was Hearst who was out of step, denounced for his isolationism. Sauerkraut had become Liberty Cab-

bage, and baseball players with German surnames were given the sobriquet of "Dutch." The Boss went on the defense, printing little American flags on the front page, acknowledging "popular sentiment in these troublous times." His employee needed no such tactics. The animation was eloquent enough.

From the opening shot, McCay exerted his mastery of unexpected angles and uncanny timing. His overview is omniscient, wordless, cold. As the *Lusitania* floats serenely on, the animation shows an underwater view. Two fish flutter out of the way as the German weapon hurtles toward its destination. In a long shot, the torpedo hits and the explosion ignites a phosphorescent sky. Smoke trails and billows, covering the screen. The tragedy plays itself out as lifeboats descend on spidery ropes. Every porthole and pennant is meticulously rendered as the ship capsizes. The *Lusitania* carried several well-known figures, and their faces pass in review: "millionaire sportsman" Alfred Vanderbilt, theatrical producer Charles Frohman, whose last words are clearly lettered: "Death is but a beautiful adventure of life." As the *Lusitania* shudders, a young mother raises her baby above the waves, hoping to save it as she goes down. The two of them sink as a trail of bubbles pass them on the way to the ocean's surface. In the final title card, McCay submits his own editorial: "The man who fired the shots was decorated by the Kaiser. And they tell us not to hate the Hun."

With "The Sinking of the *Lusitania*," McCay's film career reached its apogee. He experimented with a few short cartoons, then vanished into newspaper work for the rest of his career. His animations fell into obscurity as other more facile artists used mass-production techniques and less challenging subjects. But whether they acknowledged it or not, they would follow in his slipstream. He had proved to the world that animation could express everything, consciously or unwittingly, from understated eroticism to outright political propaganda. From here on, its limitations would be the limitations of the artist, not the medium. During his brief film career, McCay peered into the future and delighted in the view. "There will be a time," he burbled, "when people will gaze at pictures in a museum, and ask why the objects remain rigid and stiff. They will demand action. And to meet this demand the artists of that time will look to the motion picture for help and the artist, working hand in hand with science, will evolve a new school of art that will revolutionize the entire field. It was too bad that

Michael J. Angelo didn't draw for the movies. . . . The coming artist will make his reputation, not by pictures in still life, but by drawings that are animated."

About fifteen years later, McCay had reason to make a less euphoric assessment. One of Hearst's old hands, an artist who signed his work I. Klein, attended a dinner at a Manhattan restaurant in honor of the great pioneer. Many quarts of bootleg liquor had been downed before McCay took the floor. He rambled on about his methods and procedures, and the crowd grew restive. Klein recalled that the speaker rather abruptly "wound up with a statement which has remained in my mind: 'Animation should be an art. That is how I conceived it. But as I see what you fellows have done with it, making it into a trade . . . not an art, but a trade, bad luck!' He sat down. There was some scattered applause." Another veteran sadly recollected that McCay "had three strikes against him. He was a master with lofty ideals only he could reach. He had been out of the business too long. And, sad to say, he was preaching to the unconverted. An art doesn't become a trade by accident. It was a long, bitter story, and Winsor McCay didn't know the half of it."

CHAPTER TWO

WHAT WE CALL "PERSONALITY"

After watching Winsor McCay interact with Gertie, the *Chicago Examiner*'s vaudeville critic could scarcely sit still at his typewriter. "Thus the camera, that George Washington of mechanisms, at last is proved a liar," he rhapsodized. "You are flabbergasted to see the way the reel minds its master." This extravagant rhetoric was part of the time. Everything moved con brio as the twentieth century defined itself. A premium was placed on speed and overstatement. Ragtime set the foot beating to an unaccustomed pace. Inventions like the electric self-starter for automobiles were called time-savers, the rescued minutes, it was understood, to be used for gain or amusement. "Time goes, you say? Ah, no! / Alas, Time stays, *we* go," warned the widely quoted couplet. The fanciful scenarists of technology, Jules Verne and H. G. Wells, seemed to be documentarians now. The Futurist manifesto came alive: "Sabotage the adjective. Leave nothing but the verb." Daring young women considered it a compliment when their crowd referred to them as "fast"; velocity became the operative word in art, machines, conversation, classical music, show business—especially the shows at the nickelodeons, where the eye was being deceived with a rush of still pictures.

Ambitious, hurried men noticed something about those pictures. Whatever was in the newspapers could currently be found in the movies: photography, features, human interest stories, jokes—everything, it seemed, except the Sunday Funnies. McCay's experiments showed that a vast potential market sat in the movie houses, eager to see comics on the screen. To that end, a group of small studios sprung up; even Hearst made a brief, abortive attempt to produce animated shorts. One company persuaded Bud Fisher to let his white-gloved comedians, Mutt and Jeff, star in cartoons. George McManus, one of the bettors who had egged McCay on in "Little Nemo," allowed the characters in his own strip, "The Newlyweds," to caper in a series produced by Emile Cohl. Otto Messmer saw them, no doubt attracted by the advertising copy ("The Newlyweds are not real people, dressed up to imitate the famous McManus cartoons, but are *drawings that move*"). These films, and the example of McCay, whose interactions with Gertie he had seen at the Colonial Theater in Manhattan, convinced the young man he had a future in movies.

From his parents' house in Union City, New Jersey, Messmer had been sending in humorous drawings to the *New York World*. Armed with these published works, he applied for a job at almost every movie studio in New York and New Jersey—twenty in all. He had hoped to start as a set painter and climb from there. Jack Cohn, an executive at Universal, offered a shortcut. Young Otto had a nice way with pen and ink; why didn't he draw a few thousand more and make a short film? Universal would underwrite the project. Messmer might have stepped into a rarebit dream. He made the return trip by streetcar, but he could just as well have floated home. With only a rudimentary understanding of animation technique, the novice turned out a short entitled "Motor Mat," the lighthearted account of a bumpkin behind the wheel of his badly used car. Chugging along, Mat drives by some farmland and encounters his first difficulty. "I had a goat bite one of the tires on Mat's flivver," Messmer remembered. No matter. Mat "just takes his cigar out and blows a smoke ring and uses *that* for a tire. All picture gags. No matter what difficulty, he overcame it." One day Messmer would recycle these gags to the delight of a worldwide audience.

"Motor Mat" was never released to theaters. Nevertheless, Universal paid the money and liked the artist. Cohn recommended Messmer to two older cartoonists, each with his eye on a filmmaking career. The first, Hy Mayer, collaborated with Otto on "The Travels of Teddy," built around a caricature of Theodore Roosevelt. In the months it took to make this short subject, Messmer learned his new trade. He was ready to work with the second cartoonist, Pat Sullivan. There has never been an unlikelier partnership in animation, or one with greater resonance.

Born in Australia in 1885, Patrick O'Sullivan jettisoned the first letter of his surname when he peddled caricatures to the Sydney newspapers. At the age of twenty-two, he migrated to London, where he became in turn a quick-sketch artist, a music hall dancer, and a mule driver. In New York, he did a little prizefighting and then completed the circle, catching on once more as an assistant newspaper cartoonist. Sullivan's chief was William F. Marriner, owner and operator of the comic strip "Sambo and His Funny Noises." Deriding Negroes as ignorant and superstitious was a staple of prewar humor. On stage, white actors rolled their eyes and yukked it up disguised by curl wigs and layers of burnt cork. Early two-reelers occasionally used blacks as stereotypical fools; the titles give the show (and the showmen) away: *Rastus in Zululand, Pickaninnies* and *Watermelon, Chicken Thief.* In the strips, blacks were usually portrayed as a subspecies with billiard ball heads, bulging eyes, and limited understanding. Richard F. Outcault's "Yellow Kid" set the tone. America's first popular comic strip made its reputation by lampooning the speech and mannerisms of anyone outside the mainstream. In one episode, "The Kid's Great Fight," the hero knocks down a little black boy. The opponent is hit so hard he suffers multiple fractures of the jaw. A goat finishes him off, chomping at the "wool" that grows on the child's head.

"Sambo and His Funny Noises," loosely based on the 1899 children's book *Little Black Sambo,* was every bit as coarse. The title character talks in the customary vaudeville dialect ("I'se makin a noise like a two hoss truck"), and he suffers a catalog of indignities and humiliations. When Sambo dares to read a book about avalanches, for example, sneering classmates pelt him with rocks. When he comes to a passage on earthquakes, they yank the seat out from under him. Wearily, he abandons the book and concludes, "Dere aint no room on dis earth fo' dem white boys an' me!" The strip might have enjoyed a long life except for Marriner's periodic depressions and chronic alcoholism. One day in October 1914, he went to his summer home in New Jersey, set fire to the house, and shot himself. There was no way Sullivan could do a solo. His line was too thin and uncertain and his gags weak. By the end of the year, the McClure syndicate terminated the strip.

Jobless once more, Sullivan reasoned that his talents lay in drumming up trade and getting others to do the cartooning. If he was a mediocre artist, he was a persuasive salesman; soon the new Sullivan studio had contracts from the Edison company for advertising and entertainment shorts. Given this seed money, Sullivan could proceed

with plans for animating Sambo. To avoid paying royalties to Marriner's estate, he renamed the character Sammy Johnsin. To finesse his own artistic shortcomings, he hired a group of promising young artists. Among them was Otto Messmer. Although the two men were only seven years apart in age, the contrast between them could not have been more pronounced. Sullivan had a fondness for women and liquor; Messmer was a straight arrow, rooted to New Jersey where he lived with his parents. Sullivan had a loud mouth and an oversized ego; Messmer was self-effacing and unambitious. Sullivan was a born entrepreneur; Messmer was a natural cartoonist.

From the beginning, Sullivan gave his staff plenty to do. Besides the Sammy Johnsin series, they worked on a dozen cartoons built around Charlie Chaplin's Tramp character. "Chaplin sent at least thirty or fourty photographs of himself in different [poses]," Messmer later noted in an oral history. "He encouraged us and autographed all those photographs and we copied every little movement that he did." The Tramp's pantomime influenced the work on Sammy; so did Messmer's skill with sight gags. In the chase scenes, "If a lion was chasin' him, his hat would blow off, and then when he would stop the hat would come on him again. Little things like that."

As Messmer gained confidence, he grew increasingly critical of the Sambo shorts. Racism is not what disturbed the animator. He had the same problem with the Tramp episodes: The stars of the cartoons were human beings. "Why animate something you can see in real life?" Messmer asked himself. Some cartoonists "tried to make beautiful girls moving around, and men. It didn't go over too well with audiences in theaters. But if they saw even a rubber ball with a face on it—a drawing moving, doing things—it got a thrill." The insight was worth a fortune, but the fortune would have to wait until after the war.

During the time Messmer saw action in France, Sullivan was serving time of a different sort. The married Sullivan had been convicted of rape in the second degree with a fourteen-year-old girl. Taking into consideration Sullivan's "very considerable ability" as a filmmaker, the judge sentenced him to Sing Sing penitentiary in Ossining, New York—but only for a year, one tenth of the maximum punishment. In 1919, both men returned to civilian life and resumed their business relationship. Neither talked much about what he had done in the years they were apart. Messmer churned out short parodies and travelogues; Sullivan knocked on the doors of local film companies, trying to attract new business. One prospective client, *Paramount Screen Magazine,* made an offer. Its weekly compilation of live footage and cartoons was far behind schedule; could Sullivan give them some assistance? He had no interest in such a small job, but he gave his star animator permission to do a little moonlighting.

Messmer remem-
bered: "I made a little
film for them about a
cat. He was chasing
some mice around
and it was full of gags
like a mouse running
up a grandfather clock,
taking the minute
hand off, throwing it
like a spear and nailing
the cat's tail to the
floor." The title was
"Feline Follies." For
all the laughs they
engendered, "Follies"
had a melancholy
undertow just as so
many of Chaplin's
pictures did. Messmer
had learned a lot from

the Tramp, and more from the Great War. During one battle, he and a
buddy had a conversation in the trenches, then he looked away for a
moment; he turned back to see the soldier silenced forever with a bul-
let through his head. Later, a German sniper, shot from a tree, showed
Messmer pictures of his wife and children just before he died. These
experiences affected the animator in ways he did not fully understand.
Messmer never displayed much in the way of temperament or ego, and
most of his work was lighthearted and full of visual amusement. But
every now and then a bitter moment would punctuate the comedy and
throw the mood off course. The feline star of "Follies," for example, turns
out to be an unpredictable and almost tragic figure. While Tom Cat does
some hilarious back-fence dancing, the mice run wild on his home territory. Tom's owner discovers the mess and disowns her pet. Exiled, the
cat attempts to get some comfort from his heartthrob, Miss Kitty. But
when he learns that she is the mother of several black kittens, he quickly
backs away. In the end, friendless and homeless, Tom walks by a "gas
works" and inhales some fatal fumes from a hose.

Even with this glum finale, "Feline Follies" intrigued the executives at Paramount, and they asked for an encore. Messmer called it "Musical Mews." "The big gag was these four cats singing in a backyard. They became famous singers and there was one gag showing a theater. An overcrowded bus pulls up and hundreds of people get off and stream into the theater. The fat bus gets skinnier and the building grows and starts stretching at the seams." Once he had established the antic style, Messmer concentrated on the personality of his new star. By the third film, the cat had acquired a new graphic liberty and, more important, a name, given to him by a Paramount executive. "He suggested Felix," said Messmer, "which we kicked around a little bit and decided this was it. Meaning feline and felicity: good luck cat." In the next half a dozen comedies, Felix ventured into the surreal, detaching his tail and using it as a cane and wondering so intensely that question marks appeared over his head—and were promptly used as fishhooks to haul in supper, or footholds to ascend a building. Confronted with difficulties, the cat set a style, pacing back and forth, hands behind his back, the first animated creature capable of *thinking* its way out of trouble. When he hit on a solution, Felix winked at the viewer, bonding audiences to him and making them collaborators in his little plots.

From Messmer's experience on the Sammy Johnsin films, he had come to the conclusion that a solid, inky figure made the best cartoon protagonist. It amounted to a walking silhouette, easy to draw and ideal to pose against a neutral background. Felix, however, was black in more than the literal sense. The cat's speeches were never in Negro dialect (historian Donald Crafton wrote that "one could surmise from the slang language of the title cards that if we could hear Felix speak, he would have a New Jersey accent"). Nevertheless, Felix embodied the dominant racial views of the twenties. Audiences saw a dark, big-eyed, half-primitive figure, clever and improvisatory in the tradition of Br'er Fox. He dances to jazz, chases white females, and overindulges, only to be pursued by hallucinations (a string of hot dogs chases him from his home, a lamppost turns into a dragon, an antique sedan becomes a hippopotamus)

Although he customarily wins his battles with circumstance, Felix, like all great farceurs, is never far from catastrophe. One of his strangest cartoons, "Felix Turns the Tide," concerns a war between rats and cats. After bidding farewell to his white feline girlfriend, Felix the soldier goes off to battle. In an obvious recollection of the Great War, Messmer shows a landscape littered with the corpses of cats. The battle won, Felix comes home to a hero's welcome—except from his beloved. She has married another, and can be seen tyrannizing her husband and leading a long line of kittens. The untrustworthy female is one of many twenties prototypes in the Felix films. Foreigners are suspect; Jews are pawnbrokers or tailors ("Felix Trifles with Time"); blacks tend to be dupes or simpletons ("Felix Goes Hungry"). Messmer would have seen nothing unusual in this; after all, he was only giving another spin to the attitudes of his time, attitudes expressed not only on the street but in high places. In the twenties, Princeton University Press published *A Study of American Intelligence* by two respected psychologists. The book confirmed the prejudices of anyone who looked down on immigrants: "The intellectual superiority of our Nordic group over the Alpine, Mediterranean and negro groups has been demonstrated." And after a notorious race riot in the nation's capital, the *New York Times* editorialized, "The majority of Negroes in Washington before the great war, were well-behaved . . . most of them admitted the superiority of the white race and troubles between the two races were unheard of." To those two dependable springboards for comedy—race and ethnicity—the Felix cartoons added a third. In "Felix in Love," the aforementioned hippo is referred to as a tin lizzie. Infuriated by the slang word for lesbian, she demands, "Who are you calling a lizzie?" And in "Felix in Fairyland," when the cat hears a housefly claiming to be a fairy, Felix minces around until the insect adds, "No, I'm a *real* fairy."

Children laughed at the cat and absorbed his messages without exactly realizing what they meant. But their parents bought the entire package. In New York, the *Daily News* praised the films' "feline spirit incarnate. . . . We're for five reels of Felix and only one reel of other folks." The paper went on to praise the characteristics of a subsidiary player, citing "the delightful elasticity of Mr. Sullivan's elephant." Actually, it was Mr. Messmer's elephant, just as it was Mr. Messmer's cat. But Sullivan made no attempt to set the record straight. Early on, he grabbed the credit and never let go. In time, he concocted a story of Felix's birth. "My wife came into my room one day carrying a stray cat—just an ordinary, back-garden, music-making, narrow-tailed unpedigreed sort of cat. 'Everybody cartoons men. Why not create an animal cartoon?'"

He repeated the fiction to anyone who would listen, and in England, reporters hung on Sullivan's every word, for the country had succumbed to Felix fever. In 1923, a novelty number, "Felix Kept on Walking," ascended the charts in Britain ("Blew him up with dynamite. But him they couldn't kill. / Miles up in the air he flew, He just murmured 'Toodle-oo,' / Landed down in Timbuctoo / And kept on walking still"). The fever spread to the Continent. By the following year, *Film Daily* reported that consumers all over the world were snapping up "Felix handkerchiefs, Felix toys, Felix chinaware," while in the United States, "an actor in vaudeville is made up to resemble Felix and struts in the same manner as Felix's peculiar little walk."

At about the same time that Gertie transfixed Otto Messmer, other young artists caught Winsor McCay's vaudeville act and decided to try their hands at animation. Paul Terry, then an illustrator and photographer for the *New York Press,* almost immediately set to work on his own film, *Little Herman,* mixing live and animated comedy on a split screen. He showed the result to a major distributor, Lewis Selznik, who contemptuously offered a bid of one dollar per foot. "But the raw stock cost more than that," the animator protested. With some justification, Selznik informed him, "It was worth more before you drew on it." Terry's indominability was stronger than his talent. He tried to persuade Bud Fisher to let him bring Mutt and Jeff to the screen, but Fisher had someone else in mind. (A Frenchman, Raoul Barre, got the job, and even though the series was undistinguished, it contributed to animation history when a cameraman forgot to photograph some background material and made one of the leads appear to be hanging in thin air. The studio men were delighted with the accident. Soon characters were regularly walking off cliffs, continuing several steps before they realize what has happened. The routine continues, certain to outlast the century.)

Terry heard that William Randolph Hearst planned to start an animation company, and sent in his résumé. It was rejected. Finally, Terry found a job with a new concern, Bray Studios in New York City, where his first cartoon was entitled "Farmer Al Falfa's Cat-Astrophe." It starred a ungainly whiskered rube, primitive in style, elementary in humor, and one of the most durable characters ever to appear on film. Rural America had long been the butt of city humorists. The rise of the assembly line had brought thousands of unsophisticated workers into the cities. Their adjustment to urban life was awkward, their ignorance profound—ideal ingredients for comedians. Hardly a performer was without his favorite story of the farmer's daughter, and "How Ya Gonna Keep 'em Down on the Farm, After They've Seen Paree?," the Walter Donaldson song, summarized the psychology of the U.S. Expeditionary Forces. (After the Armistice, demobilized soldiers altered the lyrics to "How Ya Gonna Keep 'em Down on the Farm, After They've Seen the *Farm?*") While Chaplin and Buster Keaton found subtle ways of satirizing the innocent in the city, Terry aimed for the obvious. His Farmer Al Falfa was an extended doodle, with white beard, bald head, round nose, and choleric temper, usually exacerbated by the behavior of recalcitrant horses, cows, and chickens.

Terry, like his boss, John Randolph Bray, brought the techniques of Henry Ford into the field of animation. The artists and their assistants worked on what amounted to an assembly line, simplifying costumes, drawing only what was absolutely necessary and suggesting the rest with an outline or a brushstroke. Output increased; costs were dramatically reduced. The only casualty was quality: At a time when exhibitors demanded "product" to round out the movie program, Terry had little reason to improve or enliven the adventures of Al Falfa. During the war, he made documentaries for the army, but live-action films held little interest for him. When he returned to civilian life, he picked up where he had left off, apparently content to produce hackwork until the distributor, Paramount Studios, stopped asking for the further adventures of Al Falfa. Then, in 1920, an acquaintance suggested that Aesop's Fables might make a profitable subject for animation. Terry later claimed that he had never heard of the Greek moralist until that moment. Upon investigation—or so went the official Terry version—he saw that the tales of creatures who acted with human motives could indeed provide the basis for a cartoon series.

The fable, as Bruno Bettelheim points out in *The Uses of Enchantment,* "always explicitly states a moral truth; there is no hidden meaning, nothing is left to our imagination." The fairy tale, "in contrast, leaves all decisions up to us, including whether we wish to make any at all. It is up to us whether we wish to make any application to our life from a fairy tale, or simply enjoy the fantastic events it tells about." These definitions apply to the earliest cartoons, and they are extremely useful in considering Terry's breakthrough animations. The Fables

Fables Pictures, Inc. presents

ÆSOP'S
Fables
Modernized
Cartoonist Paul Terry

What They Are

FOR real, out-and-out humor, imagination and life-like animation these clever cartoons have got it over any animated cartoons you ever saw.

They bring wise and funny old Aesop right down to date; they prove that as a creator of clean comedy the old chap was a wonder, who would be worth a million a year today to any producer.

Your audiences will take to these cartoon comedies like a baby to a bottle.

Booked solid in the Keith houses.

one short reel each week
—every week

Pathé Distributors

underlined what Aesop and La Fontaine and other fabulists had found long ago, and what Messmer was in the process of rediscovering: People who behave like animals get ostracized; animals who behave like people become immortals. Terry's versions of Aesop were subtitled "sugar-coated pills of wisdom" and seldom rose above the level of burlesque. Even so, they contained the essence of all fables. Each cartoon ended with an instruction, usually boiled down to a punch line or a non sequitur ("He who plays the other fellows [*sic*] game is sure to lose"; "A man who cannot remember phone numbers has no business getting married"), and each was enthusiastically received. Interviewed about the films, Terry mused, "The fact that they're ambiguous is the thing that made 'em funny. Aesop said 2,600 years ago that 'The race to the altar is run in laps,' or, 'Marriage is a good institution, but who wants to live in an institution?' "

Actually, Aesop never said anything of the kind, but Terry convinced himself that he was refreshing a classic and educating America. And in a way, he was. The Fables, like the adventures of Felix, demonstrated to filmgoers that mammals, birds, reptiles, and amphibians could sustain a picture all by themselves. Without any intention other than to make money and entertain audiences, the cartoonists of the early 1920s provided new links with the classic mythmakers and tale-tellers. The Animal Powers, so prevalent in ancient societies, were reasserting themselves in clown costumes.

Not that every studio was willing to concede its cels to the animals. The Fleischers showed a particular fondness for human stars, drawn in a heightened, loopy style but still recognizable as people. There were five Fleischer brothers, and that was not their only resemblance to the Marx brothers, another group of first-generation Jews who grew up on the streets of Manhattan. Like the Marxes, who had also been born at the end of the nineteenth century or the beginning of the twentieth, the Fleischer boys displayed what Irving Howe called an immigrant "distinctiveness." It came through "most vividly in the rhythm and tone of their work, the pulsation of their nerves, the unfolding of what we call 'personality.' "

They were a conflicted group, craving recognition from the very institutions they sought to satirize or upend. The Marx Bros. introduced themselves to the public with verbal and physical assaults; the Fleischers did it with a cast of extravagant characters they spilled from an inkwell. Their father, a Jewish tailor who had emigrated from Austria in the late 1880s, had set up an eccentric tailor shop in midtown Manhattan. In order to make the very best riding habits, William Fleischer asked his female customers to mount a stuffed horse he kept in the rear of the shop. Not until they were in the saddle would he take their measurements. Between assignments, he occupied his time by producing various laborsaving devices. One of them, a button whose brass surface could be removed for easy polishing, was bought by many New York City policemen anxious to keep up appearances without getting polish stains on their uniforms.

All the children (there was also a sister) seemed to have inherited their father's ability to tinker and improvise, but while all five brothers eventually worked together, Max and Dave led the pack. Max first established himself as a cartoonist for the *Brooklyn Eagle,* and then as the art editor of *Popular Science;* Dave became a film editor for Pathé. Like Messmer and Terry, the brothers had been transfixed by McCay's vaudeville appearances. Soon after they saw "Gertie," in 1914, the young men began to experiment with animations of their own. They were convinced that the entire process could be speeded up by filming a live model and tracing its image on paper, frame by frame. Accordingly, as Max cranked the camera, Dave, dressed in a black clown's outfit, jumped and danced against a white sheet. When the film was developed, his every movement was outlined in ink. The Fleischers called their process Rotoscope, patented it, and convinced Pathé to underwrite a cartoon using this new technique.

For reasons he never explained, Max suddenly decided that the clown was too elemental; cartooning needed something more sophisticated, more political. Instead of going to his strengths, he insisted on producing a satire about Teddy Roosevelt hunting down a bird. The Pathé executives screened the Rotoscoped film, judged it to be vastly inferior to the Roosevelt short by Hy Mayer and Otto Messmer, and fired both Fleischers. Perhaps it is better to be lucky than excellent; Max ran into J. R. Bray, a colleague from the old *Eagle* days who was now running the animation studio that bore his name. After learning about the Rotoscope method, Bray invited Fleischer to produce some cartoons for a client, the *Paramount Screen Magazine.* Work had barely begun when the war put a stop to Max's activities. He became a civilian employee of the government, making films at Fort Sill, Oklahoma; at the same time, Dave joined the army and edited footage in Washington, D.C. After the armistice, Max returned to Bray and entered motion picture history.

He called his new series Out of the Inkwell. It featured the once-neglected clown, in his black outfit and white buttons, emerging from an inkwell to harass the animator, portrayed in live sequences by Max himself. The idea of a creature rising up against its maker was part of a long tradition that embraced the ancient Jewish tale of the Golem, Frankenstein's monster, the Sorcerer's Apprentice, H. G. Wells's *Island of Dr. Moreau,* and scores of folk stories. It was not even a new cartoon idea: Back in 1916, Otto Messmer had made an inventive short called "Trials of a Movie Cartoonist." The trade publication *Moving Picture World* described the film: Figures rendered by the live cartoonist "become rebellious and refuse to act as he wants them to, so he has a terrible time to make them do his bidding. They answer back and say he has no right to make slaves of them even if he is their creator." Yet after all this exposure some power still remained in the legend, and the Fleischers knew precisely how to wield it. They dubbed the clown Ko-ko, furnished him with a quirky personality and a white dog, Fitz, and in 1919 established their own studio, Out of the Inkwell Productions. Max billed himself as the producer of all cartoons, Dave as director. Success was almost immediate. By the following year, the *New York Times* reported that "The little inkwell clown has attracted favorable attention because of a number of distinguishing characteristics. His motions, for one thing, are smooth and graceful. He walks, dances and leaps as a . . . particularly easy-limbed human being might." The article proceeded to take a swipe at Fleischer's rivals: "Ko-ko does not jerk himself from one position to another, nor does he move an arm and a leg while the remainder of his body remains as unnaturally still as—as if it were fixed in ink lines on paper." The reason Ko-ko moved so fluently, of course, was because of his human origins. Dave Fleischer's Rotoscoped images supplied the original gestures. He also supplied the ideas for Ko-ko's merry pranks. In each episode, Max, appearing

live, precedes the clown's appearance. The openings rarely repeat themselves. One time, Max "draws" the clown, who abruptly springs into action. On other occasions, the cartoonist blows on an ink blob, or sketches pieces of Ko-ko and pulls them together, or creates only part of the clown costume and watches Ko-ko jump up and down until the ink flows down and completes his wardrobe. In "Ko-ko Gets Egg-Cited," the process is reversed: The clown enters first and proceeds to create Max as if Ko-ko were the real person and Fleischer the cartoon.

Ko-ko's mischief expressed the impudence of the age. Authority existed to be mocked; rules were made to be defied or canceled. Prohibition led to speakeasies, censoriousness led to licentiousness. "Bedtime" is the quintessence of the Out of the Inkwell series. After Max places him on a mountain peak, Ko-ko sets out to master his own fate. He leaps from the drawing board and lands on the artist's bed. There he inhales deeply and dilates like a balloon, growing too large for the bedroom to hold him and rampaging over the photographed skyline of New York City. Just as Max is about to be destroyed he wakes up—the entire sequence was only a vivid dream. He returns the little clown to his home in the inkwell, but there is the distinct feeling that the rebel will be heard from again, and that next time the nightmare will not be so easily banished.

Walter Lantz was another of those artistic young men whose lives were irrevocably changed by a glance at "Gertie." Like Otto Messmer, Lantz had unfocused ambitions until he caught McCay's act; like Max Fleischer, he found himself, quite by chance, sharing the screen with animated characters. A child of the century—he was born in 1900—Lantz began his career studying at the Art Student's League, then as an assis-

MAX FLEISCHER

tant to comic strip cartoonists at Hearst's New York daily *American*. In 1916, he moved to Hearst's studio, International Film Service (IFS), where he cleaned up the work of senior animators and did "in-betweening"—making the hundreds of drawings between key poses. "Those were the days before cels were originated," he recalled more than fifty years later. "We animated everything on paper. We had to pencil every single drawing. Then these pencil drawings were photographed. The background was just a strip we'd put down on pegs and then place the drawing over it. We wouldn't have anything that crossed a line. If a character walked over to a chair, you'd have to draw the chair on the drawing or it would wiggle all over the screen."

Hearst had created IFS in order to capitalize on the *American*'s biggest comic strip characters, among them Krazy Kat, Happy Hooligan, and the Katzenjammer Kids. So IFS cartoons were secondhand to begin with, unoriginal compared with Felix, and rudimentary compared with the Fleischer product. Yet the studio contributed a few influential techniques. One was "rubber hose" animation: rather than bend an arm at the elbow or a leg at the knee, characters moved their extremities as if they were elastic tubes. Liberated from the constraints of real-life anatomy, cartoon humans and animals acted with a new comic energy. IFS artists also created something they called the pan. Lantz explained: "You show a character standing in one spot and just move his legs like he's on a treadmill. But rather than a treadmill we'd have a long sheet of paper with a background on it. Every time you move the drawing, you move the pan. By moving the background you could make the character look like *he* was moving."

Lantz noticed that cartoons "weren't helping to sell any more newspapers, and when IFS folded in the summer of 1918, he signed on at Bray. The studio, like so many animation parlors, was caught in a time warp. One of its most important products was the Colonel Heeza Liar series, which had originated as yet another parody of Teddy Roosevelt. By now, however, the satire had softened. The country longed for the days of Big Stick diplomacy, before the terrors and disappointments of the war, and thus the Colonel had gone from a satiric emblem to a road company Baron Münchhausen, burbling about his exotic journeys and dragging unbelievers into the wilds to confirm his boasts.

By the mid-twenties, Lantz was playing one of the infidels in the cartoon's live sequences. "I couldn't act my way out of a paper bag," he later admitted. "Bray said, 'Walter, you're too good-looking, you need to look funnier.' So they put round glasses on me so I'd look like Harold Lloyd." As Donald Crafton points out in his pioneering study *Before Mickey,* contemporary reviews suggest that special effects were the Colonel's main attraction. "I remember one Colonel Heeza Liar in particular," said Lantz. "We were out in the forest, and I was tired. I sat down on an animated egg to rest. We animated the egg breaking open, and a live turtle came out of the egg with Colonel Heeza riding on it." *Motion Picture Weekly* reported that "Colonel Heeza Liar and the Ghost" showed "A living actor, a negro standing 5' 10", [who] shrinks until he is only half an inch in height. He is then transformed into a pair of dice which roll out of sight. Another living actor, six feet and heavy for his height, dives headlong into an ordinary waste basket."

"Colonel Heeza Liar and the Forbidden Fruit" shamelessly borrowed from Fleischer's Inkwell cartoons. Lantz and a colleague are shown in lively conversation, discussing the imminent banana shortage. The Colonel enters, disguised as a banana, and pours the contents of an inkwell onto a pad of paper. The story unfolds in animated form. At its conclusion, the two artists reappear, and return the Colonel to his home in the inkwell, plunging in the stopper to keep him from narrating yet another tale. It became obvious in the mid-twenties that Heeza Liar was an anachronism, and Lantz invented a new set of stars, a wide-eyed boy named Dinky Doodle and his little black dog, Weakheart. These failed to win a large following, and they were supplemented with a new series of "Hot Dog" cartoons featuring Lantz in his usual role of artist, accompanied by his animated sidekick, Pete the Pup. The little dog was clearly based on Ko-ko's pet, Fitz, but that was not the most blatant example of plagiarism. The Bray studio also produced "Unnatural Histories," bearing such titles as "How the Elephant Got His Trunk" and "How the Bear Got His Short Tail." There was little Terry could do; Aesop was in the public domain.

Not every Bray production had a secondhand aura. "The Lunch Hound," released in 1927, is Lantz's finest mix of live action and animation; when the human figure reaches for the animated Pete, and the pup jumps away from his hand, the illusion is flawless. But it was a last flare before darkness. The medium of animation seemed exhausted by then, and everyone knew it. When is a miracle not a miracle? asked G. K. Chesterton. Answer: When it is seen for the second time. Cartoon-

ing was running out of wonders. Audiences were no longer so amused when a dog defied gravity or a man dueled with a nest of hornets. Unlike the expanding comedies of Chaplin and Keaton and the other silent film stars, cartoons never lasted more than seven minutes. Every second counted, and yet the action stuttered and halted every time a balloon issued from a character's mouth or a title card filled the screen. The process became reminiscent of a waiter who keeps interrupting just as the speaker is coming to the point. By 1927, animation was in deep trouble. The Fleischers had gone in and out of bankruptcy. Terry was treading water. Bray had closed his studio, forcing Lantz to leave the cartoon business and head to Hollywood, seeking work as a gag writer. If the genre was to survive, it would need a fresh miracle. In the next few years, it got not one but four of them: color, sound, sex, and, most unexpected of all, a man who could build symphonies out of squeaks.

New York in the 1920s, as Ann Douglas put it in her overview *Terrible Honesty,* "celebrated excitement, danger, record-making and record-breaking, catastrophe and farce, all of it, to borrow a phrase in heavy use among journalists of the day, 'in full view of the spectators.' " Here was the epicenter of stock speculation, the home of American publishing, the location of Yankee Stadium and Madison Square Garden, the playing field of the Gershwins and Florenz Ziegfeld and the most beautiful chorines in the world, the locale of the Harlem Renaissance, the place from which Lindbergh had taken off for France and where Frenchmen came to gawk. It was a place where talent was confirmed and ambition was welcomed. To be sure, there were other glamorous towns: Hollywood, for instance. But everyone knew it was made of tinsel and fear. A scandal involving Fatty Arbuckle and a starlet had led to the creation of the Hays office, and now even a married couple could not be shown in the same bed at the same time. In New York, anything could be said and expressed, uncensored. This was truly the land of liberty. Go anyplace else—even if you were an animator—and no matter how high you rose, you were a hick.

Which was fine with Walt Disney. Indeed, in subsequent years he enjoyed referring to himself and his brother, Roy, as "a couple of rubes," and there was truth in his jest. Although he had driven an ambulance in France during the war, Walter Elias Disney kept free from the taint of cosmopolitanism. To the end of his life, he remained to the far right on the political spectrum, suspicious of foreigners, and unwilling to hire Jews or blacks in his company. More than once he announced his preference for animals over people, and called his time "the century of the Communist cutthroat, the fag and the whore." His biases, heavily masked but discernible, seeped into his work from its earliest days. None of this diminished Disney's drive or his ability to lead. Other animators drew with greater skill, were funnier, produced more original work. The world was open to them, too. But only Walt had the genius to know genius when he saw it; only Walt created a public appetite and then gratified it.

The romantic account of the craftsman rising from humble beginnings has passed into myth, and that is where it belongs. Disney's first cartoons were made in Kansas City, where, barely out of his teens, he built an art studio to produce advertisements. He learned about animation not from Winsor McCay's experiments but from a book he borrowed from the library: *Animated Cartoons: How They Are Made, Their Origin and Development,* by caricaturist Edwin G. Lutz. The author had one overriding principle: "plan the work so that the lowest possible number of drawings need be made for any particular scenario." Disney took this advice to heart. His first cartoons cut every possible corner and made much use of cycles and basic backgrounds. He borrowed from all available sources. His early work shows the unacknowledged influence of the Fleischers, complete with characters jumping in and out of inkwells; and of Felix, with a cat using his tail as a whip, a unicycle, and a ladder. Few of the films exhibited what was one day to be called the Disney touch: the glimmering scenery, the strong personalities, the whimsical tone. Occasionally, an unconventional fancy would break through. In one cartoon, for example, a bear speaks unwisely and is forced to eat his words, consuming the letters he has just uttered.

For all the industry talk of Manhattan and Hollywood, Kansas City turned out to be a surprisingly rich source of animators. Several of the locals became not only the cornerstones of the Disney empire but of the art of American cartooning: Ubbe Iwerks, Rudy Ising, Hugh Harman, Isidore "Friz" Freleng. Theoretically, Walt could have stayed in the heart of the country, turning out modest little comedies for his new company, Laugh-O-Gram Films Inc., and producing a series of fairy tales like "Little Red Riding Hood" and "Jack and the Beanstalk." He was also intent on making "Alice's Wonderland," a group of fantasies inspired by the Lewis Carroll books. The backers for these films, how-ever, were not as numerous as Disney expected, and by the summer of 1923, it was clear that Laugh-O-Gram Films was on its way to bank-ruptcy. He had a choice: stay in Kansas City or head for one of the major production centers, New York or Hollywood. At that moment, Roy was recuperating from tuberculosis at a veterans hospital in Sawtelle, California. Another consideration was that Walt's uncle Robert, a retired mining executive, owned a house on Kingswell Avenue in Hollywood. Free board, free rent, family, sunshine, film distributors—and three thousand miles between him and rivals in New York. It was too much for the twenty-two-year-old to resist. In July 1923, he left his staff behind, bought a one-way ticket on a train headed west, decked himself out in a checkered jacket, blue pants, and red bow tie, and left town. It is significant that although Walt Disney was down to his last fifty dollars, he purchased a ticket in first class.

CHAPTER THREE

FIGHTING THE MOUSE

When I sat down to play I asked for the music and were they surprised! They politely told me they didn't have any music and furthermore never used any. I then asked what key would the first number be in. I must have been speaking another language because the leader said, "When you hear two knocks, just start playing."

—LIL HARDIN

I am such a bug in accuracy in performance, about playing in tune, and with just the proper note values. In the written parts, I wanted it to sound as exact as the band could possibly make it.

—BENNY GOODMAN

At one terminal, the spontaneous outpourings of the band as remembered by Louis Armstrong's first wife. At the other, the carefully rehearsed effects produced by the great clarinetist. Both speakers are referring to jazz, but in the first third of the twentieth century, every art form was affected by these opposing philosophies: painting, sculpture, music both "serious" and popular, theater, film, and, most surprising of all, animation. Here, one would have thought, every frame had to be planned, sketched, inked, worked out to the minutest detail. Walt Disney certainly felt that way, and acted accordingly.

Otto Messmer held a different view. A staff member of Sullivan's studio used to watch him work. "There was never a script. As he worked, Otto would continually think out loud of new ideas, for this film or the next one, and when an animator would finish roughing out a scene, he would bring it to Otto and OK it. He was animating and thinking at the same time. I don't know how he did it."

Under Messmer's baton, Felix's celebrity increased every year. Intellectuals began to surround him with fulsome praise and over-analysis, as they were doing with jazz. A trade magazine called the cartoon star "The Delphic oracle and a world horoscope rolled all into one." Aldous Huxley thought the Felix cartoons best illustrated his notion that "What the cinema can do better than literature or the spoken drama is to be fantastic." Paul Hindemith wrote the score "Felix at the Circus" to be conducted at the Baden-Baden festival of 1928.

In their own way, the Fleischer brothers agreed with Messmer's approach; they were from New York and believed in improvisation as a duty. Max told his staff that "if it can be done in real life, it's not animation," exhorting them to make their work more absurd and funnier. One artist remembered Max hanging about his desk, worrying a script until it amused them both. "We'd laugh like hell at our great gags," he said, "and then I'd animate them."

At about this time, *Motion Picture Weekly* amused its readers with a close-up of a typical animation atelier. The magazine did not specify a company, but its description perfectly describes the Fleischer ethos: "God only knows what a vast number of things a movie cartoonist has to study and observe before he can do a day's work. In fact, everything from how a snake makes love, to cooking a Spanish omelet in an Irish restaurant. It is not unusual in a cartoon studio to see several artists doing high dives off their desks, or playing leap frog, or maybe doing a dry swim on the floor while several others stand by and watch to study the timing of the action."

As the Fleischer studio regained its balance, it acquired an intellectual following every bit as impressive as the one around Felix. Albert Einstein had shocked the world with his theory of relativity, and Max produced an hour-long feature, with animated highlights, to help explain physics to the general public. Einstein himself lauded the film; Max, he said, had found a way to illustrate the abstract. The trouble was that an audience of physicists was too small to be profitable. School systems turned their backs on the project, prompting Max's bitter comment: "There were supposed to be only three people who understood Einstein's theory. Now there arc four." He nourished great hopes for his next full-length project, *Darwin's Theory of Evolution,* released with metronomic timing: The "Monkey Trial" drama was underway in a Tennessee court, starring two prominent adversaries, Clarence Darrow and William Jennings Bryan. Even so, the Darwin film failed at the box office.

The Fleischers returned to their long suit. From the day Car-Tunes unreeled, they brought in profits, and the series ran for decades. The shorts amounted to sheet music on a movie screen. As the theater organist played the melody, a white circle caromed over a line of lyrics. Viewers were encouraged to follow the bouncing ball and sing along. Occasionally, the word of a lyric would change into the object it represented, or the ball would become the beaming face of an animal or a clown. The rest was as simple as a flashlight beam jiggling on a wall. Car-Tunes delighted an undemanding public; theaters swelled with music and voices, giving a hint of what might be possible if only someone could devise a way of bringing sound to film.

Walt Disney had an unshakable faith in himself as impresario; traveling first class when he was broke was a gesture to be repeated throughout his life. The trip to Hollywood had been lonely and difficult, but he wheedled some money from Roy, set up a new studio, and sent for his best animator, Ubbe Iwerks. Other Kansas City veterans followed, and together they turned out a group of films that mixed live footage and cartoon characters. In these "Alice" cartoons, very loosely based on the Carrollian fantasies, the lead character was played by a real girl dressed in Victorian clothing. Customarily, Alice was supported by a gaggle of classmates reminiscent of the juveniles in Hal Roach's Our Gang comedies. Somewhere in the first few minutes the heroine fell asleep, just as the Rarebit Fiend had done. Cartoon characters infiltrated her dream world, chief among them Julius, a cat whose lineaments were clearly derived from Felix.

More than fifty Alice films issued from the Disney studios between 1923 and 1927, not one of them notable for originality or vision. Yet within the episodes were hints of the Disney style to come. Unlike his competitors, Walt insisted on a coherent design for even the most trivial comedies. Animator Rudy Ising remembered Disney's first story conferences: "Walt would have an idea—well, let's let Alice be a fire-man in this one, or let's let Alice go fishing, or whatever it was. And then we'd work up whatever the type of thing it was, fire gags or fish-ing gags. And then Walt would put them all together to tell a story. He'd try to come up with an idea of continuity, he'd sort of work that out, figure out about how long a scene should be, and who was the ani-mator." Walt and most of his colleagues had come from farm country, and their gags smacked of the barnyard. No Fleischer impudence for them. "We never did like the New York film ideas," Ising went on. "If you look at the films, you'll see that we really developed a whole dif-ferent type of humor than back there. Back there, some of it was kind of distasteful."

While the Fleischers and Messmer used the city as a backdrop, Walt preferred a rural setting. Disney animals were simpleminded figures of fun, the cartoon children prepubescent and brimming with harmless mischief. When real trouble occurred, it was the fault of outside agita-tors, or of some mechanical device dragged into Eden. In "Alice's Egg Plant," for example, a brood of chickens abandon their conveyor belt to go out on strike, led by a Bolshevik rooster named Little Red Hen-ski. In "Alice and the Dog Catcher," puppies enter one end of a truck and emerge as a long link of hot dogs, and in a variation of the gag, "Alice's Little Parade" shows puppies forced into an official building. They emerge as canine soldiers marching in obedient columns. Silent film historians Russell Merritt and J. B. Kaufman note that in Disney's hands "the assembly-line gag seems rather perfunctory and derivative, an easy gag that all-too-obviously coasts on labor-saving cycles, clones and cross-overs. But the contraption gag became the mother's milk of Disney's comedy."

That comedy would emerge in the studio's next phase. The "Alice" films were distributed by Margaret Winkler, one of the few women executives in 1920s Hollywood. A former secretary at the Warner stu-dio, Winkler had developed an extraordinary eye for animation talent. Starting as an independent producer, she had signed up the Fleischers in 1921, and the following year entered an agreement with Pat Sullivan to produce the Felix shorts. Shortly after discovering Disney, Winkler had begun to take a backseat to her husband, Charles Mintz, a former booking agent for Warner. Mintz's marketing techniques were more aggressive than his wife's, his business practices sharper and less savory.

Early in January 1927, he wrote Walt one of the most pregnant sentences in the annals of American cartooning: "I am negotiating with a national organization [Universal], and they seem to think that there are too many cats on the market." Disney, who had never really liked Julius, got the message. He and Iwerks started to develop a new animal, a creature who might be strong enough to perform on his own. In March, Universal announced the coming of "A rabbit named Oswald to be released under the brand name of Snappy Comedies." As designed by Iwerks, Oswald was as black as Julius, with long expressive ears and a wide white face. Universal was less than enchanted with his first adventure, "Poor Papa." ("There is too much repetition of action. Scenes are dragged out to such an extent that the cartoon is materially slowed down.") Disney accepted the criticism with good grace and promised to redesign the rabbit, making him "a younger character, peppy, alert, saucy and venturesome, keeping him also neat and trim."

Universal executives screened the second Oswald short, "Trolley Troubles," and revised their opinions of Disney. The cartoon was allowed to accompany *Flesh and the Devil,* a major motion picture starring Greta Garbo and John Gilbert, guaranteeing it a large audience. By the fourth adventure, "Great Guns," Oswald had acquired a hyperactive libido and a rabbity girlfriend, later to be named Fanny. Again, Disney's gags depended on rube humor. Cannons would fire and then grow flaccid; Oswald's ears also assumed a phallic quality, and Fanny got a lot of laughs when she became excited over Oswald's prowess with a bayonet. Yet the films played as well in the cities as they did in the outlands. At the close of 1927, *Motion Picture World* indulged in a little show business exaggeration, reporting that the Oswald series had "accomplished the astounding feat of jumping into first-run favor overnight."

The Oswald cartoons observed the Hollywood dictum that a picture is only as good as its villain. The hero dueled with Putrid Pete, sometimes known as Peg-leg Pete, a threatening, indefinably hybrid figure with his eyes on Fanny. The battle of protagonist and antagonist allowed Disney to use some of Messmer's surreal techniques; at one point, Oswald leaves the room, allowing his shadow to fight on. In addition, there were other stock characters, including a dachshund who took various shapes and a comic mongrel policeman. One year younger than the century, Walt had achieved his first objective: His name was now recognizable on screens across the United States. Things could not have seemed better as he and his young wife, Lillian, boarded a train to New York. It was February 1928, boom time on Wall Street, and happy days for Oswald. Disney was going to negotiate a new contract with his distributor. Mintz had been paying $2,250 per film. Walt wanted the fee increased $2,500. It would be a fine way to begin the new year.

"Funniest Reel on Market"
—Miner's Theatre, Collinsville, Ill.

"Wish we played them every week instead of every two weeks."
—New Franklin Theatre, New Franklin, Mo.

"A cheer always goes up from audience when Oswald is flashed across the screen."
—Majestic Theatre, Memphis, Mo.

"Oswald comedies making biggest hit of any comedies I have ever run."
—Lion Theatre, Hammond, Ill.

"Best I have ever run."
—American Theatre, Johnston, Ill.

"Oswald a real hit."
—Drake Theatre, Drake, Ill.

Mintz wasted no time; he had some bad news, and he could hardly wait to deliver it. In the

Oswald is the creation of Walt Disney. Produced by Winkler Productions. Released by **UNIVERSAL**

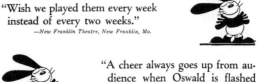

OSWALD
THE LUCKY RABBIT

first place, rather than offering Walt a raise, he wanted each Oswald film to be completed at a cost of $1,800. "But that's impossible," Walt objected. "We couldn't make a profit." The reply was just what Mintz hoped to hear. Since Walt could not produce the Oswalds at the right price, Mintz would take over, confident that the law would uphold him. Indeed, a deal had already been struck with Universal. If Walt wanted to stay with the cartoon series, he would have to list himself as a Mintz employee, along with the others. What others? Now came the coup de grace: "I have your key men signed up," Mintz declared. He was not bluffing. Without Walt's knowledge, all of his important animators had secretly agreed to work on Oswald cartoons for the Mintz studio in New York. Ubbe Iwerks was the lone holdout. Their decisions may not have been quite as underhanded as they appeared. Friz Freleng, on board since the Kansas City days, was to retain some unpleasant memories of his days with Disney: "Everybody was conspiring against the other one. Everybody had ambition; everybody wanted to be a producer and there was no one to work *with*."

Whether the animators' move was justified or not, Disney saw their departure as a collective betrayal. He wanted no part of Mintz's offer or, for that matter, of Oswald. He and Lillian bitterly headed back to California. The next sequence of events has been edited and revised so many times that even Disney may have forgotten what really occurred. All that can be ascertained is that Walt wanted to create yet another animal star, to copyright it, and do everything he could to protect it from business predators like Mintz.

Perhaps, as Walt claimed, he invented the creature on the train home. Perhaps, as Iwerks claimed, he stumbled on the inspiring picture of a real rodent in a magazine. In any case, both men acknowledged that Lillian rejected the name Mortimer. "I think," she said, "he should be called Mickey Mouse." Iwerks's original design for Mickey shows a long-snouted elastic rodent whose body and facial markings scarcely vary from Oswald's. The white area around the mouse's eyes is disproportionately large, just like the rabbit's, and his gumdrop nose and long mouth have the same dimensions as his predecessor. Both have rubber hose legs and wear shorts with oversized buttons. Only the characters' tails and ears are different. The shapes protruding from Oswald's head have the look of truncheons, Mickey's are two-dimensional circles. They give him the appearance of a toy.

Hindsight grants Mickey Mouse an irresistible appeal from the day of his birth. Actually, he had a difficult time making friends. The first short, "Plane Crazy," tried to take advantage of Lindbergh's national celebrity. A pleasant idea, but hardly new; the year before, Felix had starred in "Non-Stop Fright," with the cat as a lone pilot dueling with lightning bolts and clouds in the shape of horses. In the Disney short, Mickey transforms a jalopy into an airplane and then takes his girlfriend, Minnie, along for a joyflight, pawing her at every opportunity. The extraordinary aspect of "Plane Crazy" was not the product but the process. Some defectors had remained at the Disney studio, finishing out their contracts. Iwerks, fearful that they might carry news of Oswald's rival to Mintz, worked clandestinely in Walt's garage. There he animated every frame of Mickey's debut by himself, and he did it in two weeks. That meant an output of about seven hundred drawings per day, an accomplishment that has never been duplicated at a major studio. Disney proudly displayed "Plane Crazy" to distributors. No one made an offer. Given this gelid reception, most producers would have abandoned the project before it brought them to bankruptcy. Walt

decided to make a second Mickey Mouse cartoon. This one was called "Gallopin' Gaucho," a collection of gags from the Oswald films, with the veteran Peg-leg Pete as Mickey's antagonist. Again, Walt received no offers. Characteristically, he returned to Mickey a third time, still persuaded that the Disney studio and its mouse just needed one big break.

The flood tide of the twenties occurred in 1927. Anyone who doubted that the United States was the center of the universe could read about it in the new magazines, *Time* and the *New Yorker;* or invest in the bullish stock market; or watch one of Babe Ruth's home runs disappear into the stands—sixty times by season's end; or hear of Johnny Weissmuller's swimming achievement: one hundred yards in fifty-one seconds; or read about the ascendance of the motorcar made in the U.S.A., where pretty soon one out of every five Americans would own a vehicle, as opposed to one out of forty citizens of France or England. To crown the year came *The Jazz Singer,* a film more interesting to historians than aesthetes, but which became an essential part of cinema lore: the first talking picture.

It was nothing of the kind. The inventor Lee De Forest had been experimenting with sound film since the mid-twenties. Using his techniques, the Fleischers had produced several cartoons with a roughly synchronized sound track. The public, however, was unimpressed with a dog playing Verdi's "Anvil Chorus" on its teeth, or with human singers warbling "My Old Kentucky Home," and these experiments were abandoned. It took Al Jolson to sell the wedding of pictures and sound; after *The Jazz Singer,* in every sense the entertainment industry was turned on its ear. Just as the big Hollywood studios rushed to redo their scripts and equip their stages with microphones, the livelier animation studios hurriedly converted to sound. Paul Terry produced "Dinnertime," the first Aesop fable to feature human voices and an orchestral background. The Fleischers were deeply impressed; even before sound, Max considered Aesop's makers "the ones to beat." Walt Disney was not so sure. He had just finished an experiment with homemade sound effects. As a projector ran "Steamboat Willie," the third Mickey Mouse film, Disney and his animators improvised a score on washboard, slide whistle, and harmonica. The player of the mouth organ, Wilfred Jackson, treasured the moment: "I furnished the music ["Turkey in the Straw"] and the other fellows hit things and made sound effects. We had spittoons everywhere then, and they made a wonderful gong if you hit them with a pencil. It was really pretty exciting, and it did prove to us that the sound coming from the drawing could be a convincing thing." His boss remembered the evening's work as "terrible, but it was wonderful. And it was something new!"

Convinced that the something new would lead to fortune, Walt returned to New York in search of a sound engineer and a film distributor. En route, he had stopped by Kansas City to visit a friend, Carl Stalling, a theater organist, who agreed to set "Steamboat Willie" to music. Shortly after his arrival in Manhattan, Walt wangled an invitation to a preview of "Dinnertime." The next morning he mailed a review to his brother: "MY GOSH—TERRIBLE—A lot of racket and nothing else. I was terribly disappointed. I really expected to see something halfway decent. BUT HONESTLY—it was nothing but one of the rottenest fables believe I ever saw, and I should know because I have seen almost all of them. It merely had an orchestra playing and adding some noises. The talking part does not mean a thing. It doesn't even match. We sure have nothing to worry about from these quarters."

Walt's reaction was a mix of bravado and equanimity. He wanted to reassure Roy, his chief financial officer, but he also had an abiding belief in himself as entrepreneur. It was not misplaced. A shady, hustling promoter, Pat Powers, had agreed to record "Steamboat Willie" on some excellent equipment. By now, the film's budget was up to

$15,000. When Roy remonstrated, Walt wrote back, "Why should we let a few dollars jeopardize our chances. I think this is Old Man Opportunity rapping at our door. Let's don't let the jingle of a few pennies drown out his knock." In one sentence, the debt had been reduced from dollars to pennies. Roy replied with a test: Would Walt sell his Moon four-seater to help pay the bills? The open roadster was Walt's most cherished possession; he loved to flaunt it on Hollywood Boulevard. The owner swallowed hard and gave the nod. If Roy had any doubts about the Disneys' dependence on sound and music, they vanished at that moment. The bills were paid; the recording session took place. When the track was done to Stalling's and Disney's satisfaction, one theater, the Colony, booked the cartoon as a curtain-raiser for its feature film. That movie, *Gang War,* was to become as obscure as its stars, Olive Borden and Jack Pickford. But no one would forget the mouse at the bottom of the bill. He made his first public appearance on November 18, 1928. In its next issue, *Variety* called the cartoon "a peach of a synchronization job all the way." The *New York Times* said Disney had produced "an ingenious piece of work." Audiences burst into applause at every gag; word of mouth kept the Colony filled. Walt arranged to have the first two Mickey Mouse films set to music, and put Iwerks to work on a new project. Within weeks, critics suggested that Mickey belonged in the pantheon of American comedians. One pointed out, correctly, that "Steamboat Willie" was a bow in the direction of Buster Keaton, whose recent film was entitled *Steamboat Bill.*

Most people were so delighted with the clever amalgam of sound and comic animation that they looked past the sadism in "Steamboat Willie." The Fleischers' "kind of distasteful" comedy had nothing on Disney. In the film, Mickey not only resembles a rat, but he behaves like one. Annoyed by a cat, he swings the animal by the tail and flings it overboard. For no good reason, he rips suckling piglets away from their mother by shaking them off onto the deck. When one stubbornly resists, Mickey kicks it away and then squeezes its mother's teats, making her squeal a tune. Disney rarely allowed his own mean streak to surface, much less Mickey's, and it would never again be so apparent. Offscreen, however, vengeance was one of Walt's principal motivations. As soon as the reviews were in on "Steamboat Willie," Universal approached Disney and offered to distribute his films. If he wanted, they could supply him with the world's finest animators—the men who had gone over to Mintz. These men were professionals of an unquestionably high order. Walt could have used them; he could have smoothed things over and reconstructed his crew. Training new people took time, and Walt had no time. To spurn his old employees would be to hurt the Disney studio. Even so, he had no hesitation in telling the Universal executives, "I wouldn't have them back if they came crawling on their knees." The animators did not crawl, and neither did Universal. Disney made other arrangements for distribution, with Powers. He would live to regret them.

Meanwhile, Mickey Mouse had arrived; evidently a vacuum existed in the American psyche, and he filled it. Later, analysts would plumb the secret of Mickey's appeal. To some, it was sexual: "Mickey is made out of a series of circles," a Disney artist pointed out. "Circles never cause anybody any trouble. We have bad experiences with sharp points, with angles, but circles are things we have fun with—babies, women's behinds, breasts. . . ." A psychologist had a different take. To him, "The symbolic meaning of Mickey's figure is obvious. Symbolically, we should have to call it a phallus but a desexualized one. Mickey's actions and adventures demonstrate his lack of genital interest. His audience feels that, and although he remains a mouse and a phallus, he does not stir up wishes which have to be suppressed and consequently he does not rouse anxiety."

E. M. Forster would have none of this. The novelist surprised everyone by offering a commentary on his favorite screen star: "There is a scandalous element in him which I find most restful. Mickey is everybody's god, so that even members of the Film Society cease despising their fellow members when he appears." Whether he was everybody's god or not, Mickey was certainly Disney's Aphrodite. "I love Mickey Mouse more than any woman I've ever known," Walt was to testify, and the declaration included his mother, his sister, his wife, and his daughter. Others were less awed by Mickey—at least at the beginning. The Fleischers simply regarded him and his inventor as formidable rivals, the new ones to beat. The Sullivan studio hardly gave Mickey a second thought. After all, the London Film Society, the sort of group mentioned by Forster, had been quite blasé about the new batch of Disney films. They might be "superior in fertility of invention," but the personality of Felix "is no doubt more individual than are those of the protagonists of Mickey." Why worry about the Mouse, when the Cat was still in the lead?

*   *   *

Felix earned enough for Pat Sullivan to destroy himself in high style. In the late twenties, he drank and womanized to excess, strayed mindlessly, and paid almost no attention to the studio that had made him a millionaire. In his place, Otto Messmer tended to business; he not only directed the Felix cartoons, he drew a comic strip based on the Cat's adventures. This represented a reversal of the customary routine of comic strip into film, evidenced by Mutt and Jeff, the Katzenjammer Kids, Krazy Cat, and half a dozen others. Sullivan, who was never too big to pick up the small change, saw to it that the Felix comics were signed in his name. Visually, the Sullivan studio films retained their elegance; the feline hero paced and capered against high-contrast black-and-white backgrounds, breaking into pieces and reassembling himself, traveling in space, using props in ways no one had ever thought of before. In "Felix Trifles with Time," he spots the sign "478 Miles," removes the open figure "4," and makes it into a chair. The "7" becomes a pipe. The "8" is flipped sideways and turned into a pair of spectacles. A similar use of numbers would not be seen again until the drawings of Saul Steinberg thirty years later.

The deteriorating situation at Sullivan's was recorded, perhaps unconsciously, in Messmer's story lines. One after another of the films show Felix in a drunken state or troubled by a mate who resents the hours he spends away from home. From the cartoons and the gossip he heard around town, Walt Disney got wind of what was going on in Messmer's life and offered an escape. "He begged and he pleaded," Otto remembered. "But my home, family, and roots were in New York. And besides, it looked like Felix would go on forever." Messmer and Sullivan were not the only ones to be deceived. Felix had just inspired another popular song, this one made in America: "There's a cat, a fuzzy creature. In the movies he's a feature / He's some Cat. All the kiddies and mamas, / say that he's the cat's pajamas. . . ." And when

RCA tested its first experimental television camera, the engineers chose to beam a crude but highly recognizable image: a picture of Felix, sent from New York to Kansas City. But these were souvenirs, not harbingers. Sullivan, in a haze of alcoholism most of the time, shrugged off the implications of "Steamboat Willie"; damned if he would switch to sound, with all the concomitant expenses and details. His distributor, Educational Films Corporation, sensed the worst and neglected to renew Sullivan's contract. He was forced to lay off his staff, with the exception of the indispensable Messmer. Then, sometime in the early fall of 1920, light broke through. Sullivan signed a deal with a new producer, he rehired some of the artists and placed an ad in the October 16 issue of *Film Daily*. It showed Felix preparing himself for a new career in talking pictures. He paraphrased the words of Al Jolson in *The Jazz Singer:* "You ain't heard nothin' yet."

What audiences heard was worse than nothing. Disney carefully matched sounds to pictures. The orchestral arrangements for the Felix cartoons, as well as the dialogue, were put in afterward. The unsynchronized music was amateurish, and Felix's ill-chosen voice grated on the ear. Messmer's assistant, Hal Walker, stated what the others dared not express: "Felix was doomed because he was a silent pantomime character." The Cat was not alone; Chaplin was never the same after 1928, nor were Buster Keaton or Harry Langdon or Harold Lloyd or any of the other comic icons of the period. Voiceless, they expressed volumes; equipped with speech, they were obsolete. Nevertheless, Sullivan kept promising more and greater Felix films, bluffing the public, the press, and himself. One of the last films, "Felix the Cat Woos Whoopee," had an eerie premonitory quality. After a night on the town with females and liquor, Felix weaves his way home, helplessly drunk. The street wobbles beneath his feet; a dainty lamppost metamorphoses into a dragon; a winged elephant pursues Felix down the street. When the Cat finally arrives at his destination, he places his tail

in an umbrella stand and tiptoes upstairs, only to be revisited by hallucinations. He pummels a pillow, mistaking it for a hostile chicken.
Mrs. Felix awakens and boots him out of the house.

The following year, Sullivan was hit with a series of blows. Felix
became a has-been; his fan mail dwindled and no distributor wanted to
touch him. Everyone was talking about Mickey. Sullivan's health
began to fail. He relied on his unhappy wife to help him get through
the painful days, but she was no steadier than he. On a Saturday in
March 1932, Marjorie Sullivan leaned too far out the window of her
second-floor apartment at the Forrest Hotel on 49th Street. Was it suicide? No one could be certain. According to the *New York Times* obitu-
ary, Mrs. Sullivan had simply attempted "to attract the attention of her
chauffeur" when she lost her balance and fell to earth. Without exactly
contradicting the newspaper account, Walker offered evidence that
things were not quite as they appeared. "Pat was an alcoholic and a sex
maniac," he said. "He was taking some of his money and financed a
madam, put her in business in one of the famous hotels in New York
City and had quite a stable of females. It was quite natural that he
developed a very bad case of syphilis, which he then gave to his wife.
On a trip to England, it erupted so badly on her body she had to wear
specially designed scarves to cover her face and neck." Whatever the
arrangements and sorrows of the Sullivans' fifteen-year marriage, Pat
fell apart after Marjorie's death. By the end of 1932, banks were refus-
ing to cash his checks to Messmer because the signature had been
reduced to an indecipherable scrawl. In his final days, he failed to recognize his trusted employee. On February 13, 1933, an old man of
forty-eight, Sullivan died of "chronic alcoholism" and "terminal lobu-
lar pneumonia." Messmer had to sue for his last two weeks' wages, a
sum of $400.

As the Depression settled in for a long stay, close to a third of the country found itself on unemployment lines. And yet most Americans, no
matter how abject their circumstances, managed to scrape up enough
to attend a movie once a week. For their twenty-five cents or less, they
expected coming attractions, a newsreel, a travelogue or documentary,
and a cartoon. Disney was not the only studio to supply the animated
shorts, it was merely the best. Business picked up for lesser-known
outfits like Van Beuren and Lantz. Bigger operations, among them

Warner Bros.' animation unit and the Fleischer studio, flourished in this time of economic misery. Paramount Pictures had agreed to finance and distribute the Fleischer product, giving Max the security he had longed for. He became a paternalistic employer, radiating confidence wherever he beamed his omnipresent smile. When rumors circulated about the insolvency of the place where he did his banking, for example, the producer simply withdrew his funds and opened an account at an institution across the street. His employees copied him, standing in line at the old place, cleaning out their accounts, and following Max's footsteps. The animators conveyed so much cash they had to carry it in their hats.

Car-Tunes, the bouncing ball shorts, were now accompanied by their own sound tracks and supervised by yet another Fleischer brother, Louis. The studio's new series, Talkartoons, showed little improvement over the silents. Their characters and backgrounds seemed drab compared with Disney's; the music, based on such public domain songs as "There's No Place Like Home," was stale and ineffective. Then, for the third film in the series, Max whimsically fished Bimbo out of the Inkwell and started a chain of happy accidents. In *The Fleischer Story,* a diverting family history, Leslie Carbaga points out that Bimbo was meant "to become the Fleischers' Mickey Mouse, whose footsteps he never quite succeeded in following." One reason was his inconsistency: In some films, Bimbo was white, in others, black. On some occasions, he acted like a dog, on others, like a man in a fur costume. Still, the canine had his moments. His name derived from common argot, meaning, according to the *Crowell Dictionary of American Slang,* "A man, esp. a strong or tough man; 'These bimbos once helped pluck a bank.'. . . Dashiell Hammett, *Blood Money.*" Oddly enough, the word shifted to mean a promiscuous female just about the time Bimbo made his reappearance. But Max left no doubt about his dog's sexual preference. In an early cartoon, Bimbo is out for a drive in his sporty automobile. He spots a zaftig young woman, jiggling as she roller-skates along (the Fleischers were to pay close, not to say obsessive, attention to the female bust in succeeding films). In hot pursuit, he exceeds the speed limit and finds himself in traffic court. There he becomes the movies' first singing dog, pleading his case in song, playing a banjo, executing a few dance steps, and getting away without so much as a warning from the judge.

In the sixth Talkartoon, Bimbo was introduced to the lady who would change his life and enter the American vocabulary. Her original animator, Grim Natwick, a Hearst veteran, remembered that she "started out as a little dog with long ears, but the rest of her was extremely feminine, and she did a rather swinging dance in the first picture ["Dizzy Dishes"] which no dog could have done." After a few more appearances, "the long ears developed into earrings, and she was nothing but a cute little girl." On the debit side, the subject possessed neither chin nor neck; her catalog of assets included large round eyes, fashionable spit curls, an abbreviated skirt, a garter, a saucy figure, and an air of provocative naïveté. The studio called her Betty Boop, and after some false starts equipped her with the voice of Mae Questel, a singer-comedienne with an ability to ad-lib. She needed it. As the Disney studio made an art of recording dialogue and then creating the cartoon, synchronizing lip movements to the sound track, the Fleischers went in the opposite direction. Their films were shot first, then a "post-synch" session was organized. Actors watched the screen, inventing lines to fit the situations, much as jazz musicians played riffs

within an established melody. Questel soloed with a squeaky voice reminiscent of Helen Kane, the original "Boop-boop-a-doop" flapper of the Roaring Twenties. Audiences found Betty endearing; animators had other words for her.

A deep cynicism pervaded the Fleischer studio during its Betty Boop period. Seamus Culhane, then a promising newcomer to animation, spoke of the old days in a candid memoir. Every Saturday night a group of cartoonists "gathered for a weekly bout of sex, drinking, and bridge with a bevy of whores from a local bordello. Monday mornings were always the time for box scores of the previous weekend's exploits—alcoholic, sexual, and bridge playing—with an extra fillip of stories about the seamy side of Harlem. . . . When women were thought of in terms like 'quiff,' 'snatch,' and 'gash,' a la Studs Lonigan, there was no possibility of a story being written where Betty Boop used her charms in a light, flirtatious manner. Betty was a 'good' girl with a hymen like a boiler plate, and her sex life would never be more than a series of attacks on that virginity by unpleasant characters with heavy hands."

This is too harsh. Several Betty Boop cartoons had a curious and eerie brilliance. For all their lack of technique—no film could compare favorably with the most humdrum Disney work—they offered a cascade of visual and musical astonishments. The artists who animated "Bimbo's Initiation," an early effort, were clearly influenced by German Expressionism. (Natwick had in fact studied painting in Germany for two years.) Bimbo is out for a walk when a big-eared mouse, bearing an ominous resemblance to Mickey, steers the dog to an open manhole cover. He plunges underground, and finds himself in an Orphean underworld. Naked humanoids, with beards but without genitals, demand: "Want to be a member?" With each refusal, Bimbo is subjected to a bewildering new torment: an upside-down room, a door that promises escape but leads to further terrors, an immense knife that licks its chops in preparation for a stabbing, a bicycle that sets fire to Bimbo's pants. Exhausted, he agrees to become a member after all. A hooded humanoid accepts the surrender and removes his costume—revealing Betty Boop beneath it. A few seconds later, Bimbo finds himself surrounded by a roomful of Betty Boop clones.

None of this makes much sense today, nor did it when the cartoon was released. The story line is simply a succession of effects in the improvisatory Fleischer style. What gives it distinction is a strange undertow of melancholy—hardly the usual component of thirties cartoons—as well as a menacing palette of dingy backgrounds and looming shadows. Film historian Leonard Maltin suggests that this sort of film should be called cartoon noir, and he has a point. The genre of moody postwar features also have stark intimidating backgrounds, and they take place, like many black-and-white Fleischer cartoons, in an underworld of insecurity and dread. "Snow White," released in 1931, is even more fitting as a candidate for the genre of cartoon noir. Its six minutes contain the oddest footage ever to come out of Fleischer's studio, an onslaught of images and gags far beyond the children—and the adults—it was supposed to entertain. In the title role, Betty Boop is made to suffer a list of indignities ranging from bondage to suspended animation in a block of ice. Her enemies include cold weather, for which she is underdressed, a wicked stepmother, and a pageant of grotesques.

The weirdest cast member, Ko-Ko, is transformed into a ghostly singer with an insubstantial body and the sinuous voice of Cab Calloway. Ko-Ko moves with unaccustomed ease because his dance steps are actually Calloway's, Rotoscoped for the occasion. Ko-Ko/Calloway becomes the nouns he sings about, in the style of the bouncing ball shorts. During "Put a $20 gold piece on my watch chain," he becomes a coin; a mention of booze and he turns into a bottle of whiskey, then consumes himself like a snake eating its own tail. The dwarfs are harmless grotesques with no individuality, a flaw that Walt Disney would correct in his version of the tale some seven years later. Snow White's true helpers are Ko-Ko, restored to his old self, and Bimbo, who challenges the stepmother when she metamorphoses into a dragon and pursues the trio. Facing Betty's nemesis head-on, Bimbo takes hold of her tongue and pulls it so hard she turns inside out and goes into reverse, running in the opposite direction. Dog, clown, and the heroine celebrate in the snow. Fade out. Once again, logic eludes the Fleischers; Snow White's strength lies in the ethereal quality of its scenery and backdrops. Skeletons, icicles, furniture, playing cards, dice—almost every inanimate object seems to be touched with life. Infused with gray magic and an eccentric humor, the film proved too elusive for its audience; all the same, Betty Boop remained a star with her name above the title.

Still, she was at her best in modern dress, eluding predatory males. In the exemplary "Boop-Oop-A-Doop," Betty is cast as a circus bareback rider set upon by the slavering ringmaster. He runs his hands up and down her legs, massages her bosom, and asks the customary question: "Do you like your job?" Betty responds with a song: "You can feed me bread and water / Or a great big bale of hay / But don't take my Boop-Oop-A-Doop away." After a dramatic rescue, the heroine assures her audience that she remains Boop-Oop-A-Doop intacta. Although Betty's origins were never specified, the Fleischers left no doubt that she was a nice Jewish girl from New York. In "Minnie the Moocher," Betty's parents are immigrants with vaudeville accents, and Jewish in-jokes are scattered throughout the cartoons. In one, a speedometer is printed in Hebrew; in another, Betty imitates Fanny Brice's Yiddish intonations; in still another, a talking ape identifies a meal: "Ah, gefilte fish!" As lighthearted as these references were, they called attention to an urban scene that was defiantly, maniacally Eastern. The Fleischers and their staff were thumbing their noses at Hollywood, the new locus of show business activity. As Ann Douglas demonstrates in *Terrible Honesty*, her fever chart of New York in the twenties and early thirties, the city had lost its grip. "Hollywood was beating Manhattan to the punch . . . as the entertainment moved more and more of its branches West, it spelled the end of the city's position as curator and instigator of the nation's culture." As part of the proof, *King Kong*, the big hit of 1933, made New York an unfeeling range of stone and steel, the killer of noble animal spirits. More proof could be found at the bottom of the bill. The big Depression of finance, and the little depression of lost authority, were to be found in the dialogue as well as the lines and grit of Betty Boop's adventures. Let others move to the suburbs and chase the sun; she still lived in the Big City, with its crowds, its crime, and its melodies.

Like the backgrounds and props, like New York itself, Betty's wardrobe had a mind of its own. Garments opened up or flew off when she least expected it to reveal her bra, panties, and signature garter. After half a dozen films, she became the obverse of Paramount's other star comedienne. Mae West made herself into a living cartoon: a mocking, powerful demimondaine, flaunting her sexuality well past the point of self-parody. In each film, she went under a different name, but the character never varied. West's double entendres issued from a woman who knew her way around: "A hard man is good to find"; "When I'm good I'm very good, but when I'm bad I'm better"; "Everybody knows I do my best work in bed." When Betty Boop said any-thing, it was likely to be vacuous: "I guess the people who moved out don't live here anymore." She was reliant on masculine rescuers, and wholly unaware of her appeal. Yet her films could be just as outrageous as anything in West's repertoire. Because the Fleischers loved jazz, they hired outstanding performers to enrich the sound tracks. Cab Calloway's Hi-De-Ho numbers were only suggestive; Louis Arm-strong made no compromises. He gave gravel voice to the couplet: "You gave my wife a Coca-Cola / So she'd let you play on her vagola / I'll be glad when you're dead, you rascal you."

What linked the Misses Boop and West was the emphasis on sex, innocent and otherwise. In their costumes and contours, both women expressed the emerging spirit of the thirties. Gone was the fashionable, flat-chested silhouette of the previous decade; *Vogue*'s April 1932 issue informed its readers, "Spring styles say CURVES!" And Formfit, maker of women's underwear, announced the "Boneless Duo-Sette" that "beautifully accents the uplift bust." With this unabashed cele-bration came an increased attention to the female body; too much attention according to the Episcopal Commission on Motion Pictures and the Catholic bishops who founded the National Legion of Decency in order to contain the lasciviousness they saw and heard at the movies—particularly from the Paramount stars. They were joined by religious leaders of all faiths, and, in terrified response, the Holly-wood rulers came forth with a new Code of Production. This was far more specific than the one they had used in the twenties, before the age of dialogue. Among the precepts: "The institution of marriage and the home shall be upheld. Pictures shall not infer that low forms of sex relationships are the accepted or common thing. Scenes of passion should not be introduced when not essential to the plot. Excessive and lustful kissing, lustful embracing, suggestive postures and gestures, are not to be shown. Indecent or undue exposure is forbidden. Sex rela-tionships between the white and black races is forbidden."

The new code had a galvanic effect in Hollywood. Walt Disney was newly perceived as the unblemished midwesterner who made good, the apotheosis of good clean fun. Mickey Mouse and all his brethren were elevated to heroic status. No rutting took place on Walt's farm, no jazzmen corrupted his sound tracks. Although Mae West's movies had helped to save Paramount Studios, its executives made sure that her personality, her scripts, and even her titles were toned down. West's third film, *It Ain't No Sin,* was renamed *I'm No Angel.* Some wag said it should have been called *It Is a Sin.* Her colleague, Betty Boop, could not go it alone in New York. The studio made her over into a demure coed. Bimbo was replaced by a saccharine puppy, Pudgy, and Ko-Ko gave way to Grampy, a kindly tinkerer whose inventions were a cross between the devices of Rube Goldberg and Max Fleischer. Calloway and Armstrong disappeared from view and hearing.

Along with sex, a good deal of spirit vanished from the Fleischer studio in the mid-thirties. Producers and animators knew they had to accelerate in order to keep up with Disney, and yet they kept looking in the rearview mirror, nostalgic for the way things used to be. What the Fleischer staff felt was akin to the emotions of Charlie Chaplin on the complicated set of *Modern Times,* his protest against the new age of movie machinery and sound: "We used to go into the park with a stepladder, a bucket of whitewash, and Mabel Normand, and make up a picture." In a letter to Culhane, Max abandoned gags for a moment, and argued against the zeitgeist. "It was, and still is, my opinion that a cartoon should represent, in simple form, the cartoonist's mental expression. In other words, the 'animated oil painting' has taken the place of the flashiness and delightfulness of the simple cartoon. In my opinion the industry must pull back. It must stay in its own back yard of the 'Cartoonist's Cartoon.' " That backyard was not much of a place now that the Code was in full operation. Even so, Max refused to go to California, or to go respectable, Disney style. A cast of loopy humans had been making a splash in the Hearst papers, and Fleischer expressed an interest in transferring the Thimble Theater to film. "You know," he told an associate, "this is a nutty little creature, but I think I could do something with it. I think I could make a cartoon of this." King Features agreed with him, and several months later Betty Boop welcomed Popeye in a cameo role. Before the thirties were out, Betty and her garter had retired, and the walk-on had become a superstar. Max had found a way to fight the Mouse after all.

CHAPTER FOUR

THE WILDER SHORES OF COMEDY

International film star, principal character in a comic strip, hero of a popular song ("I'm the guy they call little Mickey Mouse / Got a sweetie down in the chicken house"), he was recognized and admired wherever he went. Yet the income from Mickey's cartoons never seemed to keep pace with his fame. Walt examined the figures, shook his head, reexamined the figures, worked up his courage, and confronted Pat Powers. The distributor refused to let him see the official records. With good reason: He had been keeping two sets of books, one for the Disneys, the other with the real earnings. For the second time, Walt's farm-boy innocence had done him in. As he looked back, the intrigues of Charles Mintz now amounted to petty theft. For Powers had not just siphoned off thousands of dollars, he had lured Ubbe Iwerks away, using Disney profits to set up the animator in his own studio.

Advisers told Walt and Roy that suing Powers would be a long, prohibitive process. Their company maintained its solvency, and the demand for Mickey cartoons was undiminished; why not push on without a backward glance? The Disneys reluctantly agreed, conscious that advancing without Ubbe was going to be like driving without a carburetor. It was a bitter thing to contemplate; the best and most industrious technician in the business had also been the most loyal. How had Ubbe been persuaded to leave? Walt demanded. As usual, he ignored the evidence under his nose.

Back in Kansas City, Ubbe and Walt had briefly set up shop as Iwerks and Disney. Although Ubbe's name was no longer on the official letterhead, the men remained as close as brothers—closer, Walt had been led to believe. After all, Roy could scarcely draw a straight line, whereas Ubbe had designed Mickey, worked ungodly hours without complaint, and had drawn practically every frame of the first cartoon to make full use of classical music. It was called "The Skeleton Dance," and despite Walt's doubts about the commercial possibilities of a graveyard ballet, the first of the Silly Symphonies had become a surprise hit. The reward for all this labor? An exchange between Walt and his wife presents some damning evidence: "Really, Walt," Lillian was heard to remark, "you shouldn't be so rough on that poor little man. The way you treat him! The things you say to him! Sometimes you're so rough on him, he looks as if he could kill you." "Nonsense," came the reply. "Ub doesn't mind criticism from me. He knows me too well to get mad with me. He's the most understanding character in the world. He'd do anything for me." Ubbe did not understand. For the last several years, he had felt humiliated and resentful. A mollifying word from Walt, an effort at inclusion might have rescued the situation, but these were not forthcoming.

Some forty years later, Ubbe's son Dave remembered the fuse burning short. My father, he said, "felt overlooked and underappreciated at Disney. He'd begun as a partner and was now an employee. When Powers gave [him] the chance to start his own studio, he jumped at it." Second to jump was Carl Stalling, the Kansas City musician who had given Disney shorts their distinctive sound. Of all the wounds Disney was to receive in his career, these may have cut the deepest. The defection of the animators a couple of years back had actually been a disguised blessing; their replacements proved to be quick learners, happy to trade a steady paycheck for anonymity and compliance. Iwerks and Stalling were different. They had been headliners on their own, praised by the boss in scores of newspaper stories. That generosity of spirit would no longer apply. From here on, only one name would appear on the company product. Walt Disney—the man who no longer drew pictures, who neither composed nor wrote scripts—would take the primary credit for everything.

Backed by Powers, Iwerks relinquished his 20 percent interest in the Disney company for $2,920. (This misdeal belongs in the same category as the sale of Manhattan for $24; today, the stock would be worth upwards of half a billion dollars.) He was only too happy to do it at the time; Powers had convinced him—and himself—that Walt could not push on alone. Within a year or so, Disney would go under, leaving the Iwerks studio as the powerhouse of American animation. The distributor had made several miscalculations. No one ever doubted Iwerks's gifts, but he possessed none of Walt's flair or commercial instinct. Seamus Culhane, who had left the Fleischer studio to join Ubbe in Beverly Hills, found his new overseer "to be colorless. He lacked showmanship." Furthermore, "by himself he was not a good gagman." One film, Culhane recalled, featured an eight-cylinder automobile motor. Ubbe "came over and looked at his drawing, took it away from me and added about 10 or more cylinders, chuckling to himself as he drew, and then he walked off smiling. It dawned on me . . . whoever heard of a car with 18 cylinders? An Iwerks joke!"

Alliteration was very much in vogue just then (Betty Boop, Mickey Mouse, Ko-ko the clown), and the Iwerks studio debuted with a character called Flip the Frog. After several episodes, Powers complained about Flip's anatomy. Iwerks took away the webbed feet and redesigned his amphibian to be more appealing in appearance and personality. Nothing helped. Flip had large eyes and a wide mouth, was dressed in well-tailored clothes, and moved with jaunty humanoid steps. Iwerks drew sharply delineated backgrounds. Stalling filled the sound tracks with an infectious ragtime beat. What the series lacked was coherence or consistency. Sometimes Flip talked; in other cartoons, he remained mute. He could be shy, then he could turn around and ogle anything in skirts. Iwerks's nonmechanical gags suggested stale burlesque routines. Flip flirts with a pretty housewife. When she hears her spouse at the door, she hides the frog. The husband barges in and suspiciously levels a pistol at the closet door. "Come out or I'll shoot," he warns. A line of men exit single file, including a butcher, tailor, and iceman. Stereotypes abound: When Flip seeks to have a facelift, he studies a group of masks. Each one speaks to him, the black face in rubber-lipped Negro dialect, the prissy face in an effeminate manner as the other masks lisp "Whoops, my dear!" In "Office Boy," one of the best-drawn cartoons, a mouse crawls in and out of a secretary's undergarments, and when a cat pulls her skirt off much is made of the lady's wiggling derriere. One or two Flip films have an intriguing premise. "The Bully" patterns itself after a Chaplin two-reeler about boxing. But Flip makes an unappealing protagonist, and his fight sequences are mistimed and excruciatingly unfunny. In "Movie Mad," the frog forces his way into a film studio—and then finds nothing comical to do. Ten years before, Otto Messmer had used the same idea for the classic "Felix in Hollywood."

In all, Iwerks made thirty-seven Flip the Frog shorts. They were produced under the best possible conditions: Powers did not stint on budgets, and Metro-Goldwyn-Mayer distributed the cartoons. Flip failed to win a following anyway; he turned out to be the wrong animal by the wrong animator at the wrong time. Iwerks replaced him with an alliterative human, Willie Whopper, a boy with a hyperactive imagination. In his first appearance, Willie conjures up Babe Ruth, and marches in a ticker-tape parade with the Sultan of Swat. During his liveliest adventure, "Stratos Fear," the youth receives an overdose of painkiller at the dentist's office. Hallucinating, he floats in a vision of outer space, meets mad scientists, watches a cow metamorphose into bottles of milk and a chunk of cheese, and confronts musical instruments that play themselves. Willie abruptly returns to earth, awakening in the dentist's chair. "Now *you* tell one" is his punch line.

With all its smooth movements and modern backgrounds, the cartoon looked backward to the images of Little Nemo. But film audiences had moved beyond dreamscapes, and Willie faded out after a year. "Ubbe kept trying to clap with one hand," says Chuck Jones, who began his career as a cel washer in the Iwerks studio. "He was a mechanical genius with hardly any comic timing, a brilliant executor of other people's notions, but an unoriginal idea man." Given all these failures, Ubbe made no attempt to cut back. He still nourished ambitions to produce cartoons in color, to invent a way of creating three-dimensional effects, to rival Disney as a major force in animation. The Iwerks studio continued to release work under Powers's auspices and, when that arrangement ended, through a series of independent distributors. Ubbe and Walt were not finished with each other as rivals and colleagues. But the films made outside of Disney's orbit were never to prosper on their own. The animator's present status can be found in video catalogs. A reel of Ubbe Iwerks's little movies is listed under the title "The Cartoons That Time Forgot."

A universe of talking animals and rubber-hose humans had little use for true life and none at all for politics. The Depression sat outside the cartoon farms and jungles and dance halls until Walter Lantz dared to introduce a pinch of reality. Since his days in New York, Lantz had written gags for Mack Sennett, replaced Disney as director of the Oswald series, and then entered animation history by directing the first full-color talking cartoon. It served as prologue to the Universal musical *King of Jazz*, caricaturing the star, bandleader Paul Whiteman, in the role of a white hunter who tames a lion by playing a violin. Whiteman's singing—voiced by a young Harry Lillis "Bing" Crosby— does the rest. Soon the entire jungle undulates to jazz. An enthusiastic monkey crowns the stout bandleader with a coconut. The bump swells into the shape of a coronet, making Whiteman look as regal as he sounds. Lantz's comic approach showed little improvement over the next three years. Then again, subtlety was never his strong point, and his schedule was hardly conducive to personal or professional growth. Universal demanded thirty-six Oswald films a year. Under enormous deadline pressure, neither director nor staff had time to think things through. Oswalds went into production without scripts or storyboards; Lantz pinned the subject of the current cartoon on a bulletin board (winter, toys, pirates), and animators were invited to contribute gags as they went along. Fred "Tex" Avery, the ebullient figure who was to become one of the most influential cartoon directors at Warner Bros., retained sharp memories of his days with Lantz. "You could just say, 'Well, a fellow goes over there and he lights a candle, gets a drink of water, and stumbles over the cat.' You'd tear off a bunch of sheets and give it to an animator. You didn't know whether you were going to have a thousand-foot picture or a five-hundred-foot picture." Finally, in 1933, Lantz made "Confidence," the one Oswald film destined to find its way into the history books. As Oswald settles down on his poultry farm, a ghastly black-robed figure rises from a nearby swamp. The apparition carries a label meant to freeze the marrow: Depression. Oswald's hens stop producing. Banks fail. The stock market plunges. The troubled rabbit consults his physician. Dr. Pill advises him to get a second opinion. "*There's* your doctor," he announces, proudly indicating a picture of Franklin D. Roosevelt. In Washington, rabbit and president confer. F.D.R. croons an optimistic song of hope and hands Oswald a hypodermic loaded with the secret ingredient, "confidence." Back on the farm, Oswald injects his hens. They resume production. The bank reopens. The economy recovers and so do the people and animals. Sunlight floods America.

That year, Walt Disney produced a cartoon on the same subject, and a comparison of the two films shows the difference between the energetic journeyman and the inspired professional. Walt had been musing about the tale of the ferocious wolf and the hog triplets who build houses of straw, wood, and bricks. The staff worked out some sequences, but he was not sure whether to proceed until he toured the studio with one of his favorite actresses, Mary Pickford. Walt stopped by the desk of a musician and inquired, "Why don't you do that 'pig' thing for Mary?" That "pig thing" was the prospective theme song of "The Three Little Pigs." Composer Frank Churchill ran through the song, "Who's Afraid of the Big Bad Wolf?," backed by his collaborators, story men Ted Sears and Pinto Colvig, later known as the voice of Goofy. The trio waited for Pickford's response. "If you don't make this cartoon about the pigs," she said to Walt, "I'll never speak to you again." Serious production began a few weeks later. Like Iwerks and Lantz, Disney relied on ethnic stereotypes to establish character. Calling upon the pig with the brick house, the wolf dresses in a black gabardine coat, a round hat, and a long white rabbinical beard. He speaks with purling villainy, in an unmistakable Yiddish dialect. This caricature was expunged later; Walt's anti-Semitism, born in the Midwest and inflamed by problems with Hollywood executives, would manifest itself in other ways, offscreen.

Besides its theme song, the cartoon had two key assets. First, it was in color, thanks to a special arrangement with the owners of the Technicolor process. Second, and more significant, it had three highly individual heroes. "Walt had made some previous cartoons in color," says Chuck Jones. "He'd even won an early Academy Award for one of them: 'Flowers and Trees.' But 'The Three Little Pigs' was the breakthrough. Until then, animated films followed the form of the silent comedies. Small creature, good guy. Big creature, villain. Cute was enough to get you by. Personality animation—characters who may look alike, but who react and move very differently from each other—begins with this little movie."

"Pigs" opened in May at the Radio City Music Hall in New York. The first response was far from encouraging. "In fact," Walt stated in a memoir, "many critics preferred another Disney film, 'Father Noah's Ark,' which was released about the same time. I was told that some exhibitors and even United Artists considered 'The Pigs' a 'cheater' because it only had four characters in it. The picture bounced back to fame from the neighborhood theaters." Audiences made "Who's Afraid" their unacknowledged national anthem, a rallying cry against despair and economic misery. President Roosevelt let it be known that "Pigs" was his favorite film, a sprightly restatement of his aphorism that the only thing America had to fear was fear itself. Just as the first reception took Disney by surprise, so the second wave of enthusiasm also found him unprepared. No one had bothered to produce sheet music. Arrangers, forced to copy the tune in darkened movie houses, rapidly scribbled the notes by flashlight and transcribed them for big bands around the country. Virtually every major publisher put in a bid; Roy selected Irving Berlin's company, and watched the song climb to first place by the end of the year. "The Three Little Pigs" was booked for a week in New York, and got held over for a month, then another month, then another, playing with various full-length features that came and went. At one movie house, the manager put whiskers on a poster of the pigs. The longer the cartoon stayed, the longer the whiskers grew.

In *The Disney Version,* Richard Schickel argues that Walt actually intended "Pigs" to be a conservative film, that its perspective is "more of Hoover than of Roosevelt . . . stressing self-reliance, the old virtues of solid, conservative building and of keeping one's house in order." But a third interpretation is as valid as the public's or the biographer's. As America foundered, Walt's company flourished as never before. His notion of depression seems to have been rather more personal than fiscal. It was only after an interval of a decade that he could speak about his severe tailspin following the business with Powers and Iwerks. "I couldn't sleep" during that period, he confessed. "I reached the point where I couldn't even talk on the phone without crying. I was in a highly emotional state." Lilly had suffered two miscarriages, and when Roy's wife gave birth to a son, Walt felt all the more inadequate. Harry Cohn provided the last twist of the knife. The head of Columbia Pictures had been distributing Disney cartoons since the Powers affair. In the early thirties, for reasons known only to him, he cut back on budgets and went out of his way to be unpleasant. Director Frank Capra remembered that Cohn "cruelly and stupidly badgered and bulldozed" Walt. Hoping to regain his balance, Walt took Lilly on a cross-country trip. They visited the nation's capital, headed south for

Florida, boarded a ship to Cuba, and then cruised five thousand miles from Havana to Los Angeles. By then, Walt appeared to be fully recovered. At the first anniversary of "Pigs," Walt's employees saw a new boss, financially secure, the owner of a big Tudor house with a pool and a gardener. He had taken up polo and played at an exclusive club with Spencer Tracy and Will Rogers. "If you didn't look too closely," said one member, "with that trim mustache and slicked-back hair, he looked like a Spanish grandee aboard his favorite mare." Walt had at last become a father, of Diane Marie. He had worked out an arrangement with United Artists, giving him greater profits and larger budgets. His characters were licensed to a merchandiser. Money came in from Mickey and Minnie dolls, watches, plates and buttons, sold in every dime store in the United States. Yet all this was not enough. He put the shoats through their paces in three sequels: "The Big Bad Wolf," "Three Little Wolves," and "The Practical Pig." This time the reception was cool and stayed cool, leading Walt to conclude, "You can't top pigs with pigs." Well, what could you top them with? his staff wanted to know. Together, he, the animators, and the story department came up with Donald, a choleric duck; Pluto, Mickey's pet dog; and the dim-witted Goofy, a creature with a canine head and a human body. All met with success at the box office.

And still Walt acted like a man with sand under his skin. At one point, he dictated his feelings about animation and sent them to one of his most respected employees. Don Graham, a college-level drawing instructor, had been hired to elevate the style of Disney's artists. His classes in anatomy and perspective were held five nights a week, amounting to a postgraduate art school on the studio premises. But Walt wanted something more, and in page after page he outlined his aims and objectives. Those who considered Disney an instinctual rather than analytical leader were disabused when they got a look at the memo. "It wouldn't be bad," he began, "if you made up a list of the qualifications of an animator in order of importance. The list would start with the animator's ability to draw; then, ability to visualize action, breaking it down into drawings and analyze the movement and the mechanics of the action. From this point, we would come to his ability to caricature action—to take a natural human action and see the exaggerated funny side of it— to anticipate the effect or illusion created in the mind of the person viewing the actions. It is important also for the animator to be able to study

sensation and to feel the force behind sensation, in order to project that sensation. Along with this, the animator would know what creates laughter—why do things appeal to people as being funny. I am convinced there is a scientific approach to this business, and I think we shouldn't give up until we have found out all we can."

This appetite for knowledge had no limits and no end. The more Walt goaded his workers, the harder he drove himself. After the initial euphoria and recovery, financial and critical recognition seemed in some strange way to deepen his insecurity, as if the rewards could all be taken away again. Just as the Disney name began to enter the American vocabulary, Walt's staff began to notice a new, restive quality about the man in the corner office. He set up a series of regulations, including a no-drinking-on-the-premises rule—and proceeded to violate them behind closed doors. Walt seemed to act in inverse proportion to his company; the more it prospered, the more peremptory he behaved. On the occasion of his thirty-fifth birthday in December 1936, the studio animators threw Walt a large party on the company soundstage. Someone set up a screen, and ran a homemade reel of Mickey Mouse and Minnie caught *en flagrante delicto*. Embarrassment and then genuine laughter greeted the film. When the lights snapped on, Walt stood up and applauded along with the crowd. Who did the terrific parody, he asked. The perpetrators identified themselves. Walt's smile dropped. "You're fired," he told them, and stalked out. A veteran commented that "it was as if they had made a film of his child being violated."

For the next couple of birthdays, Walt kept himself busy, working on new projects, involving himself in every step of production, from storyboard to final editing. Notes from a conference about a new Goofy cartoon show Disney's role in the storytelling process.

> WALT: What do you do—just come down on a pair of eyes? Maybe you come to a close-up—here's these eyes, still in the dark, and a match is struck—then reveal the elephant and the Goof. The Goof is lighting a pipe. Then, from that, let the lights come on . . . and get bird calls: *caw, caw, caw,* all kinds of funny sounds. What were you getting on that silent spot? Try twigs breaking down now and then, etcetera. Let an echo follow the roar. Then, after that, nothing but silence—a twig could snap here and there. To get silence you need contrasting things to create suspense, a few little sounds to make it sound silent.

And all this was still not enough to divert his energy. Walt kept searching for something new, something big enough for the Disney name and strong enough to support a feature film. Rip Van Winkle? Too old a protagonist. Alice in Wonderland? He had already squandered too much time with *that* young lady. He spent months pondering a classic. It had already been done by the Fleischers—unsuitably in his opinion. He would make the Disney version, the world's first full-length animated movie. Later, he remembered every step of the creative process, from the printed page to the shooting script to the first sketches to the final film. "I had sympathetic dwarves, you see? I had the heavy. I had the prince. And the girl. The romance. I thought it was the perfect story."

If Walt missed the two Kansas City veterans, Hugh Harman and Rudolph Ising, he seldom spoke about it. And the defectors make no reference to Disney—except in their work. The felicitously titled Harman-Ising Co. joined forces with Leon Schlesinger, a onetime producer of silent movie title cards. Theirs was a canny choice. Schlesinger had invested money in *The Jazz Singer,* a risky business in 1929, and the Warner brothers never forgot his act of faith. Jack Warner agreed to distribute Harman-Ising cartoons, as long as Schlesinger produced them. With this incentive, Harman and Ising fashioned their own animated star. According to Ising, Bosko, the Talk-Ink Kid, was neither human nor animal, "just a character with a Southern voice."

"BOSKO"

HUGH HARMAN-RUDOLF ISING
PRODUCTIONS
—
5653 HOLLYWOOD BLVD, HOLLYWOOD, CALIF.

Apparently, Ising was the only one who failed to recognize a Negroid caricature when he produced it. Bosko and his girlfriend, Honey, were not only black of face and limbs, they were voiced by actors who wore theatrical blackface while they read the script. Animators attended the recording sessions, studying the performers' exaggerated lip motions.

For their extraordinary catalogue raisonné, archivists Jerry Beck and Will Friedwald viewed every Warner Bros. cartoon ever made. They succinctly describe the typical Harman-Ising production as one in which "the characters are cute, the humor is gross, the visuals are uninhibited, and the music is red hot." Actually, in appearance and intent, Bosko was no grosser than the rest of thirties popular culture. Amos 'n' Andy set the tone in the burgeoning medium of radio. No matter how tastefully and sympathetically conceived, these "darkies" spoke lines written—and performed—by white men. Amos, Andy, and the fellow members of their lodge, The Mystic Knights of the Sea, lived in a different world, segregated by law or custom, communicating in a dialect meant to amuse the condescending listener ("Ah denies de allegation and Ah resents de alligator"). It was no wonder that virtually every animation studio followed their example.

The small Van Beuren company in New York briefly offered Tom and Jerry, a duet of cartoon humans. Airborne, the pair speak without inflection until they fly over Africa. Just before they land they put on blackface and chorus, "Ah sho' am glad to see you again!" In "Meller-drammer," a 1933 short, Mickey puffs away at a cigar-shaped stick of dynamite. It explodes, giving the Mouse a comic blackface. To underline the gag, Mickey and Minnie proceed to offer highlights from "Uncle Tom's Cabin," and dance to the strains of "Dixie." Their supporting cast, Pluto and Clarabelle Cow, also have burned visages, big lips, and exothalmic eyes. With Bosko, Warner Bros. inaugurated its new cartoon series, an obvious imitation of Disney's Silly Symphonies. Like Mickey and Minnie, Bosko and Honey also acquired a pet dog, Bruno. Unlike them, they spent an inordinate amount of time with comic bromides. In early Looney Tunes, blacks are cannibals or shoe-shine men or watermelon-consuming, jazz-loving simpletons; Italian immigrants go about the city streets as organ grinders with monkeys, Chinese laundrymen chatter inanely, Mexican saloons are filled with *borrachos* or overrun with roaches. In a lumberjack comedy, effeminate axmen chop down willowy saplings and beak-nosed Jewish lumberjacks cut their trees like salamis.

If this were all the Warner Bros. cartoons had to offer, they would long since have joined Iwerks's films on the back pages of video catalogs. But in the mid-thirties, the studio broke away from business as usual and took a path divergent from Disney's. Walt was the ultimate hands-on leader; Leon Schlesinger preferred to administrate from afar. He considered himself—rightly—a canny financier, and left the creativity to others. They did not disappoint him. Looney Tunes, with Hugh Harman in charge, became the venue for continuing characters. In the early thirties, the Tunes were joined by a new series, Merrie Melodies, designed to show off songs from the Warner Bros. musicals. The composers, of course, were delighted with this display window. The animators chafed under the rule, because it wrecked their timing. Decades later, one of them spoke of his overriding frustration: "We'd have a great story going along, but then we'd have to stop and have the singing."

Nevertheless, the two series provided work for dozens of artists and story men, and for a group of emerging directors. Most of them got their first break when Harman and Ising grew weary of fighting Schlesinger for bigger budgets and higher standards. In 1933, the team walked out of Warner's. With them went some fine animators and, more significantly, Schlesinger's only star. The following year, Bosko appeared under the MGM logo. Warner's was left with nothing but the names Looney Tunes and Merrie Melodies, and the signature line, "That's all folks." Schlesinger wasted no time in rancor or self-pity. He took over a Warner Bros. building on Sunset Boulevard, opened his wallet, and approached Disney and Harman-Ising animators with the promise of larger salaries and greater opportunities. Friz Freleng responded favorably, as did an ambitious young director named Robert Clampett. On Freleng's recommendation, Schlesinger hired a comic strip artist from Kansas City, Ben "Bugs" Hardaway. Several restive Disney hands were also persuaded to switch sides. Schlesinger had great hopes for his studio's initial effort, Buddy, although Clampett pronounced the bland little figure "Bosko in whiteface." Buddy came equipped with the requisite girlfriend, Cookie, and the compulsory dog, Towser. Unfortunately, the animators failed to endow him with charm or humor. After two years and twenty-three cartoons, Warner's realized that Buddy and Co. had risen without a trace, and forced them into early retirement. But during the course of those years, Schlesinger's artists and story men had edged into the territory Disney abandoned. As Walt brought animation closer to his ideal, "the illusion of life," they reclaimed the wilder shores of comedy, a place the screwball and the iconoclast were to call home.

With all its creative freedom, the Schlesinger studio still lacked an essential: its own star. In the great Hollywood tradition, his first appearance came and went without notice. The cartoon was entitled "I

Haven't Got a Hat," directed by Freleng. Along with many Fleischer cartoons, it aimed to be the animal version of a Hal Roach "Our Gang" comedy. The members of the cast included the twin puppies Ham and Ex; a shy little Kitty; a hardbacked Tommy Turtle; a bespectacled and haughty Oliver Owl; a surly black cat, Beans; and a broad-beamed Pig. "When I was a kid," explained Freleng, "I had two playmates—a little fat kid called Piggy and his younger brother, who was called Porky. I always wanted to do a comic strip with two kids with those names. But in animation everything is animals, so when I had this classroom cartoon I thought of Porky."

The scene is a rural classroom. In turn, each animal performs a number or recites a poem, with disastrous results. No turn is more agonizing than Porky's. Thrust onto center stage, the pig stutter-starts "The Midnight Ride of Paul Revere." Pure terror takes over; before he has completed one poem he switches to another, stammering verses of "The Charge of the Light Brigade." The twins sing the title song in falsetto harmony; Oliver plays the piano; a kitten does "Mary Had a Little Lamb" and forgets the color of the lamb. The bovine schoolmarm offers a hint, tossing a handful of breakfast cereal into the air. The kitten gratefully responds: "Her fleece," she tells the class, "was white as cornflakes." Other gags follow, including a battle between Oliver and Beans. All the characters are funnier than the pig, and by all rights any one of them should have made the big time. But only Porky did.

The reason, to everyone's surprise, lay in his disability. To supply Porky's voice, Freleng had chosen a real stutterer. The bit player "would begin to recite, but then he'd get stuck. He just couldn't get off certain words. We were recording on film at the time, and the film was running, and I figured, boy, if they find out how much film I used just to make a cartoon, they'll kick my ass off the lot." The kick was never applied because viewer reaction was better than anyone dared to hope. Recalled Clampett: "The audience at the same time laughed at and felt sympathy for Porky Pig. He was our first full-fledged star." Porky gained weight and acquired a piggy-bank slot down the middle of his back in his second film, "Golddiggers of '49." He also gained a new director, Tex Avery, who had just come on board, bringing with him a fresh sensibility. In addition to artistic problems at the Lantz studio, Avery had suffered from some vicious horseplay. An animator had made a catapult out of a rubber band and paper clip. The clip hit Avery full force, permanently destroying the vision in his left eye. Instead of ruining his career, the injury seems in some strange way to have enhanced it. Being half blind, argues biographer Joe Adamson, "would seem to be a serious handicap to an animator, but there are many occasions when an Avery character's apparent weightlessness or two-dimensionality is made to add to the comic effect."

Eccentric visuals comprised only a portion of the director's arsenal, and not the biggest one. As Avery's nickname indicated, he hailed from Texas. Much of his humor, visual and textual, derived from the exaggerated folktales of the West and Southwest. Jim Bridger, goes one of them, was riding a ridge in Yellowstone when his horse stepped off a cliff. The mountain man expected to fall to his death on the rocks below, but the horse merely trotted across the gulch in midair. Why? "That's just the wonder of it—the *laws of gravitation* was peetrified!" In "The People, Yes," Carl Sandburg spoke of a man so tall he had to get on a ladder to shave himself, a voyage so cold the captain's shadow froze to the deck, railroad trains so fast they arrived at the station before the whistle. And Mark Twain captured the spirit of the age with the riff of a riverboat blowhard: "I scratch my head with the lightning and purr myself to sleep with the thunder! When I'm cold, I bile the Gulf of Mexico and bathe in it; when I'm hot I fan myself with an equinoctial storm; when I'm thirsty I reach up and suck a cloud dry like a sponge; when I range the earth hungry, famine follows in my tracks!"

This broad, extravagant style showed in almost everything Avery touched. Other studios—particularly Disney's—would have found the director too special for their tastes. Schlesinger sensed that his new man might revitalize the studio and allowed him unprecedented liberties. Avery treasured the day his boss told him, "I've got some boys here—they're not renegades, but they don't get on with the other two crews. They're not satisfied working with the people they're working with." Among the dissatisfied were Chuck Jones and Bob Clampett. "We worked every night," said the Texan. "Jones, Clampett, and I were all young and full of ambition. My gosh, nothing stopped us! We encouraged each other, and we really had a good ball rolling. I guess Schlesinger saw the light. He put us up in our own little shack."

That obscure cottage had a couple of drawbacks: it was old and occupied by insects. The new group hunkered down, cheerfully referring to their new home as Termite Terrace, and worked away. Schlesinger,

Avery gratefully noted, was wise enough or lazy enough not to interfere. "He didn't disturb us. We were all alone out there, and he knew nothing of what went on." With no one hovering over their shoulders, the crew redesigned Porky, slimmed him down, gave him bigger roles and better scripts. As they went along they found themselves reinventing animation. In their cartoons, natural law was not merely suspended, it was expelled. Young Porky blows the family's last dollar on weather pills from a traveling salesman. Furious, Papa pig jettisons the pills. Farm animals anxiously gobble them up: a horse eats Fog, and his fleas report, "No visibility, ceiling zero." A chicken downs Cyclone, with dire results. A goose supplies the happy ending by coughing the Rain pill into the clouds, causing an end to the drought. Fueled with alcohol, cars weave uncertainly along the road. A villain speaks directly to the audience: "Now I'll fix the little pest so he'll be blown to pieces whether you people like it or not." The spirit of Termite Terrace caught on with other Warner animators. In those palmy days, cartoons showed King Arthur coming to life, offered parodies of film and political celebrities from Laurel and Hardy and Edward G. Robinson to Mahatma Gandhi and Benito Mussolini; allowed characters to copy the mannerisms of Groucho Marx, acknowledging the audience with a facial gesture or a wiggled eyebrow. Avery, who claimed no knowledge of thirties expressionist theater, nonetheless used its devices to break down the emotional distance between viewer and performer. "This is an electric eel folks" says a sign in a Porky adventure; a backwoods yokel comments, "In one of these here cartoon pictures, a body can get away with anything."

The animators played with language as well as visual presentation; here were send-ups of "The Petrified Florist," "Goofy-Tone News," "Owl Jolson," "Jack Bunny." In 1936, Schlesinger hired Carl Stalling to compose and conduct cartoon music; from then on, aural wit complemented the visual comedy. Warner's maintained a fifty-piece orchestra. When it was not playing the score for a main feature, Stalling took the podium, underscoring plot points with his arrangements of popular and obscure songs. Under his baton, characters chatted over the melody of "Can't We Talk It Over?," and a leak in the roof was accompanied by "September in the Rain." Late that year, Schlesinger farmed out two Porky episodes to Ubbe Iwerks. Disney's old colleague had fallen on hard times and was glad to get the work. But the years of independence had made him intractable. Even with the aid of Jones and Clampett, who had come along to advise and design, the comedies turned out poorly. The animators returned to Termite Terrace, where a man with no talent for drawing was about to change the shape of Warner Bros. cartoons.

The actors who had impersonated Ham and Ex, Porky, Beans, and the rest of the troupe assumed that oddness was synonymous with hilarity. Mel Blanc disregarded the old squeaky, weird intonations. When he gave voice to an animated creature, it suddenly seemed believable—and all the funnier in comic situations. Blanc, a radio actor with an enormous range, had been hired by Schlesinger's sound effects man, Treg Brown. The performer began by making Porky's stutter a comic device, and yet retaining the pig's sympathetic qualities. A good-bye went, "Bye—b—, uh—bye-b—, so lo—, uh-so lon—, auf Wiede—, auf Wiede—Toodle—loo!" Some fifty years and seven hundred impersonations later, Blanc looked back and commented, "anyone who marvels at how I've earned a living should consider Brown's occupation: shooting off a .45-caliber pistol to achieve the sound of a door's slamming shut, smacking an anvil to accompany footage of a cartoon character getting bonked on the head, or simulating a cataclysmic crash by dropping two armfuls of metal objects from the top of a ladder onto a concrete floor." Incongruity was Brown's specialty, Blanc said, delightedly recalling a cartoon in an operating room. The doctor asks everyone to be so quiet he can hear a pin drop. As expected, somebody drops one. But, "instead of *ping*, Brown whipped up the biggest tumult possible. So in addition to dialogue and sight gags, Schlesinger cartoons contained yet another comic element."

Frank Tashlin supplied the studio's last significant component. A onetime comic strip artist, former gagman to Hal Roach, Tashlin was among the first directors to treat cartoons as cinema. He experimented with montage, top shots, dissolves, and all the other strategies familiar to Cecil B. DeMille and D. W. Griffith. Tashlin grew famous for attending classic movies with a black book and a flashlight, noting down the tricks of the masters, and the ways of Chaplin and Laurel and Hardy. "We used to kid him about his little black book," Avery said, "because he was always looking in it for a joke. Well, the laugh was on us. He went further in this gag business than we ever did." Where Tashlin went was to the big soundstage and live action. "He wrote the Bob Hope picture *Paleface,* and he directed *Son of Paleface* and several other good pictures. What Tash did was to take cartoon gags and act them out live! And that made him a name! And they were real funny pictures." But those projects were almost a decade away. For the time being, Schlesinger's cartoonists stayed where they were, working in discrete units, but constantly sharing plots and ideas in a collegial atmosphere. "It's important to note," says Blanc, "that these weren't teams in the conventional sense, competing against each other. Such communal spirit was vital to Warner Bros.'s success, with no person ever fully responsible for the finished product."

The animators were bound to each other by an abiding affection for their work and a loathing of their common enemy, Ray Katz. Theoretically, Schlesinger's brother-in-law had been hired to take care of the financial end of the business. But he liked to fancy himself an inspector general, often touring Termite Terrace without warning to see what the creative types were doing to earn their livings. Instead of looking busy, in the manner of most office workers, the directors and their allies did just the opposite. Warned by a junior animator every time Katz entered the building, the men of Termite Terrace pretended to be on an extended coffee break. A couple of hours later, Katz would return for another surprise tour of inspection. He would open the door, says Jones, "and find the *same* person who two hours before had been shining his shoes still shining his shoes, the *same* person drinking the *same* Coke, the *same* person reading the *same* page of the *same* newspaper, and so on. If you have ever heard a six-foot blue chicken cluck in bewilderment, you will need no further explanation from me."

Schlesinger was the butt of a longer-lasting joke. The producer's speech defect was most noticeable when he gave instructions on his way to the horse races: "Put in more joketh, fellaths," but no one had ever dared to mock the boss to his face. Then, in 1937, Tex Avery decided to give a new character, Daffy Duck, a fresh voice. An animator suggested the splattery tones of Schlesinger, and Mel Blanc supplied them. "In order to save ourselves the embarrassment of being fired," Jones wrote, "all of us were careful to write our resignations before that fateful day when Leon strode into our projection room. The new Daffy Duck lit up the screen at Leon's courteous command, 'Roll the garbage!' The cartoon played to the studio audience. Then the lights went on and Leon leaped to his feet, glared around: 'Jeethus Christh, that's a funny voithe! Where'd you get that voithe?' "

Throughout his long tenure, Schlesinger gave his staff many reasons for mockery. In exchange for their liberties, he kept a tight fist on all financial arrangements. While Disney allowed budgets of up to $100,000 per cartoon, the Warner Bros. shorts came in at about $9,000. That sum included Schlesinger's profit, skimmed off the top. The only way to maintain quality at Termite Terrace was to make mistakes on the drawing board and not on film. Walt allowed his animators to experiment and reshoot; Schlesinger's crews planned their cartoons down to the last frame, leaving no room for error. It was no wonder that Schlesinger captained a yacht, and that his employees barely had enough to pay the rent. "Our relationship was revealed in a simple question and answer," Jones continued. "I once asked him if we could be guests on his yacht. He replied in his customary tone, 'I don't want any poor people on my boat.' Of course, he was the reason we were poor, but the reply made sense to him, and in an odd way to us. So we kept on working, kept on being poor, kept on having the world's best jobs at the world's worst salaries. I realize that there were equally talented people at Disney, but they were slaving away at art. We were laughing ten, twelve, fourteen hours a day. It never occurred to us that Warner's and Walt were in the same business."

Respectability and Betty Boop were incompatible. Although she continued to appear in cartoons, Betty had joined the long list of fading ingenues, unable to return to the parts that made her famous and unfit for the leading roles that were going to others. The day that Popeye made an entrance in one of Betty's adventures, her career was effectively over; she would not last out the decade. Still, the Fleischer's first superstar deserves a final tribute before she disappears into cartoon limbo. In the coming years, there would be other women in animated films, some of them demonstrating full frontal sexuality and verbal candor. But none will have Ms. Boop's universal appeal. "What Makes Betty Boop?," asks Norman M. Klein in his erudite study of American animation, *Seven Minutes.* He concludes, "She had virtually no facial expressions, except her wink, a look of dismay, and a boop-boop-a-doop. But she was designed very well for movement to music. She could sway very delicately. Her arms and shoulders syncopated much the way performers do when singing on stage. And she was a lovable victim, trapped somehow in her helpless body." We shall not like upon her look again.

Betty Boop had introduced several comic strip characters to film, among them Otto Soglow's The Little King, Jimmy Swinnerton's Little Jimmy, and Carl Anderson's Henry. Somehow, what worked in the Sunday Funnies failed to register on the screen. The members of Elzie Segar's Thimble Theater were exceptions. Popeye soloed in his second film "I Yam What I Yam" (an unconscious but effective restatement of a phrase in First Corinthians), and never looked back. The sailor outfit, the bizarre urban backgrounds, the subsidiary characters: Wimpy the mannerly schnorrer ("I'd gladly pay you Tuesday for a hamburger today"), little Sweepea, the villainous Bluto ("Lower than bilge scum, meaner than Satan, and strong as an ox"), and, most important, the whining, aggressively flat-chested Olive Oyl—all had a timeless appeal. Take away some of the modern props, notably planes, trains, and automobiles, and they could be from the epoch of Winsor McCay.

Even the voices were inspired. After the Fleischers wrangled with the original Popeye impersonator, an in-betweener, Jack Mercer, reluctantly agreed to try out for the part. He croaked on for the next thirty years. Mae Questel leaped from Betty Boop to Olive Oyl without missing a diphthong. She gave Popeye's girlfriend the dithering tone of Zasu Pitts, and her nasal cry, "Paw-poye," became a schoolyard favorite. Paramount delightedly reprinted the press notices: "Popeye the Sailor Man has stepped into a new role. He's a movie star" —*Minneapolis Tribune*. "Popeye gets just as many laughs as do any of a number of well established stars of the stage, screen and radio" —*Milwaukee News*. "Popeye is the funniest cartoon in many years. In fact, the audience thought it was the funniest they'd ever seen. Whoopee! What a guy!"—*Omaha News*. Commercial success followed, with toys, lunch boxes, and pins sold alongside the Disney toys at Woolworth's. The spinach industry credited Popeye for increasing its sales some 33 percent. The farm town of Crystal, Texas, gratefully erected a statue of the sailor puffing on his corncob pipe. Atop his perch he seemed to be the personification of the tough little guy who would not be pushed around, as much a symbol of the belligerent American spirit as the pig who built his house of bricks.

The Fleischers learned their lessons well. Double entendres would have no place in Popeye's world. The hero, heroine, and villain parodied the traits of masculinity and femininity, their remarks sexless, their skirmishes as predictable as a professional wrestling bout.

Calorific jazz also disappeared from the Fleischer cartoons; the only memorable notes were to come from Sammy Lerner's theme song: "I'm strong to the 'Finich' / 'Cause I eats me spinach / I'm Popeye the Sailor Man," followed by shrill toots from a bosun's pipe. Segar's strip had gone for comic melodrama, with plots and subplots stretching over weeks and months. Max Fleischer was out for laughs alone; he rang innumerable changes on one basic story: "I'd have him walk under a pile-driver and the pile-driver would come down and the pile-driver would break and not his head, you see? It's a funny gag, but it establishes the strength of Popeye. Then we get to the Apparent Disaster, where Bluto has got the best of Popeye and Popeye doesn't want to fight. But he can't help it. Now, the audience is ready to push for Popeye, and hoping that he fights back, and when he does fight back, they're right with him."

Because he had taken a "still" character and given him a life in the movies, Max felt compelled to keep the cast of Popeye in constant motion, even when no action was required. Staff animator Myron Waldman called these vibrations "a moving hold," and rare were the children—and adults—who could watch them without fidgeting in their seats. As the years progressed, Popeye calmed down a bit, went from black-and-white to color, and for a time to three-dimensional backgrounds, thanks to one of Max's inventions. The adventures, however, remained as inconsistent as those of the old Inkwell gang. "Be Kind to Animals" is a moral tale; Bluto cruelly misuses his workhorse. A losing battle with Popeye ends with the miscreant in harness and the horse whipping *him.* But neither Popeye nor Bluto win in "A Dream Walking." Both men follow the somnambulistic Olive as she wanders around a construction site fraught with loose girders, triphammers, and other dangers. Eventually, she sleepwalks herself back to her apartment, leaving behind a battered Bluto and a thankless Popeye. In "Never Kick a Woman," Olive catches Popeye flirting with a rival. She downs a can of spinach and, suddenly empowered, gives the sailor a sound thrashing.

When they chose, the Fleischers could be just as perverse as Tex Avery, knocking down the proscenium to remind viewers that they were watching a world of make-believe. In "What, No Spinach?," Bluto corners the spinach market, leaving Popeye helpless. Desperately he cries out, "Is there any spinach in the house?" The camera cuts to a boy in the theater audience. He rummages through his grocery bag, pulls out the desired can, and flips it at the screen. In "Goonland," Popeye battles so furiously that the film snaps, and a human hand is seen splicing the celluloid before the adventure can roll on. By 1937, the Fleischers had reestablished themselves as the preeminent animation studio in the East. Van Beuren, the studio right across the street, was going under; Iwerks had no chance of survival. In addition to Popeye, Fleischers produced Color Classics, a popular series of fairy tales filmed in a somewhat garish palette. Most of these tales reflected the family's early poverty and the boss's benign overview: starving Dickensian children are given a feast; a miser is reformed, thanks to the kindness of the very townspeople he had injured. This was not a candified version of Max's philosophy. He truly believed that a soft answer turneth away wrath, and that his avuncular approach guaranteed a happy staff. Alas, among all the characters his studio had animated, he had somehow overlooked the imp of the perverse. It was one thing to shut out presidential politics and the unpleasant news of war clouds gathering in Europe. It was quite another to ignore the clashes of labor and management that were afflicting American business. At first, Max could hardly credit the rumors of restiveness in his own shop; after all, hadn't he said repeatedly, "Anyone can come into my office with their grievances and/or personal problems and talk directly to me"? Hadn't he taken great pride in the "colored man" he had rehabilitated when a typewriter was stolen? "He said he didn't really steal it. He was in need of money, his wife was in the hospital and it was his intention to return it as soon as he got his pay. I asked him, 'what would you do with you? I leave it to you to be honest about it.' He said, 'I would fire me.' I said, 'I don't want to make things worse for you. First of all I'm going to tell the detective bureau I'm not going to press any charges. How much do you need to get straightened out?' 'About $23.' 'Well, I'll show you the difference between you and me. You would fire yourself and I'm going to try and remake you.' From that time on he would get up on the ceiling to dust, he polished up corners, etc." Wasn't the Fleischer studio continually pictured as cloud-cuckoo land, a place of fantasy and gratified wishes?

But by the middle of the year Max had to recognize that more than a hundred of his employees were discontented—so discontented that they had joined the aggressive Commercial Artists and Designers

Union (CADU). The group was protesting Fleischer's policy of a forty-five-hour week with half-day on Saturdays, no paid vacations, and no sick leaves. Some halfhearted negotiations followed, with no result. Max turned vindictive, and when fifteen union members received their pink slips, a strike was called. On May 8, 1937, pickets ringed the offices at 1600 Broadway. Placards read "I Make Millions Laugh But The Real Joke Is My Salary," and "We Can't Get Much Spinach On Salaries As Low As $15 A Week." Max issued an angry denial: "Inexperienced employees receiving the lowest pay are advanced after a short period to $40, $50 and some as high as $90 to $200 a week." Clashes commenced. A knot of strikers chanted, "I'm Popeye the union man." Fifty workers bought tickets to a show at the Paramount Theater just to razz the Popeye cartoon and yell, "Get that scab picture off the screen!" After thirteen weeks, the National Labor Relations Board intervened, and employees were asked to vote for or against the CADU as their representative. The union won. A final agreement, signed in October, allowed Max to save face. The workers won increases, but in smaller percentages than they had originally demanded. Max retreated to his office, and from then on things were never the same between the owner and his employees. One of them remarked sadly, "The family feeling was gone." It would not return.

Three thousand miles away, a full-length film was being readied for Christmas release. For over a year, people at various studios—including Fleischer's—had referred to it as Disney's Folly. Now Max was not so sure the naysayers were correct. Walt knew they were wrong. They were always wrong; they had been since the days of Oswald. Let them mock; the louder their derision, the deeper grew his faith in *Snow White and the Seven Dwarfs*.

CHAPTER FIVE

MORE HELLS THAN SWEDENBORG

Snow White began in earnest one evening in 1934, when a handful of key animators returned from an early dinner. Walt seemed unusually agitated as he led the men to a soundstage, sat them down in a circle of folding chairs, and acted out a scenario under a single unshaded work light. He "proceeded to intrigue us from eight o'clock until early midnight," said animator Ken Anderson, "acting and telling, even anticipating the songs and the kind of music, and he so thrilled us with the complete recitation of all the characters that he had created that we were just carried away." While most studio personnel continued to produce Mickey Mouse and Silly Symphony cartoons, a contingent of *Snow White* artists and writers set up shop in an office adjacent to Walt's. The preliminary work began: outlining a plot, experimenting with drawing styles, establishing the identities of the dwarfs. Walt submitted an outline suggesting more than fifty names and traits. Among them: "*Sleepy:* Falls asleep in midst of excitement, middle of sentence. *Hoppy-Jumpy:* in constant fear of being goosed but is not goosed until the last scene. *Bashful:* with a very funny bashful laugh, halting delivery, and a way of misplacing the word 'though' . . . *Sneezy-Wheezy—Gaspy:* Asthmatic inhalations and exhalations of every breath . . . *Dapper . . .* nimble dancer—quick movements stopped in mid-air by embryonic sneeze. . . . Always trying nutty cures and diets. *Biggy-Wiggy—Biggo-Ego:* A pompous, oily tongued know-it-all. *Awful:* The most lovable and interesting of the dwarf characters. He steals and drinks and is very dirty."

Walt and the writers went back to the folktale, suggesting embellish-

ments as they laid out a coherent narrative. Some ideas got dismissed out of hand. Audiences would never see Snow White confronting the Morass of Monsters. Or visiting Upsidedownland, where trees dug their branches into the ground and waved their roots in the air. Or reaching Sleepy Valley with "vast poppy fields, slumbrous music from the wind soughing through the trees." That kind of interlude would reach the screen two years later, perhaps coincidentally, in another fantasy by another studio, MGM's *The Wizard of Oz*. In the Grimm version, the Queen makes three attempts on Snow White's life. Her wicked Majesty puts the girl into a bodice so tight she has trouble breathing. Then Snow White receives the gift of a poisoned comb. When these fail to kill, the Queen tempts her victim with an apple; one tiny morsel and Snow White falls into a deathlike trance. Walt rejected the first two scenes—but not without many consultations. A transcript from a story meeting quotes him on the subject of the Queen, transformed into a crone when she visits Snow White in the dwarfs' cottage. "Downstairs she could be building up to the disguise—choosing something so that no one would recognize her. 'Ah, the old pedlar woman!' like she remembers it. . . . 'The pedlar woman—what could she sell? Combs soaked in poison—the hair will stiffen like a board. A corset—lace it tight!' So many people remember those old things from the fairy tale."

As the story department developed the script, artists worked on characterization. At first, the Queen was portrayed as fat and blunt; gradually, she became an object of refined evil with sharp eyes and fingers like the talons of a hawk. Snow White had to be human, yet not so large that she would loom over the little men. The solution was to model her on a real girl—and then render her five heads high instead of the true-to-life six. The dwarfs (three heads high) presented another set of difficulties. *Freaks,* Leslie Fiedler's study of the abnormal, points out that in ancient times dwarfs were "thought of as living underground, either just below the surface of the earth or as deep into darkness as the deepest mine. Dwarfs fuse into the figure of Pluto, the underworld rapist of the ancient Greeks, or are confused with the demons of popular Christianity."

Dickens, a master of demonology, made a lecherous dwarf the villain of *The Old Curiosity Shop.* "This creature," Daniel Quilp says, "appeared quite horrible, with his monstrous head and little body." Even J. R. R. Tolkien, whose sympathetic little Hobbit came out in the same year as Disney's *Snow White,* took note of traditional beliefs. He called dwarfs a "tough, thrawn race, holding a grudge, loving treasure—and for long, enemies of elves and men." In order to conform to such classic descriptions, the seven dwarfs had to possess oversized craniums and small torsos and legs. At the same time, they had to break with the past; Disney wanted them to be unthreatening, capable not only of cheer but love. Character designers solved the problem by creating pawky little uncles along the lines of the Hollywood standbys, Gabby Hayes and Eugene Pallette. Instead of Grimm's faceless homunculi who "delved and dug in the mountains for ore," the Disney dwarfs became miners of twinkling, multifaceted diamonds. The seven names served as labels disclosing the contents within: Grumpy, Sleepy, Happy, Sneezy, Bashful, Doc, and Dopey. All but the last were agreeable to the staff. "Some of those who worked with me," Walt remembered, thought Dopey was "too modern. But I showed them that Shakespeare had used it too, so that took care of the modernism objection. Others felt it would sound as if the dwarf was a hophead. 'That's not the way my mind works,' I told them. 'To me it's the best word I can think of for anyone who's a little off-beat.' " At this stage of his career, Walt tried to avoid yes men; he preferred the company of off-beat artists and thinkers. But such were his powers of persuasion that no one bothered to check the Shakespearean canon, where the words *dope* and *dopey* never occur. The founding father knew best; if Walt made a statement about the Bard, it had to be so.

For three years, Disney oversaw every script line, every gag, every sketch, striving for an idea he could never name. Clearly, Walt knew what he did not want. He examined two sequences, one of the dwarfs eating soup, another of them building a bed for Snow White. He laughed and applauded—and relegated them to the cutting-room floor because, on reconsideration, neither one advanced the plot. Then there was the business of the picture's palette. "I saw a Harman-Ising cartoon about spring last night," he told the staff in 1936. "They got colors everywhere and it looks cheap. There is nothing subtle about it at all. It's just poster-like. I think we are trying to achieve something different here. We are not going after comic supplement coloring. We have to strive for a certain depth and realism through the use of colors—the subduing of colors at the right time and for the right effect, not try to cram everything into every sequence." These visions and revisions proved costly, and late that year word spread through the industry that *Snow White* had more than tripled its published budget of $250,000. Rumors about Disney's Folly began to circulate. "Who'd pay to see a drawing of a fairy princess," demanded Louis B. Mayer, "when they can watch Joan Crawford's boobs for the same price?" Word got back to Walt. Distressed, he consulted Hal Horne, exploitation manager of United Artists. "What should I do about all the bad talk?" the filmmaker wanted to know. "Nothing," Horne told him. "Keep them wondering. Let them call it Disney's Folly or any other damn thing, as long as they keep talking about it."

The talk never stopped, and neither did the bills. Walt had always wanted the illusion of three dimensions in his cartoons. He got it when William Garity, head of Disney's camera department, constructed a device allowing the cinematographer to shoot various planes and levels. In essence, glass panels were painted with backgrounds and characters. As the "multiplane camera" focused on a distant object, the panels could be moved stage right or left to give the appearance of moving *into* the scene. The songs for *Snow White* were written by lyricist Larry Morey, and composer Frank Churchill, whose major credit up to then was "Who's Afraid of the Big Bad Wolf?" Their contributions to the film consisted of nine numbers, several of them excised before the final cut. As individual compositions, none measured up to the standards being set at RKO by the Broadway composers who had come west to work with Fred Astaire. But Cole Porter's 1934 film *The*

Gay Divorcee, Irving Berlin's *Top Hat* (1935), and Jerome Kern and Dorothy Fields's *Swing Time* (1936) had their roots in old-fashioned theater. When the star delivered his number, the comic relief vanished and the action halted. Disney was aiming for something very different, insisting that each song delineate a character and propel the story. His concept was so revolutionary that no one quite understood what was happening. In his definitive *World of Musical Comedy,* Stanley Green observes that "what was unique about [Rogers and Hammerstein's] *Oklahoma!* was the synthesis of its component parts into a complete theatrical entity." He had forgotten *Snow White and the Seven Dwarfs,* presented six years earlier.

Gradually, all the elements started to blend. Animated by several teams, the dwarfs interacted well with Snow White, drawn by another team. The dialogue explained what the drawings could not:

GRUMPY (leaving for work): Now, I'm warning you. Don't let nothing or nobody in the house.
SNOW WHITE: Why Grumpy! You *do* care!

The wicked Queen, animated by two teams, one who drew her when she was beautiful, another when she became a hag, had some of the most poetic moments:

Mummy dust to make me old. To shroud my clothes, the black of night. To disguise my voice, an old hag's cackle. To whiten my hair, a scream of fright. A gust of wind to fan my hate. A thunderbolt to mix it well. And now begin thy magic spell.

Close-ups, trucking shots, pans, all the effects and tricks that Frank Tashlin used experimentally at the Schlesinger studio were polished and refined at Disney. The price of perfection rose each week, and the cries of folly grew correspondingly louder. When the costs edged toward the million-dollar mark, directors of the Bank of America, backers of *Snow White,* let it be known that they wanted a look at the project. Roy arranged a screening for Joseph Rosenberg, the vice president in charge of the Disney loans. Walt was beside himself. "I can't do that," he told his brother. "All I've got is bits and pieces. You know I never like to show anybody a picture when it's all cut up. It's too dangerous." Roy overrode him. "You'll have to. The only way we're going to get more money is to show them what they're lending money for."

And so, on a bright Saturday afternoon, Walt sat in a "sweat box," company jargon for projection room, showing segments of *Snow White* to an impassive banker. Neither the sound track nor the animation had been completed, and Walt filled the gaps with his own renditions of songs and dialogue. Rosenberg watched and listened without comment as the impresario assured him: "You remember that place back there where I had those sketches? Well, before we're through that scene is going to be beautiful." Rosenberg might have been evaluating a wall. He offered no comment, and on the stroll back to his car spoke only of the weather and other inconsequential subjects. Not once did he mention *Snow White.* As he approached the vehicle, the banker shook hands, got in, and rolled down the window. Walt braced himself for the judgment. "That thing is going to make you a hatful of money," predicted Rosenberg, and drove away.

Not many people shared his confidence. At an in-house screening, the staff was asked to submit written comments. One said, anonymously, "Stick to shorts." For years afterward, every time an employee responded negatively to one of Walt's suggestions, he would reply, "I'll bet you're the guy who wrote, 'Stick to shorts'!"—even though there was a studiowide suspicion that the author was Roy himself. Roy had reason to be impatient after three years, and expenses of almost $1.5 million. In the final weeks, Walt put in a request for more cash, this time to fix the Prince's animation. The hero, who never managed to move convincingly, shimmied as he bent to kiss Snow White. "I want to make it over," Walt stated. "How much?" Roy demanded. The price came out to several thousand dollars. "Forget it," said Roy. "Let the Prince shimmy." So he did, and so he does; the footage has never been corrected.

Less than three months before the picture debuted in New York, Gilbert Seldes addressed Walt's greatest fear. In the September 1937 issue of *Esquire,* Seldes reported that he had sat through ten consecutive Disney shorts. "I wanted to see whether you could stand a great quantity of animated pictures without a break." The answer: "I should say that you can. The Disney technique is quite subtle, there are moments of suspense and moments of pure physical beauty spaced in between the great climaxes of hilarity." Copies of the article circulated through the studio and shored up morale—but only for the moment. For just as the film was being readied for its final cut, Disney's distribution arrangements with United Artists came to an end. UA announced that the contract would be renewed on one condition: Walt had to relinquish all rights for his films to be shown on something called commercial television. Walt hesitated. "I don't know what television is," he grumbled, "and I'm not going to sign away anything I don't know about." When RKO came calling, offering to distribute *Snow White* sight unseen, Walt made the deal even though he knew that studio was the least stable of the majors.

At long last, in December 1939, the tinkering stopped. The lawyers and bankers withdrew, the publicity machine paused, and the projectionists threaded the completed movie onto their machines. The houselights dimmed and *Snow White* became a new kind of legend. No hyperbole seemed too extreme to use. More than one critic wrote that Disney's leap from short subjects to this masterpiece was comparable to a sudden vault from the thirteenth century to the fourteenth, when Masaccio found new ways to create the illusion of depth, texture, weight, and expression, leading to the Florentine Renaissance. Analyzing the "profoundly pantheistic vision" in *Snow White,* historian William Paul paid particular attention to the scene of grief-stricken dwarfs around Snow White's coffin. As the little men weep, a large candle in the right foreground of the image slowly drops wax down its side, "the wax drop echoing the dwarfs' tears in both shape and movement as the tears conversely echo the wax drop. In this animated world, nature crying is given parity with human crying. Character, whether human or animal, and setting here are alike, all made from the same material."

With such extravagant appreciations, negative reactions were inevitable. The most pointed was to come from the Freudians, and many years later Bruno Bettelheim officially summed up the case for the prosecution. The very attributes so praised by animators—that the members of the cast are as individual as fingerprints—was what he found most appalling: "Giving a dwarf a separate name and a distinctive personality—in the fairy tale they are identical—seriously interferes with the unconscious understanding that they symbolize an immature pre-individual form of existence which Snow White must transcend." According to this strict (and humor-free) view, "the poet understands the meaning of fairy-tale figures better than a film maker and those who follow his lead in retelling the story. Anne Sexton's poetic rendering of 'Snow White' suggests their phallic nature, since she refers to them as 'the dwarfs, those little hot dogs.' "

Walt ostentatiously shrugged off the crossfire of artists and intellectuals. For years afterward, when the subject of *Snow White* was brought up, he spoke of retaliation rather than psychology or aesthetics. "I met a guy on the train when I was coming out," Disney remembered. "It was one of those things that made you mad. I was out on the back platform— I was in my pants and coat that didn't match but I was riding first class. I was making conversation with a guy who asked me, 'Goin' to California?' 'Yeah, I'm goin' out there.' 'What business you in?' I said, 'The motion-picture business.' Then, all of a sudden, 'Is that right? Well, I know somebody in the motion-picture business. What do you do?' I said, 'I make animated cartoons.' 'Oh.' It was like saying, 'I sweep up the latrines.' Some people make you mad, and you want to prove something to them even though they mean nothing to you. I thought of that guy when we had the premiere of *Snow White*. And then the darn thing went out and grossed eight million dollars around the world."

Actually, it grossed nearly $1 billion worldwide before it was through—if any Disney film can be said to be through. Rereleases, licensing, video rentals, and purchases have made Snow White and her friends more familiar than any ancient tale. Some of Walt's features went on to earn more over the years, but none gave Walt quite the same sense of personal fulfillment. Colleagues could see that he considered the stations of *Snow White* an allegory of his own triumph over cheats and scoffers. Meanwhile, the audiences of the thirties had another metaphor in mind. Just as the three little pigs had been made to stand against the vulpine Depression, *Snow White and the Seven Dwarfs* seemed to echo the approaching war, with its conflict of malignity and decency. Once again, history had become Walt's indispensable accomplice.

"Trend in depth'" is the way a Hollywood wag put it. If someone made a profitable western, as certain as the sunset, a dozen horse operas would clop in its tracks. Comedy, musicals, gangster movies all had their epochs, and now it was the turn of animated features. Max Fleischer was hardly surprised when Paramount, impressed with the grosses for *Snow White,* suggested that he get to work on a full-length cartoon. Universal gave Walter Lantz much the same counsel. Max responded immediately, although not in the way his employees expected. He informed the press that the Fleischer studio would indeed give the public a ninety-minute movie, an adaptation of a favorite book, *Gulliver's Travels*. However, it would not be made in New York. Max would produce the film at Fleischer's new headquarters—in Miami. He knew the territory; Max and his wife had spent many winter vacations down there. To his mind, the virtues of Florida far outweighed the expense of moving twelve hundred miles from Broadway. The state was known to be hostile to unions, raising the odds against labor strife. Better still, a new law provided tax exemptions for Florida's handful of movie studios. Max described the move in paternalistic tones; his workers would be far better off away from New York City, in a land of clean air and perpetual summer. "They need loose clothing," he proclaimed, "so their imaginations can work." The message deceived no one. Those who needed the money or wanted the sunshine came south; those with better opportunities in radio or film, like Mae Questel, remained where they were.

Seamus Culhane, one of the Disney animators who left Hollywood to sign on with Max, found himself suffering from culture shock. Years before, he had worked for the Fleischers in Manhattan. The new place was nothing like the one up north, he wrote. Culhane looked out from an impressive structure with enough space to house seven hundred artists. It had ample and well-kept grounds, a large parking lot, and a commissary. On the other hand, "every week the lawn was cut by a chain gang from the county jail. It was an all-black crew. Stripped to the waist and heavily muscled, they moved languidly about their tasks. An obese white cracker guard sat in the shade, a huge cud of tobacco bulging out one cheek and a double-barreled shotgun cradled against his belly. In the beginning, several kindhearted northerners had made the mistake of offering bottles of cold Coca-Cola to the sweating blacks, but the fat guard had promptly leveled the shotgun and warned them off—a grim reminder that they were now in the Deep South." Lou Fleischer got a further prodding when an old friend, Cab Calloway, paid a home visit. A note was slipped under the door: "Don't have any more niggers in your house." It was signed "The Ku Klux Klan." The days of Betty Boop and New York and jazz were truly over; the time of Gulliver and Miami and mainstream music had begun.

From the time of its publication in 1726, Jonathan Swift's four-part adventure had been enjoyed on two levels: as a fantasy for children, and as an adult satire of human foibles and political institutions. No profit-minded animator could hope to show the author's savage attacks on the Whig party, or on the human race ("a pernicious race of odious vermin"). That left only the lightest and most familiar of the tales, the voyage to Lilliput and its populace of tiny folk. Max wanted to retain some Swiftian bite: The novel, he stated, "shows the smallness of human beings regardless of how great they think they are." His brother, Dave, argued for a treatment that would soothe rather than scrape. He wanted a "Gilbert and Sullivan" approach and gave out the word that "whatever satire remains in our version" would be "thickly sugar coated."

Oddly enough, that approach had already been tried by Walt Disney in "Gulliver Mickey," a 1934 cartoon featuring the Mouse tied up by little humanoids and extricating himself in seven minutes. Max knew that a feature film would need a lot more. In the wake of *Snow White,* a ninety-minute movie required a highly trained staff, memorable songs, a variety of characters, a romance, and a strong narrative line. The studio began well. When the story department first discussed Gulliver, some writers suggested Popeye for the starring role, but Max had the wit to keep the hero a recognizable human being. Using the Rotoscope technique, he had his animators film the movements of a human actor and then draw over them. A subplot, the Romeo and Juliet romance of Princess Glory of Lilliput and Prince David of Blefuscu, would also use live models. All other parts would be taken by cartoon Lilliputians. Ralph Rainger and Leo Robin were hired to write the score. The celebrated Tin Pan Alley team had composed a string of hits, including the theme songs for Jack Benny ("Love in Bloom") and Bob Hope ("Thanks for the Memory"); they looked to be ideal for the job.

The book tells of a conflict between Lilliput and its neighbor, Blefuscu, over the correct way to crack hard-boiled eggs. Blefuscus hold that the fat end should be used; Lilliputians believe in the narrow end. Max felt that Swift's antiwar humor was too literary for the screen; he devised a way to tie up the film's various strands. Instead of arguing about eggs, the King of Lilliput and his archenemy, the King of Blefuscu, would oppose the marriage of their children. When young love persisted, each leader would insist upon using his country's anthem as the wedding's official melody. Gulliver would solve this dilemma by asking for both anthems to be played simultaneously. As the two national orchestras struck the opening chords, the separate songs would blend in counterpoint, causing the royals to rejoice in a rainbow finale. Max and his staff brimmed with similarly sly ideas, and many of them found their way to the screen. The track used two famous radio personalities: Lanny Ross as the singing voice of Prince David and Jessica Dragonette as his Princess. All these ingredients should have added up to a hit on the order of *Snow White*. But in the Fleischers' rush to complete the picture, they ignored several vital components, among them a thoroughly first-rate staff.

In addition to experienced professionals, Max had been forced to employ hundreds of in-betweeners, painters, assistants. He turned to the only source in town, the Miami Art School. "Instructors there tried valiantly to fill the breech," Culhane states. "They scoured the town for anyone who had even cherished the ambition to paint moonlight scenes on black velvet, or burn pictures on coconut shells for the tourist trade." The recruits were given an introductory course, and then hustled onto the production line. A few gifted ones learned their new vocation; most functioned on a barely acceptable level and lowered the quality of the picture. These shortcomings might have been overcome if closer attention had been paid to details. Max was not Walt, however, and he failed to note the underlying reasons for Disney's success. As the film neared completion, he assured a reporter: *"Gulliver's Travels* contains no horror stuff—no evil spirits or creatures to scare the youngsters." This was a reference to the most debated moment in *Snow White,* when the wicked Queen changes herself into a longtoothed, claw-handed, screeching murderess. Some educators and parents objected to this scene, and children were known to hide under their seats when the transformation began. All the same, they loved the dread they could not quite confront. They asked to view the film again, and talked about it so much in schoolyards and playgrounds that eavesdroppers begged their parents to take them to see *Snow White* even if it was scary. What G. K. Chesterton concluded in his classic defense of fairy tales, Walt had grasped intuitively: there was nothing an adult could show that the young had not already run in the skull cinema: "Alone in his bed, a child can invent more hells than Swedenborg."

But *Gulliver's Travels* lacked more than an ability to make the flesh creep. It also failed to make the foot tap. Robin and Rainger produced songs as innocuous as their titles: "All's Well," "Bluebirds in the Moon-light," "I Hear a Dream." The one sprightly number was contributed by an outside team, Al Neiburg, Sammy Timburg, and Winston Sharples. "It's a Hap-Hap-Happy Day" at least had jauntiness and a pleasant melody. With good reason; it was remarkably similar to "Whistle While You Work." The film's visuals were as disappointing as its story—with a few remarkable exceptions: the tying up of Lemuel Gulliver, complete with miniature pulleys, block, and tackle; the antics of an appealing Lil-liputian named Gabby and a trio of inept spies, Sneak, Snoop, and Snitch; the King waltzing with two of Gulliver's fingers. But these were gems surrounded by cotton batting. The film fell between two drawing tables. It was neither as well paced nor as beautiful as the Dis-ney product ("We can do better than that with our second-string ani-mators," Walt scoffed at a screening). Yet the feature lacked the outrageous, hell-bent quality of the old Fleischer cartoons.

Reviews were mixed: "Four stars. . . . That veteran of animated car-toons, Max Fleischer, has transformed the eighteenth-century cartoon into a fanciful animated drawing"—*Liberty Magazine;* "It is far more than novelty that Gulliver lacks, it is the wit, the freshness, the gaiety and sparkle, the sublety, the characterization and for that matter the good drawings that are the trademarks of the Disney factory"—*New York Times.* The public agreed with the judgment of *Liberty.* At the Para-mount Theater in New York, *Gulliver's Travels* played to some fourteen thousand people on opening day—an attendance record. The film went on to set similar records across the country. By the end of the year, it ranked among the top ten in box-office grosses. The numbers looked better in *Variety* than they did on a balance sheet. Production costs out-weighed earnings; Fleischers' fancy new buildings and large staff ate away at the revenues. Even more expensive were the processes of col-oring and editing, correcting the many mistakes, and the mixing of dia-logue and music. With foreign rights, *Gulliver's Travels* might have been lucrative. But there were no foreign rights. Edging closer to war every day, the European and Asian markets shied away from imported cellu-loid. Paramount, the Fleischers' main source of production income, demanded another, cheaper feature-length film. Several writers worked up a scenario starring the gods of Mount Olympus. Dave Fleischer's reaction was, to put it charitably, subdued. After the meeting one of the veterans scratched his head, wondering about what he had just heard.

Who were Zeus, Athena, Apollo, and the others, anyway? "Oh," Dave responded airily, "it's all in the Old Testament."

Eupeptic as always, Walter Lantz announced plans for his own animated feature film. *Aladdin and His Wonderful Lamp* would be produced by Universal for a cost of $750,000. As his skeletal staff prepared storyboards, Lantz played the jackal to Disney. The whole industry, he said, was in Walt's debt. The technical leaps of *Snow White,* the beautiful color and bright story line were exemplary. If only he had fixed the glaring faults. Never mind; Lantz would avoid them in *his* movie. The Rotoscoping of Snow White and the Prince, for instance. All that shimmying and stiffness! It was in direct contrast to the smooth movement of the dwarfs and animals, and nearly ruined the movie. None of that for *Aladdin.* If the Rotoscope was used at all, it would only be for the purpose of timing a sequence. Artists, not cameramen, would rule at the Lantz studio. In one last bow to Disney, Lantz hired Frank Churchill to write the score for his movie. But *Aladdin* never ventured beyond the storyboard stage. The enormous risks, the diminution of the overseas market, and a deep-seated lack of confidence all contributed to the stillbirth. After Lantz scrapped the movie, he pronounced it "too costly, and too much of a risk," and in a veiled reference to the Fleischers he added, "If you miss, like everybody else has outside of Disney, you can take an awful loss on it." Without a backward glance, he cheerfully returned to the medium he knew best, the animated short. For a while, he foundered. Even southern whites found nothing to like in the stories of Li'l Eightball, a stereotyped black boy with a head that matched his name. Other comic characters had similarly truncated careers. Then, almost by accident, Lantz made a cartoon about an unusual mammal. The title, "Life Begins for Andy Panda," parodied the famous Andy Hardy series, starring Mickey Rooney in the title role. The animated Andy, modeled after the Chicago Zoo's latest acquisition, began life as a furry animal. In subsequent films, he put on clothing and acquired a personality. Unfortunately, it was a phlegmatic one, and Andy never developed a comic edge. Nevertheless, he earned his place in the record books: four cartoons after his debut, the panda introduced Lantz's first superstar.

Over the years, Lantz amused his listeners with an account of the creation. On his honeymoon, he claimed, a creature kept banging his bill against the wooden roof every time the couple embraced. "I threw rocks at him but the bird would not go away. I was going to shoot him but there was a law against it." The producer related this incident to his staff—or so he maintained—and together they invented Woody Woodpecker. Actually, Woody appeared onscreen a year before Walter Lantz and Grace Stafford got married. Still, the official version made a good story, so good that it can still be found in many hardcover histories.

In "Knock Knock," Woody's first film, Andy tests the truth of an old wives' tale. Can a bird be caught by sprinkling his rear end with salt? Shaker in hand, the panda pursues the beaky, rufous Woody, who tweaks noses, pecks holes in the house, and makes a general nuisance of himself with his trip-hammer laugh: "Ha-ha-ha-HA-ha! Ha-ha-ha-HA-ha!" It was a sound most children could instantly mimic, to the distress of their parents. All too soon, Woody's peal sounded in unexpected places, including the bebop of Charlie Parker, who used it as a riff in dozens of saxophone solos. As Woody took flight, he seemed an emblem of the age. The Depression and the fear of war had raised the American voice and given it a brassy, nervous edge. It was the day of the gargoyle: Huey Long, the Kingfish of Louisiana, promising "every

man a king, every girl a queen"; Father Charles Coughlin, denouncing Jews as "wily servants of the murderous High Priests of Capitalism," publishing a weekly with news analysis straight from the Nazi World Press Service in Berlin; Father Divine consorting with his bevy of female followers with names like Quiet Love, Merry Light, Joyous Faith; Fiorello La Guardia, mayor of New York, ball lightning in a black suit, chasing fires, reading the Sunday Funnies over the radio, denouncing his own party members: "The average Republican leader east of the Mississippi doesn't know any more about Abraham Lincoln than Henry Ford knows about the Talmud." Abroad, there were the looming figures of Winston Churchill, Joseph Stalin, Benito Mussolini, Adolf Hitler, Emperor Hirohito—every one of them a caricaturist's dream, and each destined to become more familiar to Americans than the selectmen of their own towns.

Filmmakers strained to compete with history; escape in the form of musicals and romances was no longer enough. Audiences had developed a voracious appetite for tales of the unnatural, "an instinct," Edmund Wilson said, "to inoculate ourselves against panic at the real horrors loose on the earth." Vampires, mummies, zombies, and freaks emerged from their hiding places. A second generation of monsters appeared in such films as *Son of Frankenstein* and *Dracula's Daughter.* Fantasy enjoyed a rebirth in the overpowering special effects of *The Wizard of Oz* and *The Thief of Baghdad.* Humor hammered away at logic and propriety. The level of aggression was raised by the Marx Brothers in *A Night at the Opera* and *A Day at the Races,* and in W. C. Fields's salute to non sequiturs and alcohol, *The Bank Dick.* In the deepest sense, these were all protest pictures, but instead of aiming at the usual Hollywood target, social injustice, the objections were lodged against the encroachment of politics and foreign affairs. The little films that preceded the main feature made their own editorial statements. The more harrowing the newsreel, it seemed, the more imaginative the cartoon. Once again, irony made its entry: In a febrile, disintegrating world, animation spiraled toward a Golden Age.

At first, the spirit of Termite Terrace wore feathers. Daffy Duck was the studio's answer to Woody Woodpecker, an annoyance with wings, caroming off the walls, spouting nonsense, "hoo-hooing" around Porky Pig, Elmer Fudd, and other victims. Sometimes Daffy had a wife and children; sometimes he was on his own. One cartoon would find him in the Wonder Pictures movie studio ("If it's a good picture, it's a wonder"); the next would show him in the company of dinosaurs ("Our story is laid in the Stone Age—millions and billions and trillions of years ago—probably before any of you were even born"). This foolish inconsistency fit well with the moment of giddy, prewar jitters. Bob Clampett, who favored a manic approach to comedy, found Daffy an ideal vessel. In "The Daffy Doc," he put him in an iron lung, forcing various parts of the duck to inflate and deflate. In a later scene, Dr. Daffy seeks a second and third opinion. He arranges to get bopped in the head, causing him to see multiple visions of himself. Daffy can then consult with his fellow physicians. "You Ought to Be in Pictures" finds the duck selling out his friend Porky, suggesting to Leon Schlesinger that the studio needs a talented bird instead of an overstuffed ham. The blend of live action and animation is reminiscent of the Out of the Inkwell series. It also suggests the antics of Chaplin and Keaton, whom Clampett had seen rehearsing during his childhood in Los Angeles. Audiences appreciated these energized tours de force— and yet Daffy was not quite the animal of the hour. Neither was Woody. Although audiences found them amusing, these players were essentially vaudevillians in feathers. The early forties demanded a brash new character, someone or something who spoke the lingo of a nation preparing for war.

Strictly speaking, Bugs Bunny's debut occurred in the 1938 cartoon "Porky's Duck Hunt." The rabbit's name derived from Ben "Bugs" Hardaway. The gag writer had advanced the idea of a fur-covered comedian, and the model sheet referred to "Bugs's Bunny." Looking back, however, most Warner Bros. animators refused to accept the claim of Hardaway as Bugs Bunny's true father. According to Freleng, in Bugs's first films he was nothing but "Daffy Duck in a rabbit suit. Bugs Hardaway worked on formula. That's all he knew." It took several years, many directors, and the voice of Mel Blanc before the Bunny developed a stable and coherent personality. But as Joe Adamson points out in his amusing biography of Bugs, the star's origins go further back than Termite Terrace. The rabbit probably derives from "a hare named Zomo," born centuries ago in the folktales of central Africa. Like Anansi, the hero-spider of Caribbean stories, the rabbit is smaller than his opponents but far more capable of sweet talk and devious plans. When Zomo wants milk, he bets some friends that he can get it free. To that end, he persuades a cow that she is stronger than any old tree, and encourages her to knock one down. She charges ahead, and when her horns become embedded in the trunk, Zomo calmly strips her udders and collects the milk and the bet.

Slaves brought Zomo to America with them, combining him with Bro Rabbit, the impudent survivor in Gullah legends, told and retold throughout the black communities of Coastal Georgia and South Carolina. In the New World, Brother (Br'er) Rabbit became a family con man. Now when he tricked the cow, he shared the milk with his wife and children. Joel Chandler Harris heard the accounts of Br'er Rabbit during his boyhood on a Georgia plantation. It was inappropriate for a white man to speak in the accents of a slave, so he set them down in 1880 in the dialect of one Uncle Remus, an agreeable old black man. The sayings of Remus immediately found a place in the American language: "Licker talks mighty loud w'en it gits loose from de jug"; "Youk'n hide de fire, but w'at you gwine do wid de smoke?" Within a decade, Br'er Rabbit's mastery of bullies and tyrants became as familiar above the Mason-Dixon line as they were in the Deep South. Every one of the Warner Bros. animators knew of the little hero who could twist out of the tightest situation and fool the biggest enemy: "T'ain't de biggest en de strongest dat does de mostest in dis world. No, Honey, don't let nobody fool you 'bout dat. De ole elephen' may be strong, de tiger may be servigrous, but Br'er Rabbit done outdone um."

Uncle Remus's most famous tale encapsulated a character and a temperament. Caught by Br'er Fox, the Rabbit begs not to be thrown in a place of needles and thorns—only to jeer as soon as he is tossed there, "Bred en bawn in a briar-patch, Br'er Fox. Bred en bawn in a briar-patch." Half a century later, he was bawn again, this time as a Brooklyn wiseguy, using a carrot as his prop, just as Groucho used his cigar. Eventually, Bugs even echoed Marx's answer to an insult: "Of course you realize this means war!" In "Porky's Hare Hunt," Bugs came into his own. "We decided that he was going to be a smart-aleck rabbit, but casual about it," said Tex Avery. Bugs's opening line was " 'Eh, what's up Doc?' and gee, it floored 'em! They expected the rabbit to scream, or anything but make a casual remark—here's a guy with a gun in his face! It got such a laugh that we said, 'Boy, we'll do that every chance we get.' It became a series of 'What's up, Docs?' That set his entire character. He was always in command, in the face of all types of dangers."

Always in command. That was the way the armed forces liked to think of themselves, and with the war approaching they found a ready mascot. Like Bugs, they were ready to take their street wisdom and make it play on the enemy's turf. Let Elmer Fudd pursue the Wascally Wabbit with his shotgun; Bugs could outrun bullets and outtalk the enemy. Draftees made the Rabbit their unofficial mascot; his likeness sprouted on the equipment of the 385th Air Service Squadron, on the first Liberator Bomber aimed at the Philippines, on every vessel of the Motor Torpedo Boat command. Other animated figures turned up on the noses of bombers and on the sides of jeeps. But they lacked Bugs's flippant style. The GIs knew it, and so did the Hollywood studios. A Disney animator remembered being "especially jealous of how funny the Warner Bros. cartoons were" during this period. "We thought: 'All this personality stuff isn't really funny. It's cute and people kind of chuckle at it, but Warners cartoons get *laughs.*' " As the islands fell to the Japanese, and Hitler's troops sliced through Europe, laughs took on a special importance. Comedians made small fortunes, and even fictional characters took on a special kind of reality. When Chuck Jones was introduced to a little boy as "the man who draws Bugs Bunny," the child refused to accept the Rabbit as a figment of ink and paint, script and voice-over. "He does not," came the angry denial. "He draws *pictures* of Bugs Bunny."

As a national archetype, Walt Disney belongs in the pantheon alongside Thomas Edison and Henry Ford, inventive, prickly, bent on success at any cost, self-absorbed, rooted in America's heartland. And yet his early features not only originated on foreign soil, they were created in countries that were setting out to destroy the United States. *Snow White* had German origins, and Walt's second full-length feature, *Pinocchio,* came from Italy. For all of Walt's patriotic fervor and drumbeating, he suffered from the disability Henry James identified as "a superstitious valuation of Europe." It took him many years to find a local product worth animating, and even then he kept returning to the Old World for inspiration. The possibilities of Carlo Collodi's story had intrigued Disney ever since he came across the work in a bookstore, and in the late 1930s he assigned a team to explore the project.

Pinocchio was overlong; the author had been paid so many lire per word and he had been in no hurry to reach the last page. Then again, he did more than mark time in his narrative; like many storytellers of his time (1826–1890), Collodi was fond of terror and pursuit. Bad boys are turned into donkeys and their hide used to make drum skins; Pinocchio's carelessness and naïveté often result in the injury of others, including a talking grasshopper who tries to lecture the marionette and gets flattened underfoot for his trouble. Walt set out to change the picaresque and rambling tale, and to make a masterpiece in the bargain. Still smarting from "demeaning" references to *Snow White* (to him, the film was "no more a cartoon than a painting by Whistler is a cartoon"), Walt wanted his second full-length movie to be purely and simply a work of Art. That did not stop him from sweetening the narrative. The boy-puppet of the book would no longer misbehave with gross irresponsibility. He would be naughty, but no more than that. And he would move with a more human gait; that way, the audience would be able to identify with the lost little hero. Reluctantly, the animators went along with Walt's revision.

"Pinocchio started out more like a real wooden puppet," recalled animator Ollie Johnson, "but Walt looked at the footage and felt the character needed to be more appealing; so he became more like a real boy, with more squash and stretch in his movements. We would have animated the movements of the character differently, which might have been interesting." Following some frustrating story conferences and early experimental footage, Walt informed his staff that the protagonist was still unlovable. The kid needed a conscience. To that end, the grasshopper was not only revived and made into a moral guide, he became the film's narrator. Ward Kimball was put in charge of the insect, now transformed into Jiminy Cricket. The original character design had equipped Jiminy with toothed legs and antennae. Walt vetoed it. "I ended up," said Kimball, "with a little man, really, wearing spats and a tail coat that suggested folded wings; he looked like Mr. Pickwick, but with no ears, no nose and no hair. The audience accepts him as a cricket because the other characters say he is."

Prodding, wheedling, driving his staff on, Walt demanded longer hours and finer work. The pressure around the office grew so great that the artists sought all sorts of relief. Hard liquor became a staple, and this time Walt affected not to notice the too-hearty laughter and the slurred good-nights. Improvised football and croquet games, complete with tiny wickets, became a way of working off tensions; so did occasional showings of blue movies. Practical jokes, a favorite pastime at Termite Terrace, finally came to Disney. One of the animators, Bob Moore, remembered that time: "Our studios were all in a row, connected by a series of doors, and I was in the very last office in the row. So one day another artist came into my room while I was working. I heard this hammering and I turned around to see him putting up a small target on my far wall. I didn't think anything of it. Then, pretty soon, I hear this thud. There's an arrow sticking in the target. He and another animator were shooting a bow and arrow through all these doorways into the target. Somebody could have been killed. You needed to have a white flag on a stick if you wanted to get out of your room." Walt Kelly, who later abandoned animation to create Pogo, one of the most popular comic strips in the world, watched a fellow animator who had a knack for throwing his jacket across the room onto a coatrack. When the man stepped out for a liquid lunch, Kelly ingeniously sawed the rack into dozens of small pieces, then lightly glued them together so that the seams were undetectable. When the victim returned, he tossed the garment in the usual manner—and swore off liquor when the rack shattered like tower of dominoes.

Between and around the monkeyshines, Disney got what he wanted, a compelling script and an extraordinary cast of villains, saviors, and supporting players. On Pinocchio's journey from tree limb to human being, the boy encounters his saintly sculptor, Geppetto; a conniving fox, J. Worthington Foulfellow, and his henchcat, Gideon; Stromboli, the overbearing puppeteer; an innocent kitten, Figaro, and his playmate, the goldfish Cleo; a juvenile troublemaker, Lampwick; Monstro the Whale; and Pinocchio's ultimate rescuer, the Blue Fairy. He visits the purgatorial Pleasure Island and plunges into the ocean only to be swallowed by a leviathan. Walt goaded his artists: "Mountains have gotta look as if you could climb 'em, houses as if you could walk in the front door and find something cooking on the stove in the kitchen, and when we get to the whale sequence, the seas must look real wet and cold and deep and salty. As for backgrounds, they've gotta jolt the audience as never before." Disney's staff did not disappoint him. The sketched, painted, and airbrushed color had an unprecedented subtlety and richness. The detail was exquisite; models of clocks and toys from Geppetto's shop were based on working models, carefully constructed so that the animators could copy every gear and spring. The songs of Leigh Harline and Ned Washington were standouts; two of Jiminy's numbers, "When You Wish Upon a Star" and "Give a Little Whistle," voiced by Cliff Edwards (Ukulele Ike), made the charts. Most of the critics raved; the *Times* found it "the best thing Mr. Disney has ever done," and the *Herald Tribune* said *Pinocchio* was "a compound of imagination and craftsmanship, of beauty and eloquence, which is found only in great works of art." The one truly negative voice came from Paolo Lorenzini, Collodi's nephew. He demanded that the Italian Ministry of Popular Culture sue Walt Disney for libel; the filmmaker had portrayed Pinocchio "so he easily could be mistaken for an American." The objection was not unfair, but nothing came of it. Benito Mussolini had other things on his mind just then, and so did Franklin Delano Roosevelt.

That was just the trouble. The Fleischers and Walter Lantz were not the only ones to suffer from the vanishing foreign market. In Disney's case, the results were not merely disappointing, they were catastrophic. *Pinocchio* lost millions, and by then Walt had committed the studio to new projects. For the first one, he turned to the founding rodent. Mickey had come down in the world since his heyday in the mid-thirties, when his cartoons accompanied Walter Houston and Mary Astor in *Dodsworth* and Luise Rainer and Paul Muni in *The Good Earth*. Other stars had come along, and these days Mickey played the role of straight mouse to Donald Duck and Pluto. To stop the slide, Walt cast him in "The Sorcerer's Apprentice," built around the program music of Paul Dukas. This, too, was a German tale; Goethe had written it 150 years before. The role of the prankster who loses control of inanimate objects was rich with comic possibilities, and they could be played in pantomime (Walt suspected that Mickey's falsetto grated on the modern ear). The film was nearly completed when Disney ran into Leopold Stokowski at a Hollywood restaurant. Without any preamble, the conductor burst out, "I understand you are doing 'The Sorcerer's Apprentice.' I would love to do it for you. I will do it for nothing."

The monetary part of Stokowski's offer was false. But his affection for cartoons was genuine, and it gave Walt a chance to reposition "Apprentice." Made for $125,000, the cartoon was too ambitious for a short, and too short for a feature. But what if it were to be part of an anthology of classical pieces? And what if Stokowski were to conduct them all? And what if Disney were to mix live and animated footage so that Mickey Mouse and Leopold Stokowski were to shake hands? Once more the Disney factory thrummed. Walt, whose previous interest in classical music was minimal, spent hours listening to recordings of the Greats. In the end, seven other pieces were chosen for animation alongside "Apprentice": The "Pastoral" Symphony ("This'll *make* Beethoven," Walt was supposed to have predicted); Ponchielli's "Dance of the Hours"; Bach's Toccata and Fugue in D Minor; Tchaikovsky's "Nutcracker Suite"; Stravinsky's "Rite of Spring"; Moussorgsky's "A Night on Bald Mountain"; and Schubert's "Ave Maria." The result was a singular mélange—"Disney's Sacred Monster," as John Canemaker puts it, "and the strangest fusion of grossness and genius in the history of film." *Fantasia* ("Fant-ah-*zee*-ah," Stokowski called it) has elements of racism (in the "Pastoral" sequence, a black centaur acts as servant to the white ones); moments of hilarity (hippos and crocodiles perform a ballet to Moussorgsky's melodies); imaginative paleontology (dinosaurs rise and do serious battle in the Stravinsky portion); monumental character design and scenic composition (the Moussorgsky episode) and mawkish sentimentality in the Shubert finale.

On this occasion, the critical reception was not so kind. For every adherent there seemed to be a passionate and famous enemy. Frank Lloyd Wright loathed it. Dorothy Thompson used her space in the *Herald Tribune* to call *Fantasia* "a brutalization of sensibility." The collapse of the civilized world was imminent, she warned, and the impetus for the collapse was being "given by the very persons and groups most certain to be destroyed with it." As such, "*Fantasia* is a social symptom worth this column's recording." Igor Stravinsky objected on aesthetic grounds. How dare this Walter Disney, this *cartoonist*, edit "The Rite of Spring"? But didn't the maestro like the pictures? he was asked. Stravinsky gave a withering reply. "I say nothing about the visual complement, as I do not wish to criticize an unresisting imbecility." Worse still was the voice of the box office. Serious classical music devotees thought the film light-headed; mass audiences found it too longhair. *Fantasia* had cost $2,280,000, and there was no hope of breaking even, much less of earning a profit. No long lines appeared at theaters, and Walt looked in vain for new attendance records. Counting

the two flops, plus the cost of the Burbank studio, Disney currently owed $3 million to the banks, and they were about to freeze his credit. Walt began to exhibit the old tendencies to fly off the handle and cry easily. Lillian remembered the days of his breakdown, and suggested an out-of-town trip. For his part, Walt just wanted to work on his next projects. He assigned a unit to proceed with *Bambi*—another German story—and to film a semidocumentary tour of his studio, mixing live footage of Robert Benchley with stretches of animation. *The Reluctant Dragon* was for amusement purposes only; there were to be no technical breakthroughs, no spellbinding villainy or romances. It was as if Walt was calling time out, resting up for the next big battle. There was one coming, and it would not occur on screen or at story conferences, or even with the banks. The conflict was going to be Walt and Roy versus their employees, and like the bigger war outside, it would elicit the highest principles and provoke the ugliest behavior.

CHAPTER SIX

LAUGHING AT THE ENEMY

Back in the troubled days with Pat Powers, Disney employed the services of Gunther Lessing, Esq. The lawyer had been a soldier of fortune in his younger days, and Walt liked his style. Over the next decade, Lessing rose in Disney's estimation by tilting contracts in favor of his client, obtaining quantity and quality for the lowest possible costs and warning employees about the dangers of the New Deal. "You would have thought he would be a liberal-minded guy, having once worked for Pancho Villa," mused Ward Kimball. "Not Lessing! Even though many of us were politically mature enough to see how corny Lessing's doomsday rantings were, there were those genuinely frightened by his implied threat that if we did not see things his way we would not have our job at Disney." If anyone doubted Walt's resolve, he only had to look at the case of Ub Iwerks, once Disney's closest associate, who had dared to go out on his own. The venture had not been a success, some mutual friends intervened, and Ub paid a call on Walt. Disney was magnanimous; he welcomed back the most inventive animator in Hollywood—on stringent conditions. From here on, Iwerks would be an employee, nothing more. No stock, no participation in licensing rights, even on inventions he might produce for the studio's technical research division. Walt would pay Ub's outstanding debts; for that favor he demanded unwavering loyalty.

Yet there were those who refused to bend to Walt's will. They knew that no individual could win an argument with Disney, but collectively they had a chance. The power and membership of trade unions had grown exponentially since the Depression, and labor leaders had faced down the owners of sweatshops, mills, and mines. Now they were throwing their weight around in the Dream Factory, and many a Hollywood studio was experiencing problems with workers, ranging from the twenty-five-cent-an-hour carpenters to the high-priced picketers of the Screen Actors Guild. Disney was next on their list. Up until 1940, Walt had managed to keep peace with his employees, partly due to Lessing's glowering lectures, but mainly because Walt encouraged the staff to think of him as a father figure—autocratic, perhaps, but familiar with each face, willing to listen to professional grievances or personal problems. In addition to the idea that he and his staff were an extended family, he promoted the sense of mission. The animators, a basically agreeable group who disliked confrontations, went along with the company line. Kimball conceded that "even though he was prone to badger and bully us at one time or another, we knew that Walt had revolutionized the animated cartoon, and we were inwardly proud to be part of this process."

As usual in animation, there was an antic quality to all this. To demonstrate his good faith, for example, Kimball took down the sign in his car endorsing the socialist candidate for governor, Upton Sinclair. He replaced it with an old Keep Cool with Coolidge banner. Then truly hard times came to Disney—the unprofitability of the recent features, the due bills, the unwilling banks. Roy realized that there was only one way out: to raise cash the studio would have to go public. In April, Walt Disney Productions offered 75,000 units of preferred shares and common stock at prices ranging from $5 to $25 per share. Fearful that he was losing control of the company he had built, Walt discerned betrayals and disloyalties where none existed. He put Lessing in charge of labor negotiations, and urged him to bring the workers into line. In the eyes of animator Seamus Culhane, as well as many of his colleagues, "A more unwise choice could not have been made. During the preliminary seminars about unionism, Lessing's approach was too slick, too facile, and too arrogant. When some employee had the temerity to get up and ask a question, Lessing, while listening, would roll his eyes up toward heaven, in the age-old gesture of weary patience with blatant stupidity. It was a bit of action that probably was supposed to indicate Lessing's superiority over the lumpen proletariat he had to deal with. It had just the opposite effect."

Disney and Lessing hoped to create a malleable in-house union, and to persuade animators not to join the militant Screen Cartoonists Guild. They had reckoned without Art Babbit. Co-creator of Goofy, animator of the wicked Queen in *Snow White* and the dance of the mushrooms in *Fantasia,* Babbit defiantly joined the Guild and then invited a showdown by demanding a raise for his twenty-five-dollar-a-week assistant. The affront was too much for Walt. He turned down the increase and fired Babbit as a signal to anyone else who would brook his authority. The next day, May 29, 1940, three hundred strikers ringed the Disney studio. Driving his Packard past the front gate, Walt heard cat-calls. An unseen voice sounded harshly through a megaphone: "There he is—the man who believes in brotherhood for everybody but himself. Altogether now—booooooooo!" Walt applied the brakes, stepped from the car, and removed his jacket. Convinced the heckler was Art Babbit, he singled him out for a bare knuckles showdown. A studio guard intervened and Walt drove off, muttering. No one got close enough to hear him; the assumption was that Walt had vowed revenge against the ingrate. Looking back, Kimball tried to see both sides of the conflict. To be sure, Babbit had an authentic grievance, but Walt "didn't know what was going on in his own studio; he was shielded from the truth by the executives in between." Walt never learned that "there were guys making $18 a week and they couldn't even buy enough food for their families." When the studio needed additional workers, someone would go to New York and hire untrained artists. The eighteen-dollar men were then ordered "to show these new guys how it was done. And the new guys were being paid $50 a week. That sort of crap."

Despite Walt's outburst, the strike began peacefully enough. Strikers carried amusing signs: a drawing of Jiminy told passersby, "It's Not Cricket to Pass a Picket." Another compared the laborers and the boss to "Snow White and the 600 Dwarfs." As the strike wore on, however, tempers grew short. Loud shouts of "scab" were hurled at employees—more than 50 percent in all, including the indentured Ub Iwerks—who ignored the lines and entered the studio. One morning, after the dispute had gone on for several weeks, some trucks pulled up and disgorged a handful of thugs. They carried baseball bats and cans of gasoline. Circling the pickets, they poured out the fluid and threatened to set it afire unless the strikers moved away from studio grounds. The demonstration broke up, but the next day the picketers were back, accompanied by police.

"That incident seemed to be the watershed," says a Disney veteran. "Things were never the same afterward. The studio stayed open, and scores of workers still crossed the picket lines. But some of the promising artists went out in sympathy. And they *stayed* out." Walt Kelly was one of them. Sam Cobean and Virgil Partch abandoned films entirely and went on to notable careers in magazine cartooning. The greatest blow to the studio, although Walt refused to recognize it at the time, was the failure of Vladimir Tytla to side with management. In their comprehensive study *Disney Animation: The Illusion of Life,* Frank Thomas and Ollie Johnson refer to their old colleague as "the first animator to achieve strong emotions and convincing acting with the human figure." They remembered "Bill" Tytla fondly as an imposing figure with "a big mop of coal black hair, heavy black brows, and very piercing dark eyes. It was what was under the surface that made him stand out. He had great feelings churning around inside of him and tremendous nervous energy." That energy reached the screen in the Stromboli figure in *Pinocchio* and the devil in the "Bald Mountain" sequence in *Fantasia,* probably the most terrifying and truly evil personality of all the Disney villains. "It is true," the writers acknowledge, "that the basis for these characters is found in the story, but to . . . show the emotions that came from the inner feelings of his characters was one of Tytla's greatest achievements." It was also one of his last.

Whenever someone suggested that the strikers' grievances might be valid, Walt pointed to the "left-wing" organizations that had denounced the Disney studio. Some were indeed fellow travelers of the Soviet line; they had nothing to do with the reasons for the dispute or with the conduct of the protestors. But Disney refused to believe that "my kids," some of them much older than he, would rebel without the encouragement of Reds. "This entire mess," he wrote in an open letter, "was Communistically inspired and led." As Walt grew more agitated, family and friends looked for an exit. The strikers were intractable, and there seemed no way to budge Disney until Nelson Rockefeller, then coordinator of Inter-American Affairs, made an offer. Walt would journey to South America on a kind of goodwill tour. In his absence, the Roosevelt administration would arrange a settlement. Walt demanded, "You mean the unions will get what they want?" Rockefeller presented the bad news. "It's the climate of the times. This is a battle you can't win."

Vaudeville poster for "Gertie the Dinosaur": The cornerstone of
American animation made her debut in 1914 cavorting onstage with
her creator, comic strip artist Winsor McCay.

Poster for "Felix the Cat": The surrealist feline who beguiled
American audiences—as well as intellectuals like Aldous Huxley and Paul
Hindemith—was a cartoon superstar of the twenties.

Chuck Jones's Michigan J. Frog: centerpiece of the dialogue-free
1956 Warner Bros. short, "One Froggy Evening," considered by
many critics to be the funniest cartoon ever made.

A sketch from "Scrub Me Mamma to the Boogie Beat":
a Walter Lantz cartoon from the prewar years, when animated films—
and main features—employed stereotypes for easy laughs.

Gene Kelly and Jerry Mouse exchange ready smiles and dance routines in the 1944 MGM hit *Anchors Aweigh,* an intricate mix of music and color, live actor and cartoon character.

Marvin Martian and his canine sidekick prepare to face off with their
earthly enemies in Chuck Jones's 1953 parody of cold war shenanigans,
"Duck Dodgers in the 24 ½th Century."

Woody Woodpecker, whose "Ha-ha-ha-HA-ha" has sounded for six decades,
was the invention of Walter Lantz, one of the few animation producers
who could draw his own characters.

The musical that never was:
John Hubley created the cast and storyboards
for an adaptation of the Broadway show
Finian's Rainbow—only to be undone
by fifties political controversy.

The Beatles came on strong in Heinz Edelmann's full-length 1968 cartoon, *Yellow Submarine,* but the animator's influence had about the same shelf life as bell-bottom jeans.

Ralph Bakshi's feverish *Fritz the Cat* featured sex, drugs, and rock 'n' roll and provoked an X rating in 1972. It also provoked big grosses, loud applause, and a thousand imitations.

In 1965, Charles Schultz's "Peanuts" characters jumped to the small screen in "A Charlie Brown Christmas." It was so successful they went on to star in a series of specials.

Matt Groening's "The Simpsons," who began life as a small segment
of "The Tracey Ullman Show," struck out on their own to become
America's most popular dysfunctional family.

After some token protests, Disney flew off to Brazil with a bad case of what he called the D.D.'s: "disillusion and discouragement." In his absence, nonstrikers completed *Dumbo*, based on a popular children's book. With some justification, *Dumbo* has been called a Disney pastiche rather than a Disney film. Walt was not around when it was being readied, and many of the narrative techniques hark back to *Snow White*, *Pinocchio*, and *Fantasia*. The story of the lonely little elephant relies on well-worn Disney devices: the friendly narrator (a mouse instead of a cricket), the disabled hero (an elephant with outsized ears instead of a wooden boy), and simple, singable melodies—once more by Frank Churchill but with his new collaborator Oliver Wallace. Still, no other studio could have produced the best parts of *Dumbo*. Its color ranges from the stark primary statements of circus posters to the suffusions of the French impressionists. Bill Tytla's final piece of animation, the "trunk-touching" interlude in which Dumbo reaches out to his imprisoned mother, offers emotional power with none of the customary Disney bathos. The Pink Elephants on Parade sequence, filled with pachyderms who inflate, divide, evolve, carries animation technique to another level entirely. *Dumbo*'s comedy, on the other hand, is largely a matter of pratfalls and stereotypes. With the exception of Dumbo's mother, the female elephants are backbiting gossips, and the quintet of crows who sing the hit "When I See an Elephant Fly" might have stepped from a blackface vaudeville matinee. Lexicographer John Grant takes exception to those who find the yukking, eye-rolling birds distasteful. In his *Encyclopedia of Walt Disney's Animated Characters,* he argues that "The voices and appearances of the crows indicate that they are indeed black Americans but, since they are among the few goodies in a film well populated by baddies, it seems strange that racial offense should be discovered in their depiction: is it somehow all right to caricature whites but not blacks? That surely is a very deep racism." But even he concedes that "perhaps naming one of them Jim Crow was a little questionable."

More than a little to African-Americans at that time, and to almost everyone today. To be sure, the crows are neither malicious nor lazy, the standard attributes given to blacks in thirties cinema. In spirit, the quintet seems closer to the Fleischer jazz cartoons than to Amos 'n' Andy. *Dumbo* leaves no doubt, though, that these are black men in feathers, good-hearted, chuckleheaded simpletons whose skills are confined to singing and dancing. They and the rest of the cast, along with Dumbo and his mother, turned out to be exactly what the public wanted and needed in November 1941. Ecstatic notices greeted the film. Commenting on the wealth of intercutting and unusual points of

view, one critic said that *Dumbo* had "more camera angles than *Citizen Kane.*" *Newsweek* stated that this simple movie, and not the pretentious *Fantasia,* was the "real" Disney, and *Time,* impressed with the artistry of the first Disney feature to cost under $1 million, dubbed the elephant child "mammal of the year" and scheduled a cover on Disney's new hit.

By now, Walt was back from South America. Dumbo toys decorated the counters of toy and novelty stores, and the studio was back on its feet. Yet he was displeased; the strike had been settled in his absence, on what he regarded as unsatisfactory terms. Walt settled in with a vengeance. Lessing had failed to produce results; he was kept on but ignored. "Gunny doesn't know his ass," Walt would reply when anyone referred to the lawyer. Animators had been playing volleyball on their breaks; Walt ordered the nets taken down. Next came the installation of time clocks and the abbreviation of coffee breaks. The union settlement specifically stated that wages were to be frozen. Walt ignored the stricture, cut salaries back 10 percent, and issued pink slips to scores of workers, including Babbit. Here the union drew the line, fighting his dismissal in court. Frank Tashlin watched all this from his position as head of the animation department at Columbia Pictures. The Warner Bros. veteran dangled offers of better salaries and less oppressive working conditions, and some of Walt's best men responded. Disney was of course furious. When a promising young animator, David Swift, informed Walt that he had just received an attractive offer from Columbia, the boss recalled his skirmishes with the street fighter Harry Cohn. "OK, Davy boy," he snapped in a mock Yiddish accent, "off you go to work with those Jews. It's where you belong, with those Jews." It was the first openly anti-Semitic outburst from Walt; he would aim at Jews in higher places next time.

That time came shortly after December 7, 1941. War news drove all other items from the front pages of newspapers and the glossy facades of magazines. Walt was naturally disappointed that *Time* had canceled the Dumbo cover, but he could hardly have been surprised. What did astonish him was a call from his office manager the night after the bombing. "The army is moving in on us," said the shaky voice. "I said I'd have to call you. They said, 'Call him. But we're moving in anyway.' " Within hours, seven hundred soldiers occupied the Disney studio. When Walt drove up the next morning, an MP held up a white-gloved hand and refused to admit Disney to the studio that bore his name. The officer in charge politely explained that the place had been commandeered as a defense station. Mission: the protection and defense of the neighboring Lockheed aircraft plant. Antiaircraft crews and ordnance had already settled into emplacements around the lot. Crates of ammunition covered the parking lot, and jeeps occupied the lawn.

Were any other studios similarly overtaken? Walt demanded. Columbia, for instance? No, sir. Paramount? No, sir. MGM? 20th Century-Fox? United Artists? Again, no. They didn't touch the Jews, Disney told his colleagues. His was the only filmmaking organization occupied by the military. There it was for all to see. They could compliment the work and call you an American genius, but what did it mean when the band began to play? You were only a cartoonist then, the owner of a fun house, an amusement park. He went home and told Lilly and the girls he was hanging it up. The only way out of this mess was to retire while he still had his health and his sanity.

A significant Porky Pig cartoon appeared shortly before the outbreak of the war. Produced at Termite Terrace and directed by Chuck Jones, "Old Glory" begins with the voyage of the Pilgrims, moves on to Patrick Henry's "Give me liberty or give me death" speech, and then conjures up the midnight ride of Paul Revere. Here it departs from history: Instead of proclaiming, "The British are coming!" the night rider only calls, "To arms!" "To arms!" Lend Lease was under way and England was not to be portrayed as the enemy, even in fun. The following year, 1940, saw a handful of cartoons tiptoe up to the subject of war. According to the monograph "Doing Their Bit," only one of them actually addressed the subject head on. "Ants in the Plants," an allegory directed by Dave Fleischer for Paramount, tells the story of an ant colony faced with destruction by an anteater. Led by their queen, the militarized insects go on the attack. They lose each battle but win the war when they abandon tactics like the "Sewer-Side Squad" and swarm over the enemy. "Released during the so-called phony war on the Western Front," note authors Michael S. Schull and David E. Wilt, "this short may have been making allusions to the French and their Maginot Line."

In the world of cartoons, 1942 marked the beginning of full mobilization. Like the full-length films they accompanied, animated shorts turned to service comedy (jokes about getting caught in the draft, harsh sergeants, ill-fitting uniforms, etc.), as well as plugs for Defense Bonds. Only one cartoon broke from the pack. Undeservedly forgotten, Universal's "Boogie Woogie Boy of Company B" centers on the tribulations of a drafted black trumpeter, called upon by his sergeant to be "de new bugle boy." Throughout the length of World War II, this was the only American fiction film work to feature an all-black unit in the military. The rape of Manchuria, the nature of the Pearl Harbor attack, the early losses of Wake Island and the Philippines conspired to give the cinema a new stereotype: the Japanese villain. In real-life California, Nisei, native-born Americans of Japanese descent, were interned along with those who were born in the Land of the Rising Sun. Very few civil rights advocates could be found in Hollywood, the biggest complaint was about the sudden lack of gardeners. Hearst columnist Henry McLemore applauded the government's move: "Herd 'em up, pack 'em off and give them the inside room in the badlands. Let 'em be pinched, hurt, hungry and dead up against it." He added, "Personally, I hate the Japanese. And that goes for all of them." The more tolerant *Los Angeles Times* felt compelled to insist that "The rigors of war demand proper detention of Japanese and their immediate removal from the most acute danger spots."

In his oral history of the 1940s, *The Good War,* Studs Terkel comments dryly that "Paul Douglas, the liberal Illinoisian, volunteered for the marines at fifty 'to get myself a Jap.' True, it did no harm to his subsequent campaign for the United States Senate. There was nothing unusual in Mr. Douglas's pronouncement. 'Jap' was a common word in our daily vocabulary. He was a decent, highly enlightened man caught up in war fever as much as fervor. It was the doyen of American journalists, Walter Lippmann, who urged internment for Niseis and their fathers and mothers." The studios magnified the local hysteria. Warner's built a bomb shelter to house its top executives in case of emergency. During mock air raids, Jack Warner would sit in what he called "this underground haven playing checkers with Jesse Lasky, Mervyn Leroy, and others [cartoonists were never included among the occupants], and expecting to have the game broken up any moment by Japanese bombs." On screen, a number of Asian actors—most of them Chinese and Korean—made good livings playing Nipponese. Blinking out from Coke-bottle lenses and smiling enigmatically in the accepted style of the Yellow Peril, they created an impression that was to endure for generations. Yet scripts and performers had to stay within the limits of reality and taste. No such strictures applied to characters who were drawn; throughout the war, if newsreels became the cinematic equivalent of the front page, animated shorts were the editorial cartoons.

An able seaman, Popeye starred in adventures like "Scrap the Japs." During a ferocious battle at sea, he croaks, "I never seen a Jap that wasn't yeller." By the fadeout, he has locked the Asian enemy forces in a cage, where they squeal like rodents. In "You're a Sap, Mr. Jap," he fights bucktoothed Japanese in kimonos, and sinks their battleship. Below decks of the sinking ship an officer declares that he must "save face," and commits hara-kiri by drinking fuel and swallowing firecrackers. The boat explodes to the sound effect of a flushing toilet. The Office of War Information had mixed feelings about jeers directed toward the Japanese. The agency's official reviewers endorsed the notion of a humiliated foe, yet they disliked the Japanese to be dismissed as comic victims. In the end, they turned thumbs down on Popeye's cartoon: It contained "propaganda on the absurd side [because] it laughs at the enemy in such a way as to discredit the real danger." The Fleischers enlisted Superman in the war. Leaping from comic books to the screen, the Man of Steel showed what he was made of in Paramount's "The 11th Hour." Disguised as Clark Kent, he and the intrepid Lois Lane pursue a story in prewar Yokohama. When Lois is threatened with death for being an American, her rescuer flies in, thwarting the Japanese—portrayed as grinning caricatures or ominous shadows. The OWI review: "It seems to have a bad influence. The Japs are not to be beaten by a mythical Superman, but by the men of the United Nations."

Bob Clampett's animation techniques reached their apogee during the war. His films moved with the leaping congruity of fever dreams, and specialized in nose thumbing, particularly at Disney ("A Corny Concerto" reduces *Fantasia* to rubble) and flaunting the Film Code ("An Itch in Time" finds Elmer Fudd's flea-ridden dog dragging his rump on the ground and stopping to remark to the camera, "Hey, I better cut this out. I might get to like it"). Clampett's humor was rich and quirky, as "Coal Black and De Sebben Dwarfs" showed in abundance. The brilliantly paced sendup of *Snow White* was not some hastily composed parody. Clampett spent hours in the black sections of

Los Angeles, listening to the jazz he loved and attempting to capture the looks and sounds of the community.

"Coal Black" has an enormous cast for a six-minute film, ranging from the Mammy and the zoot-suited stud to the innocent young thing, Coal Black, and the scheming Wicked Queen. An overweight hoarder of items needed for defense, the Queen hires thugs so lethal they kill "Japs for Free". The men are to "black out" So White, but the heroine avoids their clutches, thanks to the aid of the "Sebben Dwarfs"—caricatures of a very rotund Fats Waller. Two of them are in uniform, and So White sings "I'm Wacky over Khaki Now" before the happy finale. From the beginning, objections were hurled at this extraordinary short. (The year it was released, the Office of War Information labeled it a "vulgar parody." Yet even these assessors had to concede that there was "excellent boogie-woogie background music.") Oddly enough, through the years some of Coal Black's most vigorous defenders have been African-Americans, including Tom Bradley, the first black mayor of Los Angeles.

Initially, American movies had not gone after Germans in the same way they had hounded Asians. The Hollywood Production Code forbade

moviemakers from urging American involvement in the European war, and as late as 1941 Louis B. Mayer told director William Wyler that he was uncomfortable with the early rushes of *Mrs. Miniver.* He thought they demonstrated a clear anti-German bias. Wyler protested: "Mr. Mayer, you know what's going on there, don't you?" Mayer answered grandly, "This is a big corporation. I'm responsible to my stockholders. We have theaters all over the world, including a couple in Berlin." Only after Germany declared war on the United States was Wyler allowed to complete his film without interference from the front office. In contrast, said producer Joseph Mankiewicz, "Warner's had guts. They hated the Nazis more than they cared for the German grosses." But hate was not enough. When the Warner film *Confessions of a Nazi Spy* was released in 1939, the German government lodged an official protest with the State Department, and the German-American Bund filed a $500,000 lawsuit for damages. Letters threatened the lives of Jack Warner and the star, Edward G. Robinson. These had the desired chilling effect. Other producers paid attention; it would be quite a while before the Germans were perceived as safe subjects for attack—particularly in animation. According to Tex Avery, when he planned to caricature Adolf Hitler in "Blitz Wolf," producer Fred Quimby urged him to be circumspect: "After all, Tex, we don't know who's going to win the war."

Termite Terrace was not so craven. The studio offered a wild, barely coherent short called "The Ducktators." A rotten little egg bears a swastika on its shell. Out of it hatches a duckling with a Hitler mustache. He quickly invents the "heil" salute, attempts to paper walls with swastikas—a swipe at Hitler's early years as a frustrated artist— then bombinates to all the birds in the barnyard. A squat Mussolini duck breaks away from yo-yo twirling to join him, spouting in an Italian accent: "He's a smart-a fellow with brains, like-a me." The Duce duck gives his own rabble-rousing speech and flashes an "Applause" sign. A little bird obediently claps as the camera pans to show him chained to the ground. A toothy, squinting duck completes the Axis trio, chanting "I'm a Japanese Sap-man." A peace-loving dove tries to stop them all from going to war, but they trample him down. Furious, the pacifist changes his tune, rolls up a sleeve, and leads the other birds in a vigorous beating of the fascist fowl. A title card provides the moral. "If you'd like to make this true, this is all you have to do: For Victory Buy War Bonds and Stamps."

Cartoons like these prompted the armed forces to revise their visual aids programs. Official training films, made by some of Hollywood's top directors and actors, had failed to impress the troops. Whatever the subject—hygiene, strategy, technical instruction—GIs tended to close their eyes as soon as the lights were snapped off. Those who stayed awake greeted the movies with catcalls and Bronx cheers. "The government had a real dilemma," observes Chuck Jones. "If they used real soldiers, they lost because the kids couldn't act. And yet if they used real actors, the guys in uniform saw right through the fakery. By some miracle the army got one thing right very early in the war. Some genius—it might have been Frank Capra, the great civilian director who became Major Capra, the great military director—had the inspiration to try something different: animation."

Artists and technicians were drafted, put through a perfunctory basic training and then sent to the Hal Roach Studio in Hollywood. "They irreverently called the installation 'Fort Roach,' " recalls Seamus Culhane, "and the inmates 'The Foreskin Fusileers.' There were no barracks, so everybody went home after work, appearing in the morning just in time for roll call, in a state of disarray that would have given General Patton the vapors." Attempts at discipline were few and futile; the snappy salute soon degenerated to a casual wave, and the chain of command to a series of hallway conferences. The army sent a strict disciplinarian to take charge; he was wise enough to go along with the gags and invent some of his own. During a white-glove inspection the colonel reached under a drawing board and swiped at the underside. Out came his glove with a dark smudge, enlarged when he touched the underside of a storyboard. A horrified silence followed. The staff braced itself for an eruption. Studying the stain for a dramatic moment, the officer turned to his aides and inquired, "Does anyone here have a black glove?" The animators understood: As long as they produced first-rate work, and a great deal of it, the military would look the other way.

It was a wise move. John Hubley, who had left Disney during the strike, directed a highly successful cartoon for the navy called "Flat-Hatting." The title was fliers' slang for putting a plane into an almost vertical dive at some terrified group, usually on a beach or farm, and then pulling up at the last minute. Far too often the plane and pilot were lost. Hubley's film turned the flat-hatter from a daredevil hero into an unattractive and dangerous idiot, someone to be mocked rather than imitated, and just about stopped the prank. Theodor Geisel, already famous under his civilian nom de plume, Dr. Seuss, helped to produce a character called Private Snafu. The name came from a favorite GI acronym, Situation Normal, All Fucked Up (Fouled Up for civilian consumption). Geisel furnished Snafu with bright story lines and bumptious verse. Chuck Jones, establishing himself as a master director at the age of twenty-six, helped to give Snafu a face and body. Now every recruit, no matter how oppressed or inept, had someone to look down on. While the soldiers were laughing, the most ungainly enlisted man in the world taught them the value of discipline, hygiene, and the keeping of military secrets. The prototypical cartoon, "Gripes," is a fantasy of the armed forces under the command of Private Snafu. He and the rest of the boys in the barracks indulge themselves with booze, women, and late hours; meanwhile, the fort goes unprotected when the Germans mount an attack. In shorts about espionage and rumor, Seussian rhymes supply the comic energy. Snafu brags, "The military secret that I carry in my brain / I keep in safe deposit with a pad-a-lock and chain." A few drinks at a nightclub and that pad-a-lock is loosened. Snafu begins babbling to his sexy date (a spy whose capacious brassiere houses two recording machines), endangers his troopship, and ends at the bottom of the ocean wondering, "Now, who in hell you s'pose it was who let my secret out?" Hitler appears, completing the verse in German intonations: "Vot vos dot I heard you say, my liddle sauerkraut?" Another spirited cartoon finds Snafu in the tropics. Here the foe is not the Axis but the mosquitoes, a highly trained air corps whose weapons are their proboscises, and whose target is the Private's privates. He has forgotten to take his antimalarial pills and winds up alternately burning with fever and freezing with chilblains, the fate of soldiers who refuse to take precautions.

All along, animators enjoyed a liberty denied to all other military personnel. The well-chosen four-letter word was acceptable, along with selected double entendres. Jones, a lifelong enthusiast of word games and puns, particularly enjoyed Geisel's Snafu script about survival in the Arctic. As the camera moved over a cartoon tundra, the announcer's voice intoned, "It was cold enough to freeze the nuts off a jeep." The film then cut to a cartoon jeep and its nuts loudly dropped off the bolts. Not to be outdone, an animator named Bill Hurtz used sex to save lives. Fliers hated the unwieldy garment that was supposed to keep them afloat in case they had to ditch in the ocean. Happily, someone noticed the similarity between Mae West's buxom figure and a man in a life jacket. The star was approached, she agreed to lend her voice and body to the war effort. Posing for Hurtz's cartoon, West purled: "I'm happy to think that the life jacket is gonna be called the Mae West. It kinda gives the woman's touch while the boys are flyin' around nights."

Less than two months after his self-imposed retirement, Walt Disney had found a reason to go back to work. The Naval Bureau of Aeronautics asked him to make twenty animated instructional films. The fee: $80,000 each. With a mixture of patriotic fervor and boredom with hanging around the house, he reentered studio grounds. Ignoring the occupying soldiers, Walt, working with a handpicked crew, produced such successful cartoons that other agencies clamored for their own Disney films. These new assignments kept him busy, and by cutting corners Walt was able to make $8,000 profit on each short. His satisfaction was short-lived; the government proved to be more irritating than the banks and the unions. Not only did Secretary of the Treasury Henry Morgenthau complain about costs, he tried to fire Donald Duck. Walt had planned to star Donald in a film urging Americans to pay their income taxes. Morgenthau took exception: "I'd always visualized you creating a little character here that would be Mr. Taxpayer." An assistant secretary added: "I don't like Donald Duck." Walt counted to ten. "Maybe you don't," he replied between his teeth. "But there are a lot of people who do." He turned to Morgenthau. "I've given you Donald Duck. That's the equivalent of giving you Clark Gable out of the MGM stable."

This was pure sophistry. When MGM donated Gable for a propaganda film, the studio received no compensation. Many stars took great risks for the government; Carole Lombard died when her plane crashed during a war bond tour. Walt took no chances, and he was paid for everything he did. Nevertheless, Disney got his way: "The New Spirit" did star the Duck after all. He plays the part of a contentious tax avoider who learns that his $13 annual payment will be used "to beat to earth the evil destroyer of freedom and peace." The cartoon did what it was supposed to do; Americans filled out their tax forms with greater alacrity than ever before. But Walt nursed his grievance. He told associates that Donald had become a mere puppet of the government, with "that Jew" Morgenthau playing the part of Stromboli. To show who was in charge of casting at the Disney studio, Walt offered "Der Fuhrer's Face," again starring Donald Duck. A miserable citizen of the Third Reich, Herr Donald lives in a Hitler-shaped house, awakens to the ring of an alarm clock with Hitler's face, and works in Hitler's munitions factory. He is forced to give the Nazi salute even while tightening the fuses on shells. Each moment is worse than the last, and Donald comes close to a meltdown. A ersatz vacation—sit-ups before a bucolic backdrop curtain—fails to restore his mental health and he goes beserk. The tantrum fades and he awakens in an American bed, embracing a model of the Statue of Liberty: The fascist nightmare was exactly that and nothing more. As always, precise timing and attention to detail marked it as a Disney product. So did Oliver Wallace's title song: "When Der Fuhrer says, 'Ve iss der master race, ve heil (Bronx cheer), heil (Bronx cheer), right in Der Fuhrer's face / Ven Der Fuhrer says, 'Dey'll never bomb diss place,' Ve heil, heil, right in Der Fuhrer's face." Cliff Edwards sang the number on film; a new novelty band, Spike Jones and his City Slickers, performed its own rendition complete with rubber "razzer" for the heils. The juicy sound caught on, the record sold more than a million and a half copies and announced the arrival of Jones and his madcap musicians. They were to remain famous for the next forty years.

Disney produced three other significant propaganda films during the war. "Education for Death" had none of the absurdist humor of Donald's cartoon. In a fairy-tale format, it examined the methods of Nazi indoctrination. Young Hans learns the story of Sleeping Beauty, with Hitler as the Prince and a bulky Germania as the leading lady. Later, Hans sees a fox pursue a rabbit, and gets called down for sympathizing with the victim. He obediently parrots the party line: "I hate it. It is a coward." Hans grows up to be a classic storm trooper, burning books, sacking churches, and showing contempt for culture. "Education" was the only cartoon to acknowledge the Nazi policy of euthanasia for physical "defectives": When Hans falls ill, his mother is warned that a sickly child will not be tolerated by the Third Reich. "Reason and Emotion" contrasted the primitive, irrational person easily swayed by emotional appeal, and the sensible, thinking individual able to separate truth from fantasy. Hitler's emotional appeals are used to fan the flames of resentment and prejudice. The average American, in this case the cartoon figure of one John Doakes, is cautioned not to be swayed by rumor and scare headlines.

Shortly after the bombing of Pearl Harbor, Walt had come under the spell of a book, *Victory Through Air Power.* The author, Major Alexander de Seversky, argued for the importance of long-range bombing, then a new and untried strategy. Training films and war cartoons had begun to pour out of the Disney studio, but the major's work seemed to demand a more ambitious treatment. Walt's 1943 version was made independently, mixing animation and live action to sell the public— and the Pentagon—on the importance of winged victory. The hour-long film traces the beginning of air war circa 1914 by using two cartoon pilots. Pierre and Fritz hurl bricks at each other from their planes. The argument soon escalates to full-scale war, with the airmen mishandling their primitive machine guns and shooting off their own propellers. After that comic interlude, *Victory* switches to a live presentation of Seversky's thesis, starring the major himself. With animated visual aids, he recounts Hitler's use of airpower to gain the advantage in 1939, and asserts that Allied long-range bombers could cause a turnabout, breaking the German supply lines and releasing Japan's grip on the South Pacific. To underline Seversky's point, an American eagle swoops out of the sky to attack a Japanese octopus, tearing at it until the eight tentacles weaken, withdrawing from the islands it has ensnared. Elemental, melodramatic, simplistic, *Victory* nonetheless had a striking effect. Disney's director, H. C. Potter, later testified that "The British thought this was the greatest thing that ever came down the pike. When Churchill came over to the Quebec conference, they were trying to get Roosevelt interested in the long-range bombing idea, and Roosevelt didn't know what the hell they were talking about. Churchill said, 'Well, of course, you've seen *Victory Through Air Power.* And Roosevelt said, 'No, what's that?' Roosevelt put out an order to the Air Corps to fly a print up to Quebec. Churchill ran it for him, and that was the beginning of the U.S. Air Corps Long Range Bombing."

It was when Walt brought his attention to civilian projects that he ran into trouble. *Bambi,* yet another German story, was supposed to be Walt's greatest film to date, but that was not the way it turned out. The Felix Salten novel, translated by a *Time* editor named Whittaker

Chambers, seemed to have all the requisites for a hit: charming depictions of natural scenery, a spectacular forest fire, a love story, and a sprinkling of appealing animals. The Disney version capitalized on all of them, making the death of Bambi's mother into as heartbreaking a scene as Garbo's farewell in *Camille,* and adding Thumper, a rabbit who piped the message of the film: "If you can't say somethin' nice, don't say nothin' at all." Those words went unheeded by the critics. Although the *New York Post* reviewer praised *Bambi* as a "serious showing of nature," he wondered about its suitability for children. The *New Republic*'s critic was full of scorn: "In an attempt to ape the trumped-up realism of flesh and blood movies [Disney] has given up fantasy, which was pretty much the magic element. Mickey wouldn't be caught dead in this." A Disney executive later acknowledged that "*Bambi* was a sweet little story about please don't kill the deer, when we were talking about killing human beings, and it just didn't sell."

Saludos Amigos, the result of Disney's voyage to South America, includes footage of Walt and his entourage, along with four animated sequences. The first stars Donald Duck, now riding high in Walt's esteem, on the shores of Lake Titicaca in Peru. Most of the adventure is taken up with physical byplay between the always furious Donald and a balky llama. The second follows a little airplane, Pedro, from his birth (he nurses from a nipple at a gas pump) to his fogbound adventure carrying the mail (one postcard). The third, "El Gaucho Goofy," is done in the style of the Goofy How-To series, in which the star sets out to demonstrate a process and gets hopelessly entangled. Here, caparisoned like an Argentinean cowboy, he tries to bring down a wild animal with his deadly bolas—ropes with metal weights—only to bring down his horse and conk himself on the head. The finale reprises Donald and a new South American friend, the parrot Jose Carioca. Together, they tour the lands south of the border with the aid of a paintbrush, filling in the backgrounds as they samba along. *Amigos* enjoyed a warm reception in South America. The air was chillier in the United States, where even the most lenient critics had trouble with Disney's Hands-Across-the-Panama-Canal gestures. And James Agee, newly installed at the *Nation,* had no use for any of it. The "self-interested, belated ingratiation embarrasses me," he wrote, "and Disney's famous cuteness, however richly it may mirror national infantilism, is hard on my stomach." Agee would have been interested in the objections of an Argentinean artist Florencio Molina Campos, hired by Disney as an adviser. When Campos got a look at the Goofy segment, he was so distraught that he wrote a formal protest. The letter, which landed on the desk of Secretary of State Cordell Hull, had nothing kind to say about the film or the producer. " 'Goofy Gaucho' was brought to my office so that I might study it and arrange the gaucho dialect that was to accompany the version destined for Spanish-speaking America. I tried to find a way of fixing it, but I found all my efforts so hopeless that I told them I didn't see any way at all; such was the conglomeration of errors."

A complaint to the boss went nowhere. Disney "had no real answer, making a vague gesture, like a child caught in some prank." Attached to the letter was a memo from a government official: "If we want to sell phoney gauchos to the Americans that is Disney's business, but I believe we should put a stop to the insulting of our neighbors and the revealing of ourselves as having little knowledge of their lives and habits, while we pose as good neighbors." Neither the State Department nor Walt responded except through intermediaries who repeated the everlasting shibboleth of Hollywood: You can't argue with success. *Saludos Amigos,* one of Disney's few profitable ventures in the forties, returned grosses of some $1.3 million. Better still, it proved that the combination of live action and cartoons could play in Buenos Aires as well as Peoria. Walt made ambitious plans for the postwar period. There was no more talk of retirement.

"To be an animator in the war years was to be somewhat schizoid," observed a Hollywood veteran. "Disney actually separated his units: some artists did government films; others concentrated on strictly civilian stuff. The rest of the studios weren't so neat about things." MGM worked both sides of the street with its two new stars, Tom Cat and Jerry Mouse. In "Yankee Doodle Mouse," Tom acts as a stand-in for the Axis and Jerry for the Allies. Predictably, the rodent defeats his traditional antagonist, all the while paraphrasing celebrated quotes from war heroes ("Sighted Cat, Sank Same"; "Send More Cats"). Most of the other Tom 'n' Jerry cartoons of the period made no reference to the war. They were too busy with their own one-on-one conflict, bombarding each other in deliberately irrelevant pantomime. At Paramount, Dave Fleischer directed "Slay It with Flowers," following a fox as he seeds his Victory Garden ("Artichoke Hitler . . . Beet Mussolini . . . Squash the Japs"). As the seeds hit the ground, a predatory crow snatches them in his beak. The fox uses a variety of methods to keep the bird at bay, including a Hitler scarecrow. None of them work until the crow learns that the garden is a home-front weapon and politely withdraws. The OWI greeted "Flowers" with a pan: "In view of the present shortage of film, this cartoon is an irresponsible waste of footage," and it was small wonder that Fleischer spent the greater part of his career on civilian Popeye and Superman shorts.

Paul Terry, Columbia Pictures, Walter Lantz, and other producers also moved uneasily between propaganda and entertainment. None of them operated a faster shuttle than the one at Termite Terrace. One week, a group might be assigned to Snafu, the next it would be completing "Tortoise Wins by a Hare," seeing to it that Bugs Bunny lost a footrace. ("A turtle beating me, a rabbit. Why, I'm in the pink! I'm an athlete. I've got athlete's legs! I've even got athlete's foot!") As the war turned in the Allies' favor, the OWI attempted to soften Hollywood propaganda. The agency now looked with favor upon cartoons aimed at lifting home-front spirits, rather than broadsides aimed at the enemy. An easy kidding of gasoline rationing and food shortages, of draft boards and wartime slogans ("Is this trip necessary?," followed by a character falling downstairs)—these should be the concerns of animators. Warner Bros.'s "The Weakly Reporter" served as a model. The presidents on Mount Rushmore wear Civilian Defense helmets. The Statue of Liberty has a CD armband. An ambulance screeches up to the scene of an automobile accident, the stretcher bearers pass by the human victim to rescue his precious rubber tire. As soldiers guard a pound of butter, a narrator intones, "While there is sufficient food for all, many items fall into the luxury class." When women are shown, it is usually with amused derision: WACs learn commando tactics so they can fight their way through crowds at a hosiery sale. A longhaired and supposedly alluring blonde sits behind the wheel of a taxi—then turns around to reveal an abrasive gorgon with a well-chewed cigar and a voice like a diesel engine. Weightier subjects, in the agency's view, would best be left to newsreels and "serious" filmmakers. For if cartoons continued to present Japanese troops as fools, what did that imply about the boys who were fighting them? It also occurred to the OWI that our Allies in the Far East were just as Asian as the Japanese.

Those peoples were currently being presented as "our gallant friends." So the caricatures of Yellow Devils were passé. As for the silly portraits of the Germans, they might be toned down as well.

If the OWI's logic persuaded most studios, it failed to sway the wilder minds of Termite Terrace. Leon Schlesinger sold his studio to Warner Bros. in the summer of 1944, but that seemed to make no difference to the inmates. Late in the war, the house Rabbit was still making sport of the enemy in "Bugs Bunny Nips the Nips." Adrift in a wooden crate, Bugs lands on an island occupied by Japanese. Recognizing him from the movies, a soldier says, "What's up, honorable Doc?," and gives chase. Rabbit and man take flight in separate airplanes, and when the Japanese bails out, Bugs flies by to hand him an anvil: "Here's some scrap iron for Japan, Moto! Happy landings!" Returned to earth, he knocks out a Sumo wrestler and hands out exploding Good Rumor ice cream sticks to an enemy platoon. "Here's one for you, Monkey Face! There's plenty for all. Here you are, Slant Eyes' Business is BOOMing!" Ethnic jokes only seemed to go on tiptoe around the Reich. Having folded, Italians were no longer fit subjects for satire, and cartoonists considered the mass of Germans too "civilized" for low comedy. Mockery was saved for the leaders, not the herrenvolk. Only three months before Hitler committed suicide in his bunker, "Herr Meets Hare" was still twitting the Fuhrer and his entourage. On an underground route to Las Vegas, the ubiquitous Bugs makes a wrong turn and surfaces in the Black Forest. Hermann Göring stands in his way. Bugs declares that the Field Marshall's medals are ersatz, and "Fatso" fulminates against his leader—until Bugs shows up in a Fuhrer disguise, complete with toothbrush mustache. Bugs next appears as a Wagnerian "Brünhilde," and Göring captures him in a sack, taking his prisoner to the real Hitler. The two men peek in the sack and run off terrified, screaming, "Ach! Evil!" For Bugs has disguised himself as Joseph Stalin, now with a pushbroom mustache and the Generalissimo's signature pipe.

As the war wound down, both the cartoonists and the public grew weary of the predictable style and comedy of animated shorts. Disney had created nothing new in years, and Warner and the other studios seemed to be running in place. Everything had a slightly used air, like guests who were once charming and entertaining but who had overstayed their welcome. Only a handful of filmgoers saw that Chuck

Jones had already indicated a new path with "Hell Bent for Election."
Moonlighting with a crew from Fort Roach, he had directed a cartoon
encouraging voters to reelect Roosevelt. F.D.R. was represented by a
streamlined train, the opposition by the Defeatist Limited, a puffing,
out of breath old coal burner with cars like the Business as Usual
sleeper and a caboose labeled the Jim Crow Special. Because of a
severely curtailed budget (the animators had donated their time), the
animation for "Hell Bent" was limited and the backgrounds austere.
And yet the film had verve and style; the humor made its point succinctly and well. There had been nothing like "Hell Bent" before—
except in two forgotten shorts, also by Jones: "Aristo Cat" and "The
Dover Boys at Pimento University." The first used highly abstract
backgrounds to show a day in the life of an overindulged feline; the
second was a spoof of 1890s dime novels. In their sibling rivalry for the
heart of Dainty Dora Standpipe, the upright heroes and the villainous
Dan Backslide "popped" from position to position, with a few frames

of "smear" action between poses. Jones noticed that audiences filled in the gaps without complaint or comment. "They thought they were taking a peep at the past," he came to realize. "Instead, we were all of us looking at the future."

WHO'S DIRECTING THIS PICTURE?

The fortunes of the Fleischer studio took an irreversible slide after the debut of their second full-length film, *Mr. Bug Goes to Town*. It came out in the winter of 1941, and several critics saw the movie as a "New Deal melodrama," noting that more than its title was evocative of Gary Cooper's *Mr. Deeds Goes to Town* and Jimmy Stewart's *Mr. Smith Goes to Washington*. Like those plainspoken individuals, the Fleischers' grasshopper hero, Hoppity, opposes plutocrats wherever he finds them. Chief among the film's villains is C. Bagley Beetle, a land developer with an exoskeleton for a heart. Beetle gets Hoppity out of the way by kidnapping him, and then makes a move on the winged ingenue, Honey. The good bugs are saved by a true deus ex machina: a crane operated by the "human ones." The device frees Hoppity, flattens the neighborhood, and destroys Beetle's plans. Like Okies in *The Grapes of Wrath,* the file of insect refugees wanders to new turf, a penthouse garden far above the old slum.

Mr. Bug came with extraordinary assets: a three-dimensional background with over ten thousand tiny glass windows, humans rendered in striking Art Deco style, and a score by Frank Loesser and Hoagy Carmichael. Once again, though, the Fleischers had neglected the story and, worse still, centered it around the wrong sorts of animals. One bug per film seemed to be the limit for moviegoers of the forties. They could accept Jiminy Cricket as Pinocchio's conscience, but a whole cast of six-legged creatures seemed a bit much. Like *Gulliver's Travels,* the film flopped. Shortly afterward, Paramount assumed control, fired Max and Dave, and renamed their place Famous Studios.

Animation's Jewish uncles were out of business. Word went out that only Disney knew the secret of making profitable animated features. No one at Paramount—or at any of the other majors—seemed aware that Walt had lost his touch.

Disney's *Three Caballeros,* released after the European victory and only a few months before V-J Day, once again showed Latin America as an apolitical land, full of loud colors and syncopated music. Throughout the forties, whether by design or sloth, South of the Border was portrayed in a series of postcard formulas: the sun constant; the peasants simple, happy, and lazy, always ready to do a task mañana; the mustachioed leaders uniformed popinjays; the music hot; the women likewise. For this second South American tour, Donald Duck and Jose Carioca did nothing to break the stereotypes. Accompanied by their new friend, Panchito, a Mexican Rooster, they offered bogus Latino songs by many hands, none of them distinguished. The frenzied script takes everything literally. If an announcer says a blanket of fog moved in, the weather resembles bedclothes; when a runner speaks of a race so fast that "we passed them as if they were standing still," the opponents are frozen in place. Animators compensate for narrative shortcomings by dazzling the eye: With the aid of new techniques developed by Ubbe Iwerks, the members of the trio pass in and out of a pop-up book, ride swirls of color, board a flying serape, and dance with live South American entertainers.

Walt had his new picture promoted as "the most startling advancement in motion picture techniques since the advent of sound." Even in a town where hyperbole is dispensed like bottled water, this was an absurdity. If *Caballeros* announced any kind of watershed, it was one in which the water flowed backward. From this point on, intellectuals began to downgrade the Disney product. *Three Caballeros* "dazzles and numbs the senses," said the *Times,* "without making any discernible sense." *The Saturday Review* asked why "Mr. Disney and his staff should have tried to mix human beings who are only real with drawn figures who are pure fantasy," and added, "compared to this unhappy mixture, the home life of bromo and seltzer is bliss itself." The White House may consider Disney an ambassador of goodwill to South America, but "the portfolio he carries turns out to be a strange grab-bag." Two magazines analyzed the contents of that bag. "Donald whizzes from one Latin American beauty to the next like a berserk bumble bee," observed *Time.* "Since he remains at base a combination of loud little boy and loud little Duck, his erotomaniacal regard for these full-blown young ladies is of strictly pathological interest." The *New Yorker* remarked on the film's "mixture of atrocious taste, bogus mysticism, and authentic fantasy, guaranteed to baffle any critic not hopelessly enchanted with the word 'Disney.' " The worst of it was "a somewhat physical romance between a two-foot duck and a full-sized woman, though one happens to be a cartoon and the other pleasantly rounded and certainly mortal." This union was "one of those things that might disconcert less squeamish authorities at the Hays office." Then came the Freudian coup de grâce: "It might even be said that a sequence involving the duck, the young lady and a long alley of ani-mated cactus plants would probably be considered suggestive in a less innocent medium."

Walt replied to the cavilers in 1946 with *Make Mine Music.* Planned as a pop companion to *Fantasia,* the film ranges from Benny Good-man's jazz quartet to Prokofiev's "Peter and the Wolf," from cartoons about "Casey at the Bat" and a backwoods feud between the Martins and the Coys, to Dinah Shore singing "Two Silhouettes in the Dark" as dancers from the Ballet Russe leap and twirl in a background of lace valentines and floating cupids. Frost formed on the reviews: "pot-boiler" was one of the kinder critical terms. *Theater Arts* led the high-brow assault: "Suppose you go to visit a friend. You know that he has a warm heart and is kind to animals, that his sense of humor is infec-tious, his professional skill beyond compare. But when you enter his house you find to your dismay that his walls are festooned with second-rate art; romantic scenes of white doves against lush blue back-grounds; vapid landscapes; tinsel hearts and stars of assorted sizes. You would not therefore cease to love the man, to laugh at his jokes or admire his skill; but you would have to admit with regret that his taste is deplorable. On similar internal evidence, this is the reluctant con-clusion of a visitor to *Make Mine Music.*"

Time weighed in with a premonitory note. The Martins versus Coy episode, with its mockery of hillbillies, might amuse children and uncritical adults. But it would surely "offend those who think such car-icature as insulting as the hush-ma-mouf kind of comic contempt for Negroes." No major periodical would have made such a remark in Dis-ney's heyday. Indeed, five years earlier, *Time* had found the Black

Crows portion of *Dumbo* "hilarious, eminently crowish, typical of the good circus humor that babbles through the picture." Now the magazine vigorously opposed the use of racial stereotypes. Three months later, *Time* renewed its assault when Walt presented his version of Joel Chandler Harris's folktales. In the live portion of *Song of the South,* a chuckling Uncle Remus addresses a group of enchanted black children. As he talks, cartoon versions of Br'ers Rabbit and Bear appear, acting out the little anecdotes. *Time* would have none of it: "Tattered ol' Uncle Remus, who cheerfully 'knew his place' in the easygoing world of nineteenth-century Georgia (author Harris, in accepted Southern fashion, always omitted the capital from the word 'Negro'), is a character bound to enrage all educated Negroes, and a number of damyankees." That he did. The NAACP called the film's "idyllic master-slave relationship" a "distortion of the truth," and the National Urban League decried *Song*'s "stereotype casting of the Negro in the servant role, depicting him as indolent, one who handles the truth lightly."

The combination of black objectors and mainstream carping left Walt confused and glum. Filmmaking ceased to invigorate him; he seemed to discern moral decay wherever he looked. Along with John Wayne, Robert Taylor, Gary Cooper, and a phalanx of like-minded actors, screenwriters, journalists, and executives he founded the Motion Picture Alliance for the Preservation of American Ideals (MPA). Within

their industry, the organization would oppose and weed out "domination by Communists, radicals and crackpots." One of the most influential members of the MPA, the widely syndicated columnist Hedda Hopper, found a kindred spirit in Walt. They lunched several times a week at the Brown Derby restaurant, talking over the latest tactics of the House Un-American Activities Committee (HUAC).

As the Committee closed in on the movie colony, ten writers were singled out for suspected membership in the Communist party, or for fellow traveling. Columnist Murray Kempton, ruefully watching the West Coast circus, listed the products of the radical scenarists. Then he quoted the ratings assigned to the films, several years before, by the staid Daughters of the American Revolution. *Rich Girl, Poor Girl:* "Good." *Confessions of a Nazi Spy:* "Excellent. No sentimentalized patriotism." *Sorority House:* "Wholesome." In New York, Kempton brought down the house. Hollywood was not amused. Its terrified leaders searched for exemplars of probity in Hollywood, and placed Walt at the top of their list. A lifelong promoter of hard work and family life, he had already been given twelve Oscars and the prestigious Irving Thalberg Award. They were not enough. Hopper endlessly boomed him, and upon the rerelease of *Bambi,* he was hailed as "Hollywood's Rembrandt."

Yet all this was praise for the past. What about tomorrow? Walt was closemouthed on the subject. He preferred to speak of politics, preparing himself each morning by going through reports of the HUAC hearings as he breakfasted on doughnuts dipped in Scotch. Afterward, he played with his model trains, an elaborate setup dominating his office. Slowly, the founder of the greatest animation studio in the world distanced himself from day-to-day operations. One of his fondest admirers, critic Bosley Crowther of the *New York Times,* dropped by one morning. He was dismayed to find Walt "totally disinterested in movies and wholly, almost wierdly concerned with the building of a miniature railroad engine and a string of cars. All of his zest for invention, for creating fantasies, seemed to be going into this plaything. I came away feeling sad." Crowther would not have found much cheer at the other cartoon studios. The *Hollywood Quarterly* noted that in the last few months the town had "periodically been reading the Requiem over the animation industry. Hat on breast, it waits reverently at the yawning grave."

Given these conditions, Walt could easily have retired once again, this time permanently, had he not found a new freshet of energy. The Art Babbit lawsuit, long tied up in the courts, was finally decided in the artist's favor. Over Walt's protestations, the National Labor Relations Board forced the Disney studio to rehire its dismissed employee at a higher salary. As Seamus Culhane saw it, "Two tragic heroes butted heads together like moose in rutting season, and Walt lost." The setback was unacceptable, and an elaborate psychodrama began. Walt sent a notice around that Babbit, unforgiven for his role in the strike, was to be greeted with "the silent treatment." Recalled Babbit, "Anyone caught talking to me was to be summarily fired. When Disney came down the hallway, he would always get coughing fits when we passed, so he could cover his face and not have to look at me. Besides constant anonymous threats of physical violence, they'd sometimes put pretty girls in my room, where I worked, in order to distract me, to catch me in some sort of compromising position. But I was one tough sonofabitch and wouldn't fall for it." Still, the stifling corporate atmosphere ultimately consumed all the oxygen in the room and Walt got his wish after all: Babbit quit to pursue what he called "a sane career." Once the hated employee was gone, he became a nonperson in Walt's eyes and on his records. Disney ordered the animator's name expunged from the credits of *Snow White* and all the other films he had worked on, as well as any related printed materials and publicity documents. Stalin could not have been more thorough.

The heat of battle seemed to warm Walt's blood. He looked up from his miniature rolling stock to consider new projects. The *Adventures of Ichabod and Mr. Toad* would be another anthology film, a two-part feature based on Kenneth Graham's *The Wind in the Willows* and Washington Irving's *Legend of Sleepy Hollow.* After that would come *Cinderella,* then his old favorites, *Alice in Wonderland* and *Peter Pan.* These features would take a great deal of money to make, and Walt thought first of his old benefactor, Joseph Rosenberg, at the Bank of America. But conditions has changed since the old days. America's postwar prosperity had yet to reach the Disney studio: It was actually $4 million in debt. The banker advised his client to look elsewhere for money: What about the new owner of RKO Pictures, a venture capitalist and aviator who liked to dabble in films? Perhaps Howard Hughes would come up with the funds. A meeting was arranged and to everyone's surprise, including the participants, Disney and Hughes hit it off. They were never to be close friends, but each recognized the other as an eccentric in the same mold, autocratic, chain-smoking, nostalgic for the uncomplicated nation of his boyhood. Hughes thought he could do something with the Disney inventory; schools and private exhibitors might pay sizable fees to rent the classic cartoons and features. If Walt would let RKO have the nontheatrical, nonbroadcast rights, Hughes would grant the Disney studio an interest-free loan, repayable from the newly opened foreign markets. Walt jumped at the chance. Early in 1948, he called a press conference to announce the deal and spread the euphoria. That day, he said, "As you walk down Dopey Drive and turn left on Mickey Mouse Avenue to the studio gate, the sunshine seems a little brighter."

In June 1946, the National Broadcasting Company had made a telecast of the Joe Louis–Billy Conn heavyweight championship fight. Not many Americans owned sets and only a few newspapers bothered to comment on the new electronic medium. One of them was the *Washington Post*. "Television," it told readers, "looks good for a 1,000 year run."

Hollywood ignored the forecast. A character on Fred Allen's show had just spoken of his unwillingness to own even one radio because "I don't hold with furniture that talks." What was a television set but furniture that glared? Robert Taylor and Olivia De Havilland loomed like Isis and Thoth in the motion picture palaces; you could cover the figures on the television screen with your hand. What reason was there to fear such a paltry achievement? A year and a half later, producers found new reassurance in a study by the Twentieth Century Fund. "Movie going has become a fixed habit with the American people," said the report, "and it is unlikely to be shaken by the advent of television."

The complacency lasted about six months. Then a series of events conspired to change the town and the studios forever. First, in the case of *United States* v. *Paramount et al.,* the Supreme Court decided against the major studios. All were ordered to divest themselves of their theater holdings. They could produce whatever they wished, but they could no longer control the retail end of the business—there would be no more "block booking" with the same film simultaneously running in a thousand subservient movie houses. During this period, Britain, France, and Italy, in an effort to stem the outflow of currency to the United States, imposed heavy quotas on imported films. Just as the studios tried to adjust to the new realities, more bad news arrived in the form of demography. The postwar recovery allowed veterans to realize a dream they had nourished all the years they were in uniform: owning their own homes. More than half of these dwellings were in just-bulldozed developments outside the city limits, and few planners had thought to equip the tracts with theaters. A young husband spoke about the situation to the *Saturday Evening Post*. "First I have to change my clothes," he said. "Then I have to hire a babysitter. I drive downtown in heavy traffic, fork up 50 cents at a parking lot, and walk about seven blocks to pay two dollars for two tickets. It's too much trouble and it costs too much."

Individual ticket sales plummeted; by 1949, they had fallen 14.2 percent. That year, Americans spent a smaller share of their incomes on movies than at any time since the Depression. Sam Goldwyn was the first studio head to face the truth: "People will be unwilling to pay to see bad pictures when they can stay home and see something which is, at least, no worse." Warner continued to play the ostrich, petulantly banning TV sets from the lot. A screenwriter wryly predicted, "The swimming pools are drying up all over town. I do not think I shall see them filled in my generation." The movietown jitters were not only the subject of gossip on the set and in the corner offices, they worked their way into feature films. On one level, *All About Eve* is the backstage tale of a ruthless ingenue befriending a headliner in order to betray and replace her. But it is also a story of ambitious youth, contemptuous of tradition and social place, trampling the past in pursuit of glory. For Margo Channing read Hollywood, for Eve read the voracious newcomer, TV. *Sunset Boulevard* presents contemporary Hollywood as a thicket of predators. No one denies that the old town was notorious for its pushcart peddlers turned moguls—Poland to polo in one generation. Still, the place had its loyalties and standards. In 1950, these were swept away. Even 10 percenters sold out their clients: "Maybe you better get another agent," says Joe Gillis's representative, shunning the writer who dares to ask for a loan to tide him over. Then an obsolete silent film star takes pity on Gillis in order to feed her self-delusions. Norma Desmond stands for Hollywood in extremis. When Gillis observes that the aging actress used to be big, Desmond replies with the one of the most quoted lines in cinema history: "I *am* big, it's the pictures that got small."

To remind people that even the worst films were bigger than the best TV shows, the industry took out ads that no one believed: "Movies Are Better Than Ever"; "Get More Out of Life, Go Out to a Movie." When these failed to bring in a sufficient crowd, it fell back on the reliable old nostrums: Size and Significance—big musicals like the Gershwin romance *An American in Paris;* or such extravaganzas as *The Greatest Show on Earth* and *Around the World in 80 Days.* Interspersed with these overloaded features were stark Broadway dramas: *A Streetcar Named Desire; Death of a Salesman; Come Back, Little Sheba; The Country Girl.* The important films of the fifties tended to go heavy on metaphor: the blacklisted Carl Foreman's *High Noon*—one man against the malefactors, with no help from the indifferent townspeople; *On the Waterfront,* Elia Kazan's defense of those, like him, who had cooperated with the Committee—sometimes you had to name names. Comedy retreated into puerility, typified by the emergence of Jerry Lewis on film and Milton Berle on television. Both were veterans of the Borscht Belt; both made new reputations by becoming human cartoons. Lewis, ten years younger, played and replayed a spastic loser who somehow manages to get the girl. Berle was the brash and shameless tummler who never grew up, mugging, overacting, horning in on other acts, reviving ancient routines, like the miming of a fat woman putting on a girdle, which other comedians had abandoned long before. Envious rivals dubbed him the Thief of Badgags. "Milton is responsible for more television sets being sold than anyone else," said Joe E. Lewis. "I sold mine. My father sold his. . . ." While the comics threw rocks, Berle rose to unchallenged prominence as a new generation greeted him in their living rooms as Uncle Miltie and Mr. Television.

During this fallow period, James Thurber defined his fellow humorists as those who have, "nobody knows why, a genius for getting into minor difficulties; they walk into the wrong apartments, they drink furniture polish for stomach bitters, they drive their cars into the prize tulip beds of haughty neighbors, they playfully slap gangsters, mistaking them for old school friends." These unfortunates can always be spotted in a crowd, talking "largely about small affairs and smally about great affairs, ears shut to the ominous rumbling of the dynasties of the world moving toward a cloudier chaos than ever before." Yet now Thurber's home base, the deliberately, proudly insular *New Yorker,* had published the entire text of John Hersey's *Hiroshima.* Except for a few brand names, the wild old humor was gone from its pages. Small wonder that critics mourned the disappearance of polished, headlong, joyously irrelevant American farce.

They were looking in the wrong places. That kind of humor was not to be found in the magazines anymore, and not in broadcasting, books, or movies—except for the little films with names like "Ballot Box Bunny," "Johann Mouse," "Duck Amuck," and "Mice-Capades." While the cold war put a layer of ice on the outside world, and gross comics underlined the obvious, polished screwball comedy found a home in cartoons. At MGM, Tex Avery learned how to produce mayhem in miniature. Routines that once consumed thirty feet of film were squeezed down to eight. "I found out," he said, "the eye can register an action in five frames of film at one twenty-fourth of a second. So it's roughly one fifth of a second to register something, from the screen to your eye to the brain. I found out if I wanted something just barely to be seen five frames was all it needed. Say we had an anvil falling. We would bring it in perhaps four or five frames before the hit, that's all you need—Djuuuuuu . . . Bam! It's there and you don't know where the hell it came from. It makes that gag that much funnier. If you saw a thing coming down, and you panned down with it, and it hits—uh—uh."

When he was not absorbed with violence, Avery jubilantly turned to sex. One of his favorite characters, Red Hot, made her first appearance at MGM during the war. The redheaded singer, animated with enormous gusto by Preston Blair, excited an audience of howling wolves wherever she performed. The Hays office was forever demanding cuts, and Avery saw its point. "Showing body heat, the steam coming out of the collar, and the tongue rolling out—it's suggestive stuff, in a way. Sometimes we would just stiffen [the wolf] in mid-air; he'd make a take and his whole

body would stiffen out like an arrow!" Too phallic, said the guardians of public morals, and out it went. But by the late forties, Avery and his crew had mastered the art of evading censorship. "If we had one suggestive gag there, or one that was particularly suggestive but we felt was very funny, then in there we would inject perhaps three that we knew we couldn't get by with. And then it'd come back from Hays, well, they'd check out in the red pencil, 'This goes . . . this has to go!' And hidden in there is this little one that we liked. They'd say, 'Well, this is pretty bad, but we'll let this one slip by.' "

"Little Rural Riding Hood," released in 1949, provides a case in point. A country wolf visits his cousin in town. The two repair to a nightclub to watch Red gyrate. The performance is too calorific for the yokel; his eyes spring from their sockets, his tongue drops to the floor, he ignites his nose instead of his cigarette, all the while babbling "Wanna kiss the girls, where's the girls, sure do love girls!" Appalled at his cousin's behavior, the supercilious city wolf knocks him unconscious, packs him into his car, and drives him back to the sticks. There he sees a shapely milkmaid and explodes with all the libidinous gestures of his country cousin. . . .

Blair remembered that Fred Quimby—the same producer so careful of Hitler's feelings a few years back—never shared the wolves' affection for Red. "He didn't like the character because I could only animate about 15 feet of her a week, and we were supposed to do 25." So Avery turned his attention to other characters, among them Droopy, a dog with a depressed, baggy voice and low-slung jowls, who always managed to defeat larger antagonists; and Screwy Squirrel, who was everything his name implies: crazy, aggressive, loud, unalleviated by Bugs Bunny's panache or Tweety Bird's gentler comedy. "The genius of Tex lay more in his graphic approach than in his characters," observes Chuck Jones. "While the rest of us were getting more involved with the personalities of our creatures, Tex was bending and breaking rules, taking the screen to places it had never been before." In Avery's postwar cartoons, animals and people habitually defy natural law and cinematic rules. They race to the edge of the frame only to get caught in the sprockets; telephone to someone on the other side of a split screen— and then reach through the dividing line to touch the character on the other side. At any time, a dog or cat may break away from its role to demand, "Who's directing this picture?"

Inventive as he was, Avery never received the recognition or the financial rewards of two MGM colleagues. William Hanna preferred an entry-level job in animation to the uncertainties of a career in structural engineering; Joseph Barbera was trained as a banker. They came to MGM in the late thirties, where the pair seemed to mark time until they were assigned to "Puss Gets the Boot." It featured a cat called Jasper vainly trying to annihilate an unnamed mouse. Quimby disliked it so much that he forbade them to do any more pictures with felines and rodents. "We might have made fish pictures, horse pictures, and any number of other failures," conjectured Barbera, "continuing on the studio's infernal tangent to nowhere until some executive would finally have the decency to put the cartoon department out of its misery. But then a single, miraculous letter appeared in Fred Quimby's mail. It was from a leading Texas exhibitor: 'When are we going to see more of those charming cat-and-mouse cartoons?' Instantly we were directed to make more." The animals were renamed Tom and Jerry, given sharper outlines and more emphatic personalities, and supplied with a cornucopia of sight gags. Essentially, the cat was the pursuer who became the victim; the mouse was the allegedly helpless target whose cruelty knew no bounds. Avery's restless spirit always kept his cartoons from getting stale, and their manic violence from edging over to the brutal or the sadistic. The same could not be said of Hanna and Barbera. They knew a mediocre thing when they saw it, and for more than a decade devoted themselves exclusively to Tom and Jerry. In most of their cartoons, brutality is only a frame away (Jerry's idea of a good time consists of driving a golf ball through Tom's teeth, and if a waffle iron is heating on a stove, it can only be a matter of moments before the cat's tail gets trapped in it.) And there is worse: As Tom chases Jerry around the baseboards of a suburban house, the pursuit is frequently interrupted by a human, "Mammy Two-Shoes," a galumphing black domestic who can only be seen from the hemline down. Naturally, Jerry terrifies her and as Mammy fusses and scampers away, dice, watermelon, switchblade knives, and other supposed appurtenances of the ghetto tumble from her capacious housedress. The saddest part of Hanna and Barbera's early history is that they had no reason to use such cheap inducements. At their best, the collaborators produced seven Oscar winners, including the classic "Cat Concerto," in which Tom performs Liszt's Second Hungarian

Rhapsody. Asleep on the Steinway strings, Jerry awakens, stirs, and seeks revenge, furiously conducting Tom, leading him astray with all sorts of incorrect tempi. A chase ensues, always within reach of the keyboard, and not a note is missed. Tom and Jerry even stepped out of their own cartoons to stir up the live film *Anchors Aweigh,* dancing with Gene Kelly. But there were too many times when Hanna and Barbera went for the repetitious routine and the cheap joke. As long as the cat-and-mouse game continued, their lack of real wit was masked by fluent animation. It would be revealed soon enough, and it would make them the butt of dedicated cartoonists who derisively referred to products made by Hanna and the Barbarians. It would also make them extremely rich.

At Warner, an executive almost as unsympathetic as Fred Quimby was brought in to oversee production. Edward Seltzer became notorious at Termite Terrace for viewing footage and demanding in one cascade, "Theresomethingnewtakeitout." This was his usual response to any unprecedented routine, sequence, or character. Writers especially cherished a remark Seltzer made when he found them chortling over a storyboard: "Just what the hell has all this laughter got to do with the making of animated cartoons?" If Seltzer thought his admonitions would bring about a change of routine, he was right. The tighter the strictures, the more inventive were the attempts to circumvent them. "Eddie once appeared in the doorway while the writer, Mike Maltese, and I were trying to come up with a premise," Chuck Jones remembers. "Without any provocation, he said, 'I don't want any gags about bullfights, bullfights aren't funny.' Then he disappeared. Seltzer had once said the same thing about camels, whereupon Friz Freleng made a hilarious cartoon called 'Sahara Hare.' So Mike immediately responded, 'I never knew there was anything funny about bullfighting until now.' And we had our idea. 'Bully for Bugs' turned out to be one of our most successful works." Seltzer also provoked Jones to greater heights after a showing of "For Scentimental Reasons," starring the priapic skunk Pepe Le Pew: "Seltzer predicted, 'Nobody'd laugh at that shit.' But never let it be said that Eddie couldn't change his mind. Although he had found nothing funny about a skunk talking French and fought its use, he gracefully accepted as his right the Oscar when the cartoon won."

In the early fifties, all but the actual Warner brothers, Jack and Harry, realized that a comic genius lurked on studio grounds. Jones had begun his career by imitating Disney and concentrating on small, shy characters such as Sniffles, a mouse who slept in a matchbox. By Avery's account, "Chuck tried to compete with Walt. Did the little fuzzy things for a while there, then he got off it, finally saw the light." With that illumination, Jones joined the small group of highly original talents whose ambitions stretched the limits of their budgets and storyboards. Yet there was a difference between Jones and the others. The work of Freleng, Warner's first master of comic timing, derived from the strange admixture of Disney and vaudeville. Although Clampett had watched the makers of silent films as a child, his sensibility seemed closer to the puppets and toys he had designed early in his career. However brilliant his cartoons, they always had the faint suggestion of Punch and Judy, raucously trying to pound one another into splinters. Jones was also a child of Southern California, and he, too, had watched the Keystone Kops rehearsing in the orange groves. But his strongest sources came from the world of literature. As a child, Jones read every volume in the furnished houses his entrepreneurial father kept renting and quitting.

The adolescent art student peppered his conversation with references to Mark Twain and George Santayana, and with allusions to natural and human history. The love of books increased with age. "Chuck always read the encyclopedia as if it were the latest best-seller," observed his old friend, novelist Ray Bradbury. "Whenever he called me up and asked, 'Did you know that the male whale swims around the Atlantic with a permanent erection?' or 'Did you know that when the engineers on the trans-Egyptian railway ran out of fuel they burned mummy cases?' I knew he'd been at the Brittannica again."

Jones wore his scholarship lightly; the characters in his films never spout strange facts or quote the classics. Instead, they exhibit true personalities and native wit. "I learned," the cartoon maker said, "that I could not animate a character I could laugh at but not understand. Bugs Bunny, for instance. Those were giants who had gone before me, and they had done wonders with him. Still, a wild, wild hare was not for me. What I needed was a character with the spicy, somewhat erudite introspection of a Professor Higgins, who, when nettled or threatened, would respond with the swagger of D'Artagnan as played by Errol Flynn, with the articulate quick-wittedness of Dorothy Parker—in other words, the Rabbit of My Dreams, something I could never be.

"This Bugs Bunny is too strong a character to behave as an early Daffy Duck or a late Woody Woodpecker. It is no part of his character to go out and bedevil anyone for mischief's sake alone." In contrast, Jones's Daffy became the swaggering loser, a "preservationist," in his creator's word, who would betray a friend at the drop of a coin, and run from danger pleading, "I'm not like the others. I can't stand pain."

As Jones's career developed, a question arose. Manifestly, he could fill out and modify someone else's invention. But could the animator invent characters strong enough to last, as Freleng had invented the durable Yosemite Sam and Clampett the I Tawt I Taw A Putty Tat series with Tweety Bird and Sylvester Cat? To some degree, Pepe Le Pew provided an answer. But it was "Fast and Furry-ous" and "Beep Beep" that established Jones as a maker of superstars. He drew his inspiration from Mark Twain. In *Roughing It,* the author describes the coyote as "a long, slim, sick and sorry-looking skeleton with a gray wolf-skin stretched over it, a tolerably bushy tail that forever sags down with a despairing expression of forsakenness and misery, a furtive and evil eye, and a long, sharp face, with slightly lifted lip and exposed teeth.

He has a general slinking expression all over. The coyote is a living, breathing allegory of Want. He is *always* hungry." In the long life and hard times of Wile E. Coyote, the luckless mammal (*Carnivarious vulgaris*) pursues a permanently elusive roadrunner (*Accelerati incredibulis*). In their debut, the first of more than forty episodes with the same pair, the filmmakers discovered that eleven gags—not ten, not twelve—comprised a Roadrunner cartoon. These would come to include an exploding glass that backfires, a magnet that accidentally attracts a container of TNT, a boomerang that attacks the Coyote instead of the Roadrunner, quick-drying cement that splatters on the Coyote instead of the Roadrunner, dehydrated boulders that crush the Coyote instead of the Roadrunner, a swarm of bumble bees that goes after the Coyote instead of the Roadrunner, and scores of other items from the Acme catalog of instruments guaranteed to disable birds but which always manage to undo the buyer. According to Jones, "The Coyote is a history of my own frustrations and war with all tools, multiplied only slightly. I can remember that my wife and daughter would start to weep bitterly and seek hiding places whenever they saw me head toward the tool drawer." He remembered an attempt to get "a spiky thing out of the drawer, but found out that the last time it had fallen on a tube of glue, puncturing the tube and affixing it to the drawer for all time. I have tried lackadaisically from time to time to remove it, and have succeeded in breaking a rattail file, a kitchen knife, three fingernails, a nailfile, a pair of manicure scissors, an eggbeater (in one of my more fanciful efforts) and a window, when the tail of the rattail file separated from the rattail file."

Here, another *New Yorker* tradition was being assumed, three thousand miles from its birthplace. The magazine's resident humorist, Robert Benchley, had staged a long and famous war with inanimate objects. He exaggerated, of course, but the ineptitude was genuine. His family had heard him pleading, "Somebody get this away from me!" as he tried to unfold a beach chair; and Nathaniel Benchley wrote of the time his father packed up to leave town: "As he was walking across the room with an armful of shirts, he stepped into an open suitcase; the knee buckled, and he fell forward and closed his fingers in a dresser drawer. It was several minutes before he was able to extricate himself, and he made the train with only seconds to spare, but his real regret was that nobody had been there to witness his fall. He figured

LLOYD VAUGHAN

that he must have looked unbearably funny." Benchley died in 1945, and now, in an unexpected location and in a new decade, Jones had picked up the fallen banner.

The fifties were an extraordinary fertile period for the director. In "What's Opera, Doc?" (first on the list of *50 Greatest Cartoons*), he simultaneously parodied Wagner's Ring Cycle and Disney's *Fantasia*. Elmer Fudd, costumed as Seigfried, hunts his traditional game. To escape, Bugs gets himself up as Brünhilde, complete with blond braids and curvaceous gold breastplate. Elmer is immediately smitten, and he and Bugs sing a love duet to Wagner's melodies: "Oh, Bwünhilde, you're so wovewy"; "I know it, I can't help it." The idyll continues until Elmer discovers that he has been duped. Standing on a crag, he furiously summons forth wind, lightning, and a lethal smog. As a suddenly remorseful Siegfried walks off with the limp body of the "wabbit" in his arms, Bugs suddenly rouses himself for a dying line: "What did you expect in an opera, a happy ending?" In addition to Michael Maltese's spare, funny script and the inspired lunacy of the characters, "What's Opera" displayed a baroque gelding, and elaborate backgrounds that out-Disneyed Walt's most pretentious footage. The scenery was the work of Maurice Noble, one of several key artists who altered their time cards, stealing time from a less complicated Roadrunner short. As the *50 Greatest Cartoons* notes, "Obviously, they knew they were working on a classic."

A handful of those fifty employ Daffy for a wide range of parts. "The Scarlet Pumpernickel" features the Duck as a starving screenwriter *and* as the star of his own swashbuckling scenario, conjured up as he makes a pitch to Jack Warner. By day the Pumpernickel is a sixteenth-century fop; by night, a masked daredevil who bungles every exploit ("This never happens to Errol Flynn," mutters the bewildered hero as he leaps from a window, misses his horse, and crashes to the ground). His notion of a thrill-packed climax includes a dam bursting, an erupting volcano, a cavalry charge, and a shortage of kreplach. In addition to satirizing Warner Bros.'s overstuffed costume pictures, Jones sent up the studio's insistence on using the same character actors in film after film. "There were a lot of in-house jokes," he remembered. "We put in the Mother Bear from the early Three Bears cartoons, 'Henery' Hawk appeared as a messenger, and, of course, we had Sylvester as the heavy and Porky as a bewigged aristocrat."

In "Duck Dodgers in the 24th ½ Century," Daffy is a space explorer sent to Planet X in order to claim the last supply of "alludium, fozdex, the shaving cream atom." After a false start, backing deep into the earth ("Had the silly thing in reverse"), he tries to locate the mysterious Planet X. His space cadet, Porky, suggests that they start with planets A, B, and C and work their way up the alphabet. Sure enough, there it is. ("Gad!" exclaims Daffy. "How do it I do it?") Moments after they land, a rival rocketship zooms in. The pilot: Marvin Martian, with his own ideas about galactic imperialism. A showdown takes place on another intricate Maurice Noble set, with the opponents firing every comic weapon in their arsenals until the entire planet is reduced to a sliver of soil. Desperately clinging to it, Daffy triumphantly claims it for the Planet Earth. Desperately clinging to Daffy, Porky surveys the damage and stutters the curtain line: "B-B-Big Deal." This commentary on the futility of cold war rivalries is as close as Warner ever came to an editorial cartoon. Unlike most topical films of the period, it survives because the slapstick and the dialogue occur outside their era, as timeless as the two-reelers of Chaplin and Keaton.

"Duck Amuck" represents Jones's venture into the cinema of the absurd. Here Daffy enters again with cape and sword. "Stand back, Musketeers, they shall sample my blade!" But the background and the music have vanished. "Hey, psst," he asks in a stage whisper, "whoever's in charge here, the scenery, where's the scenery?" A moment later a paintbrush draws a barnyard setting. Daffy alertly jettisons his swashbuckler's suit for overalls and hoe. But by that time the background has been altered anew. Now he's in the North Pole. The confusion has only begun. By the finale, Daffy has been dragged to Hawaii and made to wear a sarong; given a guitar that renders him mute; put in a sailor suit and nearly drowned; painted as a surreal, web-footed animal with flower petals growing out of his head; split in half, precipitating a quarrel with himself; put in a plane and forced to bail out, at which point his parachute is weighted with an anvil. An unseen hand is doing all this, as mysterious as Godot and as cruel as Fate. Only at the last moment is the auteur revealed: Bugs at an animator's drawing board, looking down and musing, "Gee, ain't I a stinker?" More than any other film, "Duck Amuck" reflects the studio's aleatory nature: "The idea began with Daffy running out of background," said Jones. "The rest of the cartoon happened right there on the board. Mike Maltese and I didn't have a story as such. I came up with the opening, and we just went from there. We didn't hit upon the Bugs Bunny ending until the last week of layout. That was the way inspiration was allowed to work in those glorious days."

As the mainstream cartoon studios worked in what was to later to be recognized as the Golden Age, a nucleus of animators were busy drawing outside the lines. They had split off from Disney at the time of the strike, and several of them had worked on "Hell Bent for Election," the minimalist 1944 cartoon dedicated to keeping Franklin Delano Roosevelt in office for a fourth term. After the war, the most talented of the group organized a new studio, Industrial Films and Poster Service. One of its early efforts, "Brotherhood of Man," showed an even more advanced graphic design. (It also contained more advanced political content: The United Auto Workers Union, which had produced both films, wanted to encourage blacks and whites to join the same southern locals. At the time, this was considered a revolutionary idea, and union officials thought that a little humor might help to make the sale. They were right.) Subsequent work was known for bright primary hues, lonely appealing protagonists who seemed to have leaped from *New Yorker* cartoons—particularly the bold linear designs of Saul Steinberg—and a jaunty disregard for perspective and realism.

During the late forties, Industrial Films and Poster Service was reorganized and renamed United Productions of America. In its early struggles for recognition, UPA suffered as much from internecine strife as from battles with outside forces. Sides were drawn up. Within a year, the original owners, Zach Schwartz and Dave Hilberman, sold off their interest and opened a studio, Tempo Productions, in New York. Tempo enjoyed some quick success in the field of television commercials, but neither man was to be an influence in the New Wave of Hollywood animation. That was left to their principal opponent, Stephen Bosustow. The winner of the battle for control of UPA was criticized for egotism and mismanagement, but no one ever accused him of lethargy. Unable to issue regular paychecks, he kept the nucleus of his staff in place by offering stock to favored employees, including the Disney veterans John Hubley and Dave Hilberman, who had been with UPA from the start. Meanwhile, Bosustow tirelessly banged on doors until he convinced Columbia to distribute his company's cartoons. There was a catch: UPA had to use the studio's established characters, the Fox and Crow, mediocre stars of some earlier shorts. UPA gamely turned out "Robin Hoodlum," starring the Fox as Robin Hood and the Crow as the Sheriff of Nottingham, and used the pair in two other cartoons with promising titles but conventional executions, "The Magic Fluke" and "Punchy De Leon." Even though "Robin" and "Magic" received Academy Award nominations, Hubley told friends he was "sick to death of people dressed in furs and feathers." He wanted to draw a human acting like a human in a human situation. The animator got his wish in 1949, when he was assigned to "Ragtime Bear." Just as Porky Pig had been a walk-on in his first role, Quincy Magoo began as a minor character, snorting and bombinating as he walked through the woods with his nephew, Waldo. Magoo had two major attributes. Hubley gave him the bulbous nose and tiny squinting eyes of W. C. Fields, allowing for a chain of sight gags (mistaking a bear for Waldo's raccoon coat set the pattern for reels to come). And Magoo had the good fortune to be voiced by Jim Backus. Like Mel Blanc, Backus came from an extensive career in radio and a budding one in films—four decades later, he was still complaining that more people remembered him as the voice of the nearsighted Mr. Magoo than as James Dean's father in *Rebel Without a Cause*. Freely ad-libbing in the recording studio, he made the old man apoplectic and lovable at the same time. The character took off; he became popular enough to star in some fifty cartoons, and he won two Academy Awards. All the same, while Quincy Magoo was UPA's largest star, he was not its most influential one. That title belonged to a character born when two veterans from Fort Roach met at a casual lunch. Philip Eastman had just joined United Productions of America, and he was sounding off for Theodor Geisel. "All the cartoons being made are obsolete," he claimed. "Mice keep outsmarting cats, and rabbits are always wiser than foxes. UPA has a fresh outlook. You must have a story idea for us."

As it happened, Dr. Seuss did have something in mind. Capital Records was about to come out with an instructive little fable about those who ostracize the "different." He thought he might polish it up a bit, change a few things, make the victim "a little kid who didn't speak words but only weird sounds." The boy's name was Gerald McBoing-Boing, and he was to become the centerpiece of an entirely new way of animating the human dilemma. Just as Eastman had promised, UPA swept away the conventions of animal comedy. Gerald was portrayed as a real boy in real pain, derided in school and deprecated by his family. Audiences found themselves laughing with a catch in their throats because Gerald's comic affliction was the cause of misery and misunderstanding. In the first of a long series built around the boy, director Robert Cannon and designer Bill Hurtz used tints and odd perspectives to convey a child's sense of dislocation. Jettisoning the customary cartoon devices—cuts, dissolves, wipes—they kept the character in view at all times; it was the backgrounds that did the moving. In "Gerald McBoing-Boing," no demarcations exist between walls and ceiling and floor. Chairs and sofas seem to float in air. Gerald starts his adventure feeling chipper, and the colors are primary and bright. As the jeers increase and his sense of isolation grows stronger, the palette gets dark and melancholy, abetted by minor chords and an intimidating background (a slow, sad walk up the unsupported stairway of Gerald's home was inspired by *The Fallen Idol,* the Graham Greene film about a child with a dreadful secret and no friend to confide in). By the time the boy runs away, only to be stalked at the town depot, the screen turns as dark as night. When the stalker turns out to be the manager of a local radio station, and the man offers him a job as director of sound effects, the rainbow hues return.

UPA's portrait of the Little Man Against Circumstance came at precisely the right moment. David Reisman's *The Lonely Crowd* was in vogue, its Inner Directed and Other Directed readers discussing the author's proclamation that people "are created different; they lose their social freedom and their individual autonomy in seeking to become like each other." As the political climate grew more gelid, as performers went on the blacklist and the pressure to conform increased, small symbols of rebellion were treasured. The Loner had always been the centerpiece of westerns and film noir, but now a different kind of hero emerged. The self-abnegating figure was matched against a faceless Establishment; withdrawn and shy, he went through the worst of times with a secret smile and an air of forbearance. He was Alec Guiness in *The Man in the White Suit* and *The Lavender Hill Mob;* he was Pogo, the title character in the most widely syndicated comic strip in America, matched against the vicious polecat Simple J. Malarkey, a stand-in for the red-baiting Senator Joseph McCarthy; he was the hollow-faced loser in De Sica's *The Bicycle Thief* and the adolescent

Holden Caulfield in *The Catcher in the Rye,* all characters who emerged in the first years of the fifties, along with Gerald. Having deserted Disney, *Time* embraced the new studio and the "understated motion" of its title character. "Little Gerald's talents are too specialized for many other stories," said the magazine, "but in its own way, his 'Boing' may prove as resounding as the first peep out of Mickey Mouse." A most excessive prediction, as it turned out, but significant all the same: "Gerald McBoing-Boing" won the 1951 Oscar for best animated short subject. The reviews kept coming in, and they were all hortatory. *Theater Arts* delighted in the proof that "cartoons need not be all cuteness or all violence . . . they can be artistic and intelligent and still be popular." Gilbert Seldes, tireless explainer of the popular arts, took up the cause. Disney's attempts at realism were passé, he decided. Walt had "subtly violated the character of the cartoon (which is a drawing on a flat surface) by giving it depth and, in a brilliant combination of artwork and machinery, substituted movement—remarkably lifelike— for animation." In contrast, UPA's attempts had turned a liability into a virtue. Its work was deliberately, self-consciously flat. No need for the multiplane camera in this new era: "Because they use one drawing for every two or three frames of the film, instead of Disney's one for each frame, the figures move less smoothly, they have a galvanic animation." Result: pure delight prompted by an "impudent and intelligent approach to subject matter and a gay palette, a cascading of light colors, the use of color and line always to suggest, never to render completely, a great deal of warmth, and an unfailing wit." To be sure, not every scene was original: "some of the cartoons recall stock episodes—tubas grunt and Mr. Magoo steps off a girder into thin air—but most of them are as fresh in concept as in execution."

Secure aesthetically, if not yet financially, UPA embarked on a number of breakthrough cartoons. In 1952, Hubley's brilliant "Rooty Toot Toot" retells the Frankie and Johnny ballad with fresh imagery and a score by Phil Moore, one of the first black composers to be given screen credit. Later that year, Hubley and designer Paul Julian produced seven short pieces of animation to bridge the scenes of *The Four Poster,* starring Rex Harrison and his then wife, Lilli Palmer. Some made a comic point—the husband's egomania was neatly punctured. Others offered an acute portrait of tragedy—their son's death in the Great War is commemorated with a view of Flanders Field, soaked with rain and covered with useless muddied helmets. Oddly enough, this, rather than the Magoos and McBoing-Boings, was the first UPA work to play in Eastern Europe. These breaks from traditional cat-and-mouse cartoons astounded a group of young cinema and art students, and they founded their own animation studio in Zagreb two years later. They would make their films come alive "not through the copying but through the transformation of reality," a deep bow to United Productions of America. Praised on both coasts and on either side of the Atlantic, the studio confidently sought out properties Disney would never have touched. James Thurber's drawings reminded many people of unbaked cookies; in order to preserve his line, UPA assigned its most unsophisticated draftsmen to "A Unicorn in the Garden." The author/artist's whimsy remained intact. Ludwig Bemelman's delicate watercolors jumped easily from the page to the screen in "Madeline." "The Tell-Tale Heart" used limited animation, gothic backgrounds, and James Mason's haunting narration to heighten the effects of Poe's story. In 1955, the Museum of Modern Art saluted the revolution in animation by mounting an exhibit of drawings, cels, and films called UPA: Form in the Animated Cartoon. Meanwhile, commercial offers kept the company's New York office so busy that TV spots soon accounted for over 40 percent of the yearly gross of $2.5 million. There was talk of a full-length animated Gilbert and Sullivan operetta, *Don Quixote, Volpone.* In 1956, CBS commissioned a half-hour series, "The Gerald McBoing-Boing Show." There seemed to be no end of possibilities as UPA rowed on to greater appreciation and rewards. It was only later that the cartoonists realized that what they heard in the distance was not applause; it was the sound of a waterfall.

CHAPTER EIGHT

WE COULD GET AWAY WITH LESS

One by one the giants succumbed. Joseph Barbera described the day the music stopped at MGM. "By the late 1950's, television was cutting deep inroads into traditional Hollywood's bottom line. Studio heads were desperately groping for corners to cut. One corner they found was ours." Examining the books, chief financial officer Arthur Loew Sr. had come across an interesting discrepancy. Each new cartoon could cost between $30,000 and $60,000 to produce, whereas rereleasing an old Tom and Jerry would bring in 90 percent of the income without any expense at all. His reaction was immediate and sulfurous. "At the time," Barbera adds, "Bill Hanna and I ran the MGM cartoon studio. But the call—and it was just a single phone call—came down from the front office, not to us but to our business manager: 'Close the studio. Lay everybody off.' With that phone call, conveyed to us secondhand, a whole career disappeared.

"Or so Bill and I thought—at the first shock of it."

At Warner, the ax fell with similar results. Chuck Jones wryly spoke of the time he, Friz Freleng, and their fellow director Bob McKimpson met Harry and Jack Warner at the studio's private dining room. "Harry set the tone of our day in court by observing that he had no idea where our cartoon division was, and added, 'The only thing I know is that we make Mickey Mouse.' We were proud to hear that and assured him that we would continue to keep Mickey at the top of his popularity. Jack Warner suggested that it would be healthiest for our future if we did so. Friz Freleng later contended, "the Warner brothers implicitly believed we did indeed make Mickey Mouse, until, shocked to dis-cover that we did not, they shut the studio." Jack Warner proceeded to do further damage, this time to himself. He sold off the rights to all the pre-1948 cartoons—some four hundred in all—for $3,000 apiece. Each one would go on to earn an average of $5,000 per year in rentals. "Jack had closed the studio before," Jones remembered. "In 1955 I had a short stint at Disney when 3-D hit the screens. Everybody wore those special glasses for a few months, and Warner was convinced that all babies would soon be born with one green and one red retina. So he shut our doors. The fad passed and Jack came to his senses. But not the second time. Then it was 'That's all folks' for Termite Terrace."

United Productions of America might have been expected to weather these economic conditions; its films had become so modish that even Disney animators were being instructed to put some UPA style into their backgrounds and figures. But the studio's bright facade was a mask for some serious predicaments. In testimony before the House Un-American Activities Committee, Walt Disney had blamed the strike at his studio on "a Communist group trying to take over my artists." He fingered Dave Hilberman as one of the culprits, a man who, "number one has no religion, and number two, had spent considerable time at the Moscow Art Theater." Although Hilberman left UPA, the Committee still regarded the upstart company as a haven of fellow travelers. Director William Hurtz was at the office when HUAC investigators dropped by and demanded to see the payroll book. "They went through the names of anyone who worked there, checked some off and gave it to Columbia, who came back and said these people have to be out of the studio or we yank the release. Most of the guys resigned rather than torpedo the studio." UPA's most original talent, John Hubley, was listed as one of the volunteers. That was not the way his widow Faith remembered it. "John didn't quit," she insisted, "he was kicked out." The HUAC was not finished with Hubley. In the early fifties, he turned his attention to an adaptation of the Broadway musical *Finian's Rainbow*. The songs by Burton Lane and E. Y. Harburg, "How Are Things in Glocca Mora?," "Old Devil Moon," "That Great Come and Get It Day," "If This Isn't Love" had made the Hit Parade, and a stellar cast kept the show at the 46th Street Theater for 725 performances—this despite notices that derided "the most elaborate plot since *War and Peace*." They had a point. *Finian's* offered a potpourri of Irish mythology and American history, atomic energy, a pot of gold, a leprechaun and his pretty daughter who turns a segregationist into a black man until the bigot sees the error of his ways—and, of course, the complications of romantic love. An enterprising film producer, Michael Shore, recognized that the musical was clotted and ambiguous: "It tells you that a terrible person turns black because he's so bad, and then redeems himself and they reward him by making him white again. It occurred to me that the story line could be made more palatable if it were done in animation."

At another time, the majors would have bid for a property with so many hit songs and production numbers. Now they were silent, unwilling to tackle anything with the slightest hint of political controversy. With no one to outbid him, Shore took an option and began to confer with Hubley. "John was in love with *Finian's Rainbow*," said Faith. "It was to be the work of his life." A new company, DCA, headed by Fred J. Schwartz, was brought in to raise funds and arrange distribution. Storyboards decorated the walls of Hubley's new studio in Los Angeles, and plans were made to hire the best talent in the business, including the old Disney strikers Art Babbit and Bill Tytla. Frank Sinatra, then at the peak of his bel canto phase, was attracted to the project. He would be singing voice of the male lead; other parts would be taken by Ella Fitzgerald and Ella Logan, one of the stars of the original Broadway production. Several songs and pages of dialogue were recorded on the Samuel Goldwyn lot; attendees told their colleagues that *Finian's* would surpass anything dreamed up at Disney, Warner, MGM, or UPA. Creative problems arose, but these were surmounted. (Shore, who had conceived the animated film project in the first place, found himself "on the outside looking in. I couldn't even get into the office" until a lawyer negotiated a rapprochement.)

Then one morning Schwartz received a phone call from Roy Brewer. In addition to his job as leader of the International Alliance of Theatrical Stage Employees, Brewer held high office in the Motion Picture Alliance for the Preservation of American Ideals. This was the outfit that Walt Disney had founded to keep leftists from sullying the film industry, and few production houses escaped its scrutiny. Brewer informed Schwartz that he had an unspecified "problem," and suggested a private meeting. The problem turned out to be Hubley; Brewer called him "suspect," underlining the animator's refusal to testify before the Committee. "If he doesn't appear and clear himself," Brewer warned, "you lose your money, you lose everything." With the picture at stake, Schwartz confronted Hubley: "I have to ask you a question. I have to swallow hard before I ask it. I want you to know I don't believe in it, but I'm faced with a terrible situation with many individuals at risk. Were you ever a member of the Communist party?"

Hubley indignantly replied, "No. Definitely not! I will admit that like many other artists in Hollywood, I belonged to some organizations that had high-sounding names and when I found out they were fronts for the Communist party, I left them. That's as far as I ever went."

"John," Schwartz continued, "we have $365,000 in the project. There are other people involved. Go before the Committee and clear yourself, so we can go ahead."

"I would be happy to," the animator told him—then added, "but they're going to ask me to name other names, and that I won't do!"

Hubley's position could not be kept secret for long. DCA's parent company, Century Film, and their lender, Chemical Bank, dropped their support of *Finian's Rainbow*. Scrambling for new money, Schwartz persuaded RKO to put up $75,000. He went back to Century, hoping to change a few minds. The executives shook their heads. The next day, Chemical Bank gave Schwartz their final judgment: "If your own company turned you down, we can't lend you the money." That effectively ended the project. DCA abruptly shut shop and the employees dispersed. All that remained were some luminous drawings, and Sinatra's recordings, both prized by collectors. More than a dozen years would go by before *Finian's Rainbow* came before the cameras in a live adaptation. Miscast and charmless, it had only one distinction: It was Francis Ford Coppola's worst picture. "The blacklist was that powerful," Schwartz concluded in a reminiscence. "This is an example of what happens when you squelch talent. Which is directly against everything we stand for, such as freedom of speech. This could have been a classic." On the other hand, as one of the artists suggested, "it could have been one of those art house movies, by animators for animators, the kind that never play outside New York and Los Angeles and gets rented two generations later by film students. Who can tell? That's the hell of it. We'll never know."

Hubley's former base, UPA, buoyantly entered the television market with "The Gerald McBoing-Boing Show" on CBS in December 1956.

Accustomed to the rhythms and demands of the movie business, Bosustow and his staff walked into a wall. The gentle whimsy of Gerald; the show's central segment, "Dusty of the Circus," about a boy who could converse with lions and tigers; the educational portions, "Meet the Artist" and "Meet the Inventor," were made for a selective audience, not the mass of television watchers—and certainly not for ratings-hungry programmers. The kiss of death came when the *Los Angeles Times* praised the show's "remarkable ability to tickle the funny bone of a philosopher." Those who lived the life of the mind were the last people advertisers wished to reach. "The Gerald McBoing-Boing Show" went off the air October 1958. That cancellation marked the beginning of a long slide downhill for its creators. UPA shut its unprofitable London office, and when the market for commercials dried up, closed its New York headquarters as well. Bosustow and his staff made one last creative effort: They hired Aldous Huxley to work up a treatment of *Don Quixote*. UPA's bank refused to back the project; according to one executive, they had never heard of the Don. They had, however, heard of the Arabian Nights, and underwrote an adaptation starring Quincy Magoo. The full-length project retained some of the studio's old graphic style—and that was its trouble. Nothing rusts as rapidly as fashion, and the UPA style lacked the ability to astonish. The humor, based on a curmudgeon's confusion of objects, had run dry. *Newsweek* encapsulated *1001 Nights* in a sentence: "In the first minute of the movie, Magoo remonstrates with a flock of birds which he thinks are schoolboys, puts the coffee pot on the fishbowl instead of the stove, mistakes a camel for his nephew, and pats a stool thinking it is his cat (which is named Bowzir because to Magoo it is a dog)." The public had fallen out of love with myopia, and after a short run the picture was withdrawn. UPA's brightest talents got the message and sought jobs elsewhere. At the end of the decade, Bosustow sold out to Henry G. Saperstein, who would drain the lifeblood out of all the old cartoon characters. The graphic revolution was over.

Throughout the fifties, Disney's critical reputation continued to slip. *Cinderella*, released in 1950, ran seventy-four minutes and reminded many of the great days when Walt turned out radiant, full-length features, picking up awards along with the profits. The public approved; *Cinderella* grossed over $4 million, putting the studio in the black. Reviewers were not so sanguine. In the *Saturday Review*, John

Mason Brown expressed bewilderment at his own dissatisfaction. "Is it because I have grown older? Is it because repetition is bound to have robbed his work of its novelty? Is it because Mr. Disney at present fails me or I fail him? Or is it because of the very nature of the medium at which he excels? Is this because it is a medium that, in spite of his courage and success of his attempts to alter and enlarge it, is nonetheless limited?" *Time* found the central characters "drawn in an attempt at literal likeness that the best technique of animation never brings off without a certain stiffness."

Walt lost more ground the following year when *Alice in Wonderland* appeared in theaters. He, too, had kept Aldous Huxley busy on an adaptation. The arrangement had not worked out, and Walt had settled for a collective scenario credited to thirteen writers. For all the fathers, the film was something of an orphan. Alice did display some remarkable footage, notably the Caterpillar puffing on a hookah and making smoke rings in the shape of the words he spoke. But as a whole the thing was a hodgepodge, chiefly because Disney rarely trusted Lewis Carroll to speak for himself. The mushrooms, the threats of beheadings, the tumbling through tunnels, the compound absurdities of the Alice books had provoked shelves of interpretations—Freudian, Jungian, and literary. Walt wanted no part of them and may have been embarrassed by the Carrollian symbols of sex and aberrant behavior. Certainly, he kept as many as he could from reaching the screen. In their place were novelty songs, disfiguring the classic every frame of the way, along with the inappropriate voices of comedians Jerry Colonna as the March Hare and Ed Wynn as the Mad Hatter. Walt expected the worst from English purists; just before the London opening, he warned his office about "a certain handful who can never be satisfied." In fact, the British objections surprised everyone with their mildness. Only one critic remarked that the film missed the "sense of summer peace, the comfortable drowsy Victorian quietude that used to brood over these magic stories." Americans had far less tolerance. The *New Yorker* called the picture "a dreadful mockery," pointing out that "in Mr. Disney's *Alice* there is a blind incapacity to understand that a literary masterwork cannot be improved by the introduction of shiny little tunes, and touches more suited to a flea circus than to a major imaginative effort." After years of admiration for practically everything Walt ever produced, *Life* remarked that "the leering, loony faces he has concocted will be a shock to oldsters brought up on the famous John Tenniel illustrations." Yet none of these reproaches could have stung as painfully as the dressing down Roy gave his brother. When it became clear that the feature was not only an aesthetic but also a financial disaster, he reminded Walt, "I kept telling you that *Alice* would never catch on. You only made it to puff up your goddamned ego."

Neither Roy nor the reviewers were kind to Walt's next project, *Peter Pan,* another favorite of the English nursery. Bosley Crowther complained, "Mr. Disney has completely eliminated from his film the spirit of guileless credulity in fairy that prevails in the play." In *Sight and Sound,* cineaste David Fisher went further: "As expected, Disney brings to Barrie's tale his comic strip mind and sentimental vulgarity." (This curiously antiseptic and evasive approach could be seen not only in the animated feature but in the studio's commercial work. At the same time *Peter Pan* went before the cameras, the studio produced "The Story of Menstruation" for Kimberly-Clark. In the short film, noted one commentator, "the menstrual flow is not red but snow white." Although Disney and Kimberly-Clark advise exercise during the period, the exercising girls are drawn without feet; bicycles magically propel themselves down the street without any muscular or mental direction from the cyclist. The film ends happily ever after, with a shot of a lipsticked bride followed immediately by a shot of a lipsticked mother and baby.)

In a discerning essay on *Peter Pan,* Donald Crafton postulates that the Disney version is best understood as a moral tale directed toward an adult audience, the parents of the children in the theater: "It was very much a part of its time," says the historian, "and its concerns, which were the concerns of its storywriters, its animators, and its guiding intelligence (Walt Disney), were specifically addressing immediate social preoccupations during the time of the film's planning and execution." The reason so few have bothered to go beneath the surface of the film is "our tendency to separate animation in general, and Disney in particular from mainstream cinema (and society as a whole). But there is in fact no reason to separate the productions of that studio from the others of the postwar period." Using the established figure of the young heroine, Wendy, *Peter Pan* pushed the Hollywood agenda. The villains are the antifamily groups of mermaids, pirates, and, most important, the gang of Lost Boys. Presumably, says Crafton, "if they did not grow up, they would become delinquents as in some 1950s teen pic." The more desirable alternative, suggests the film, is to inculcate the values that bring families together. And prime among those values is participation in a common experience. "What better way to share your children's fantasies than to take them to a feature-length animated film (the modern equivalent of reading a story)? Well, perhaps there might be one better way—taking them to an amusement park." Less than two years after *Peter Pan* appeared, Disneyland opened to enormous fanfare and press coverage. Whether by design or unconscious imitation, the place seemed closer to Barrie's original conception than anything Walt had allowed on the screen. "The delectable island," the author wrote, was "not large and sprawly, you know, with tedious distances between one adventure and another, but nicely crammed." Fantasyland was one of the prime attractions at the nicely crammed amusement park in Anaheim, and one of its prime attractions was Peter Pan's moonlit flight over the streets and towers of a plastic London.

Disney's exploration of new revenue sources, among them theme parks, commercial shorts, nature films, and live movies like *Davy Crockett* and *Johnny Tremain,* was prompted by the same motives that encouraged MGM and Warner's to shut their animation divisions: profit and fear. "Television," as a Warner executive admitted, "was something we treated like a terrier yapping at our heels. By the mid-fifties it was an 800-pound gorilla." The tube, as it was derisively called, altered nearly every aspect of American life, from sports to politics. President Dwight Eisenhower campaigned on it; his vice president, Richard Nixon, defended himself, family, and dog in his notorious "Checkers" speech. The downfall of Senator Joseph McCarthy, the heavy threats of Nikita Khrushchev ("We will bury you"), the quiz show scandals, the World Series were all television events of the fifties; so was the rise of Sid Caesar, Jackie Gleason, Lucille Ball, and Ernie Kovacs. The novelty had not worn off, as the studios had blindly predicted; adults could scarcely tear themselves away from their sets. Children often sat alongside, entertained or confused, depending on the program. Conscious of the need for preschool programming, the networks produced some shows exclusively for the young, most of them worthless. On a typical day, an ex-schoolteacher prattled down to the young on "Ding-Dong School"; a gross marionette, Howdy Doody, bounced around the stage spouting idiocies; and scores of local announcers, usually dressed as clowns or animals, auditioned for the role of national baby-sitter. After some fatuous patter, they reran antique cartoons, and Paul Terry's Farmer Al Falfa and Warner's Bosko romped once more. All the intervening years of taste and technical proficiency went by the boards. On the bright little screen, it was 1935 again, complete with basic rubber-hose animation, cruelty to animals, and race-based comedy.

CBS added more antiques when it purchased all of Paul Terry's assets for $3.5 million. Terry retired happily, pocketing all the proceeds without a thought for his animators who received little in the way of bonuses or payouts. Having done nothing very remarkable in his field except survive, Terry continued that accomplishment, boasting that the only exercise he got was acting as pallbearer for his friends who worked out. The Terrytoons library inaugurated the "Mighty Mouse Playhouse" and the "Heckle and Jeckle Show." That they were hits in the early days of commercial television says less about their quality than about the willingness of children to watch any drawing that moved. The network, hoping to energize Terry's demoralized staff, brought in one of UPA's hottest young talents, Gene Deitch, as supervising animator. He, in turn, hired Ernest Pintoff and Jules Feiffer; both would establish their names in other places and at other times. So would Deitch. Resented by Terrytoons's veterans, he lasted only two years. The Terry studio, he said in a bitter postmortem, "must have surely ranked the next-after-last on any roster of cartoon studios. For thirty years they had been making the crassest of unadulterated crap. I was trying to make a renaissance out of the most moldering foundation to be found anywhere." He enjoyed only one victory before moving on: Tom Terrific. The five-minute cliff-hangers starred a little boy who wore an inverted funnel on his head, and who could metamorphose into objects and animals. Accompanied by his apprehensive pet, Manfred the Wonder Dog, Tom engaged in a daily battle with Crabby "rotten to the core" Appleton and other scoundrels. The scripts and animation had a dashing, stripped-down quality reminiscent of Gerald McBoing-Boing's better days, and served to enliven the soporific atmosphere of the "Captain Kangaroo" program. The condition was not to last. CBS pronounced Tom too "different" from his surroundings, and like his creator, the boy with the funny hat left after a two-year run.

Animators found CBS's rival, ABC, a bit less oppressive—but only a bit. Disney commissioned some new animated sequences for the "Mickey Mouse Club," and Walter Lantz appeared live on the "Woody Woodpecker Show" to explain the process of animation from story conference to storyboard to finished film. As lucid as he was, though, Lantz could not explain the problems of censorship to his young audience. He left that to the *Hollywood Reporter.* As he explained it to the trade journal, advertising agencies were attempting to out-Hays the Hays office. In all of his cartoons, references to black people had to be removed even if they flattered the subjects. "The agency reasoning was that if there was a question at all on a scene, why leave it in?" Lantz was also forced to excise any scene with a liquor bottle in it. "In one we showed a horse accidentally drinking cider out of a bucket and then, somewhat pixilated, trying to walk a tightrope. On TV you'll see the tipsy horse on the tightrope, but since we cut out his drinking the cider, the TV audience won't understand why he is groggy." Agencies demanded more changes: "The entire 'Abou Ben Boogie' film was rejected on the grounds it showed a little harem girl wiggling her hips."

The censors had next to nothing to say about the other television fare. Had they bothered to look, they would have found much to occupy their energies. The producer of an ABC program advised a writer, "I wish you would come up with a different device than running the man down with a car, as we have done this now in three different shows. I like the idea of sadism, but I hope we can come up with a different approach to it." And in Los Angeles, a watchdog group tabulated the results of one week's worth of nighttime TV: "144 murders, 143 attempted murders, 52 justifiable killings, 14 cases of drugging, 12 jailbreaks, 36 robberies, 6 thefts, 13 kidnappings (1 of a small boy), 6 burglaries, 7 cases of torture, 6 extortion cases, 5 blackmail, 11 planned murders, 4 attempted lynchings, 1 massacre scene with hundreds killed. . . . These figures do not include the innumerable prolonged and brutal fights, the threats to kill, the sluggings or the many times when characters in the crime programs manhandled the victims, the forced confessions, and dynamiting to illegally destroy."

These crimes to person and property continued unabated. Meanwhile, the law was vigorously laid down to animators. Some had wide experience with evasion; every week a collage of their uncut work opened with a team hoofing and puffing "Overture and curtain lights /

this is it, the night of nights / no more rehearsing and nursing a part / we know every part by heart." Bugs and Daffy had made prime time, and while adults became reacquainted with the best works of Termite Terrace, a new generation sat at their sides, joining in the laughter. (It has never stopped. From its first half-hour episode in 1960 to the present moment, "The Bugs Bunny Show" has always been on one station or another, the longest, continuously scheduled program in television history.)

Yet reruns and short-lived characters could not fill the intense demands of network schedules. In animation, as in live programming, TV needed an unending parade of new faces to accompany their familiar standbys. Crusader Rabbit had begun the parade, conducting a private war on crime with his hulking partner, Ragland T. "Rags" Tiger. "We wanted to get the effect of an animated comic strip," said Crusader's creator Jay Ward, and that was exactly what viewers saw. Using far fewer cells than the standard twenty-four per second, Crusader depended heavily on scripts rather than visual effects. Self-conscious gags abounded: Asked to whistle "Dixie," a character demanded, "Is it in public domain?" The comic villains had names like Dudley Nightshade, the Brimstone Brothers, Bigot and Blackheart and the titles were heavy on puns, the more labored the better—"West We Forget"; "A Midsummer Night's Scream." Art Clokey produced the adventures of Gumby, a clay, pointy-headed male who rode the range with his orange horse, Pokey. This kind of stop-motion animation had been tried many times before, notably in the Puppetoons by a Dutch puppeteer, George Pal. But they had never quite won the hearts of the audience. Gumby did, and carried on for more than three decades, first as an eccentric comedian, then as a rubberized toy, and finally, when he got religion, as a medium of moral instruction for the National Council of Christian Churches. Bob Clampett recycled the stars of his forties puppet show, Beany Boy and Cecil, the seasick serpent, giving them new lives in a cartoon format. Small budgets forced him to use limited animation, and verbal play substituted for Clampett's visual surrealism—Beany and Cecil went searching for the prehistoric singing lizard, the Dinashor, and followed the frontier insect Davy Cricket. It was all blithe, cheery, and completely devoid of the old Warner esprit. That was to be revived in an unexpected quarter.

Jay Ward had once experimented with a satire, "The Frostbite Falls

Review," about a North Woods TV station run by animals. "Frost-bite"'s cast included Blackstone Crow, Sylvester Fox, Oski Bear, and two lesser personalities, Rocky, a flying squirrel, and Bullwinkle, a French-Canadian moose. Somehow the last two exerted the greatest appeal, and they formed the nucleus of a new show, "Rocky and His Friends." Ward's partner, Bill Scott, an animation writer with experience at Termite Terrace and UPA, impersonated Bullwinkle. June Foray, the most gifted of Warner's female voice-overs, played Rocky. William Conrad, more familiar to viewers as one of the heavies in *The Killers* and to listeners as the radio voice of Marshall Dillon on "Gunsmoke," was the hot-tempered narrator. Puns detonated here as well, but it was the personalities of the characters that carried the day. Rocky was a piping, continually worried rodent and Bullwinkle a serenely foolish creature who always managed to land the pair in unexpected trouble. A typical adventure found Rocky and Bullwinkle on the moon after they mixed Grandma Moose's cake recipe, accidentally manufacturing rocket fuel, and stuck it in the oven. The two mammals were harassed by a trio of bipeds: Boris Badenov; his girlfriend, Natasha Fatale; and their spavined boss, Fearless Leader—who proved to be funnier and more memorable than the heroes.

Bullwinkle's tribulations were punctuated by interludes far above

the heads of small children. "Fractured Fairy Tales," narrated by Edward Everett Horton, retold fables in the spirit of James Thurber. Rather than wake Sleeping Beauty, for example, the ambitious Prince constructs a theme park around her. Other segments included "Peabody's Improbable History," incidents from the past narrated by a time-traveling dog with the gifts of speech and a high IQ, and "Aesop and Son," a parody of the ancient tales.

In its comparatively short run, "Bullwinkle" had several distinctions, one of which was that it aroused children to vandalism by suggesting that they twist the knobs off their sets. "NBC was furious," Ward said many years later. "Seems about 20,000 kids did pull the knobs off their sets. Well, we fixed it. We had Bullwinkle come on and say, 'You can put them back now. Use glue—make it stick.' " Other stunts followed. To pique the sponsor, Badenov suggested that capitalism could be toppled by counterfeiting box tops. General Mills saw to it that the first such impudence would be the last.

Bullwinkle was also the first consequential "runaway" show. The term signified the use of foreign labor for domestic programs; in this case the labor was done in Mexico at a saving of $500,000. Technical quality dropped precipitously; too late for alterations, one scene arrived with Bullwinkle walking in midair. "His feet," said a director, "were the equivalent of four feet off the ground. But that didn't seem to bother the audience." Indeed, nothing seemed to trouble Bullwinkle fans. They were everything a producer could want: loyal, enthusiastic, consistently amused by the satires of Saturday afternoon serials, politics, advertising, and television in general—everything, that is, except numerous. Discouraged by low Neilsen ratings, NBC pushed the show from prime time. Ward reacted by sending out his own press release: "It is with great ennui and profound personal apathy that the National Broadcasting Company announces the renewal of 'The Bullwinkle Show' for the 1962–1963 TV season. 'The Bullwinkle Show' will air at 5:30 on Sundays. . . . Oh, well, it's in color." The network allowed Bullwinkle a marginal existence before terminating it in 1963. By that time, said Scott, the show had "affected people, especially bright kids growing up. I'm fond of saying that we corrupted an entire generation."

Not many other animated programs could make that statement, or wanted to. A mild send-up of popular music and family life, "The

Alvin Show," arose from novelty hits by Ross Bagdasarian, who had simply speeded up a tape recorder to get a series of funny voices he called The Chipmunks. Simon, Theodore, and Alvin, the irrepressible Chipmunk brothers, appeared on CBS in the early sixties, along with their humanoid manager/guardian, David Seville, a pseudonym for Bagdasarian. They were voiced with virtually no nuance or timing. In between misdeeds that drove Seville to screaming rages—always ending with the cry of "Allll-vin!"—the scamps plunged into odd projects: teaching an eagle to fly by having it hold cymbals and clang them together rapidly, visiting foreign lands where they sang one of their celebrated numbers to cheering crowds. "Alvin" made no lasting mark; even the most avid fans had to admit that these rodents were toothless.

In the sixties, the field remained open for anyone who could produce original shows with limited, quality-controlled animation, simple scripts, and strong characters. Experience counted, and Bill Hanna and Joe Barbera rushed to fill the void. They assumed that their track record with Tom and Jerry, coupled with a willingness to try the new medium, would make them hot properties. They were quickly disabused when the sole offer came from Screen Gems, and that took the form of a paltry $2,700 advance for five minutes of animation—about one-twentieth of what they usually received for a theatrical short. Assuming grateful attitudes, the partners prepared "Ruff and Reddy," a limited animation series about a dog and cat. In the middle of their labors, Harry Cohn, head of Columbia and Screen Gems, demanded to know what he was getting for his investment. "We took the film to the suffocatingly hot screening room at Screen Gems and set it up," Barbera wrote. They and their advocate, John Mitchell, Screen Gems vice president in charge of sales, sat silently while Cohn viewed the work in progress. "Without punctuation, let alone ceremony, the lights came up again, and White Fang, accompanied by his entourage, left the room without uttering a word or cracking a smile. . . . I waited within reach of a phone for as long as I could stand to wait, then finally dialed John Mitchell myself.

"What did he say, John?"

"He said, 'Get rid of 'em.' "

As they prepared to depart from the business forever, Hanna and Barbera learned that one slim chance remained to them. NBC was looking for animated "bookends" to place before and after a children's television show. Network executives took a chance on "Ruff and Reddy." The Hanna-Barbera era had begun. "Ruff" was followed by a series of energetic, derivative shows like "Huckleberry Hound." The title character, Barbera admitted, came in large part from "my recollections of Tex Avery's great MGM character Droopy—a deadpan, droop-jawed basset hound who would greet his public with 'Hello, you happy people'—uttered in a forlorn monotone." What was remarkable about these cartoons was not their secondhand humor but their bargain rates—the episodes cost $3,000 each. "Disney-type animation is economically unfeasible for television," observed Hanna, "and we discovered that we could get away with less." So much less that animation became a secondary consideration; for comedy and character delineation, the Hanna-Barbera factory relied on actors and scriptwriters. "Yogi Bear" and "Quick Draw McGraw" suffered from the same shortcomings, and when Chuck Jones described them as "radio with pictures," the professionals, recalling the days of real cartooning, nodded in sad agreement. And there was worse to come.

Like most animators of the early sixties, Hanna-Barbera tired of creating shows about humans in animal suits, so, as an alternative, they produced a show about bromides in human suits. In the beginning, "The Flintstones," set in the prehistoric land of Bedrock, had trouble finding a home. An advertising executive "distinctly remembered how Joe Barbera had all the storyboards everywhere and did every voice. I was amazed. I went back to the agency and they asked me what I thought. I said, 'Well, I wouldn't watch it but I think it'll be a hit.'" His endorsement helped to persuade ABC to make room on its schedule and One-A-Day vitamins and Winston cigarettes to sponsor the show. Principal personalities, animated or otherwise, were expected to plug the product, and while America's families looked on, Fred Flintstone and his friend Barney Rubble puffed cigarettes on demand. Unlike Gerald McBoing-Boing or Mr. Magoo, Fred, Barney, and their wives, Wilma and Betty, seldom showed more than a scintilla of originality. They were the unacknowledged offspring of "The Honeymooners," a live show about the comic frustrations of a booming, insecure bus driver, Ralph Cramden (Jackie Gleason); a dim sewer worker, Ed Norton (Art Carney); and their wives (Audrey Meadows and Joyce Randolph). This was not the first time the comedian and his supporting cast had been used as the basis for a cartoon. In 1956, Termite Terrace openly caricatured Gleason, Carney, and Meadows in "The Honey Mousers." But Hanna-Barbera had no intention of recognizing the Flintstones' antecedents. Several decades would pass before Barbera wrote, "There have been no shortage of people to tell me that 'The Flintstones' borrowed (or stole) very heavily from 'The Honeymooners'—an observation (or accusation) I always take as the highest compliment possible, because The Great One really was, and 'The Honeymooners' was a landmark in the history of television comedy." Translation: When plagiarizing, always steal from the best.

Barbera was quick to point out that whatever had been borrowed from Gleason & Co., "The Honeymooners" did not have a Stoneway piano, and "certainly did not have access to the Stone Age technology we made available to Fred and Barney. Barney invented a helicopter, foot-pedal-powered and resembling nothing more than a very large eggbeater, to transport Fred and himself to and from the bowling alley without the wives catching on. Nor was Neolithic bowling quite the sport that Ralph and Ed would have been familiar with. . . . When Fred rolled a split, it really was a split. His rock-ball would break in half, each half knocking over a pin and thereby scoring the spare."

Anachronisms became the Flintstones' hallmark: crabs strapped to boards and made into lawnmowers; a mastodon's trunk turned into a vacuum cleaner hose; a round piece of granite used as a long-playing record, with a long-beaked bird for a phonograph needle. The cast looked as flat as playing cards. It was the backgrounds that seemed three dimensional: mounds of rubble in the shape of rock candy. Elementary sight gags coupled with some bright vocal acting by Mel Blanc, Bea Benaderet, and others gave the program a professional veneer. The first generation to be raised by television confused Hanna-Barbera animation with the real thing, and propelled the show to unparalleled popularity. The pros knew better; their code word for shoddy animated shows was "Hannah and the Barbarians," and the *New York Times* called "The Flintstones" an "inked disaster." The paper found the masculine figures "unattractive, coarse and gruff and the women nondescript." Bill Hanna and Joe Barbera saw no reason to pay any attention to their detractors; a 1961 story in the *Saturday Evening Post* was all they needed to read. "Four years ago," it ran, the two men "were has-beens, bounced out of the movie business with no prospects for future employment. This year . . . they will gross an estimated $9,000,000."

Gross was the operative word. Hanna-Barbera's next significant show, "The Jetsons," exhibited the same compromise with quality. This time the characters lived in a future world where everything and everyone seemed to be made of Tupperware, the plastic merchandise being peddled in America's suburbs. By now, the Hanna-Barbera formula and style was unmistakable. Neilsen ratings underlined a truth that all broadcasters knew: Sell 200,000 copies of a book, and you had a best-seller. Show a movie to only 200,000 people, and you were through in Hollywood. Show a movie to 7 million people, and you had a box-office smash. Show a television program to only 7 million people, and you had better look for a job in children's ready-to-wear. With an eye to what Groucho Marx called "the lowest common dominator," Hanna-Barbera produced the shallowest characters and the most obvious gags. George Jetson, a middle-management type, lived in Orbit City with his nuclear family—wife, Jane; space-age children, Judy and Elroy; and their dog, Astro. George commuted to his office at Spacely Space Sprockets, passing signs that read "Speed Limit: 5,500 MPII," while Jane gave orders to the family domestic, hired from the U-Rent-a-Robot Maid Service. The tired jokes were easy to produce, and the so-called planned animation cut costs even further. A body needed to be drawn but once: Only moving its parts required a series of drawings. To mask the ungainly result, characters wore collars and ties so their heads could be swiveled without sitting directly on their shoulders. Lips moved from vowel to vowel; consonants were ignored. It was not to be expected that Hanna-Barbera would honor the old Warner Bros. standard of having a character move in different ways depending on the situation. Once a run or walk was filmed, it was cataloged and recycled at every opportunity.

"The Jetsons" could not have picked a more appropriate moment to arrive. "The Flintstones" had been resolutely working class, expressing the nature of American politics in the late 1950s, when, as historian Samuel Eliot Morison detailed, "the great federations of union labor [had] probably been greater than the government." Instead of hunting and gathering, as a true Cro-Magnon might have done, Fred worked for the Rock Head and Cave Construction Co. Yet he was always getting entangled in some get-rich scheme or other, and this, too, fit in with the spirit of the times. Morison speaks of a Polish Communist visiting San Francisco, where he found "dock workers going to work in Cadillacs, and was shocked to hear that they did not want their union newspaper mailed to their home addresses, as it might injure their middle-class status with the neighbors. Which only confirms a fact that has puzzled socialists and communists for a century—the American workman is an expectant capitalist, not a class-conscious proletarian." The Jetsons, on the other hand, expressed the collective feelings of the early sixties, when the young President John F. Kennedy pushed space exploration as "the last frontier." Eyes had shifted from immediate gratification to future possibilities. In April 1961, the Russians had put a Cosmonaut in space and demoralized America. The following month, Kennedy had called for a plan to have an American walk on the moon's surface by the end of the decade. From there on, space probes would reach out to Mars and beyond. Space itself would be colonized. Anything was possible. The slick, optimistic Jetsons entered 1962 assured of national acceptance. Historian Norman M. Klein described the show's overall design as one of surburban convenience. "I mean household conveniences, shopping for convenience, the myth of the four-day week, labor-saving devices, a democracy by microwave, with wall-to-wall carpeting, dishwashers, and smooth surfaces that can be wiped off with a damp rag."

Something else also ran beneath the gloss of Hanna-Barbera productions. The early sixties marked the decline of craftsmanship, the speedup of planned obsolescence, of deliberate shoddiness, of products meant to end in a landfill. It was the time of *The Man in the Gray Flannel Suit* and the *Hidden Persuaders,* the authors warning about superfluous products sold to an unsuspecting public, of automobiles with fins and portholes, Insolent Chariots guzzling the world's supply of fossil fuel. These were counterbalanced with signal achievements in technology, and now and then in the arts. But overall, a deterioration of standards could be seen wherever people looked, and they looked most often at their television screens. The head of the Federal Communications Commission, Newton Minow, made a speech to that effect in 1961. The members of the National Association of Broadcasters had no idea what to expect of the new commissioner. He was bespectacled and professorial; they sat back for a mild pep talk. Minow began on a reassuring note. When television was good, he stated, there was nothing better—the great debates between candidates Nixon and Kennedy; the documentary of World War II, "Victory at Sea"; the fine dramas presented by "Playhouse 90." Then the bomb struck. "But when television is bad, nothing is worse." The speaker invited them to stare at their sets for a whole day. "I can assure you that you will observe a vast wasteland. You will see a procession of game shows, violence, audience participation shows, formula comedies about totally unbelievable families, blood and thunder, mayhem, violence, sadism, murder, western badmen, western good men, private eyes, gangsters, more violence, and cartoons. And, endlessly, commercials—many screaming, cajoling, and offending. . . ."

Used to having their way, the broadcasters professed shock at the style of this upstart. "He's bucking for a bigger government job," they told reporters. Here was "a naïve young man who has read all the books but hasn't had to meet a payroll." And most mendacious of all, "I can watch any TV station all day long and enjoy it." Unhappily, Minow had simply stated what everyone already knew but no one could bear to hear. Because the broadcasters attacked or ignored him, the wasteland spread. The cartoons Minow deplored, and the commercials he derided, were about to merge into one cynical and sordid presentation. They would be so execrable that, in time, Hanna-Barbera would come to be regarded with nostalgia as one of the better producers of animation. Perhaps that was the saddest aspect of all.

CHAPTER NINE

AKIN TO STATUTORY RAPE

In 1966, American animation entered its Great Depression. To begin with, the greatest name of all, the leader responsible for the long climb from novelty to diversion to art form, lost a long sad battle with lung cancer. *Jungle Book,* the last full-length cartoon to be supervised by Walt Disney, displayed all the attributes and faults of his late style. Technically proficient, filled with sinuous panthers, tigers, and snakes, the film had almost nothing to do with its source. The central character, Mowgli, made a cloying rather than feral hero, and a host of irrelevant characters were shoehorned into nineteenth-century India, some of them with accents of the modern American south. The spirited songs could not disguise a banality of ideas and a vulgarization of animal and human personalities. It could hardly have been otherwise after Walt instructed a writer, "Here is the original by Rudyard Kipling. The first thing I want you to do is not to read it."

Sentimental obituaries came in from all over the world, all sounding the inarguable note that we would not look upon Disney's like again. On the "CBS Evening News," Eric Sevareid offered something more—a double portrait of the deceased, and of a tormented America that would crucially miss him. "By the conventional wisdom, mighty mice, flying elephants, Snow White and Happy, Grumpy, Sneezy and Dopey—all these were fantasy, escapism from reality. It's a question of whether they are any the less real, any more fantastic than intercontinental missiles, poisoned air, defoliated forests, and scraps from the moon. This is the age of fantasy, however you look at it, but Disney's fantasy wasn't lethal." Sevareid did not know, or would not say, that

193

cartoon fantasy had become a mere fraction of the Disney enterprise. For all the carefully timed rereleases, the occasional new features like *One Hundred and One Dalmatians,* the Mickey Mouse Club, the ice shows featuring the dwarfs, Disney's name was now more synonymous with live action films. *Mary Poppins* led the pack; before and behind her came a procession of tame, picket-fence comedies like *The Shaggy Dog; The Absent-Minded Professor; The Parent Trap;* and *Monkeys, Go Home!* In the months before his death, Walt had abandoned cartoons altogether, his dwindling energies devoted to the denatured theme park rising in Orlando, Florida. Epcot (Experimental Prototype Community of Tomorrow), as he envisioned it, would have "no slum areas because we won't let them develop . . . there will be no retirees, because everyone must be employed." This is what the free spirit of Walt Disney had become, and yet as long as the man remained alive, animators told themselves that somehow, some time, he would stop the social tinkering, return to his roots, and save them all. After the funeral, they regrouped and thought about other ways to make a living. "Well," said one mourner, hiding his desperation with a smile, "there's always television."

He had a point. The year of Disney's death marked the first time all three networks presented cartoons on Saturday morning. For animators with sensitivity as well as ambition, the good news ended there. Hour after hour swarmed with superheroes ("Gigantor," "The Fantastic Four"), futuristic extravaganzas ("Space Ghost and Dino Boy"), fantasy-horror ("King Kong," "Frankenstein Jr. and the Impossibles"), and leftovers from radio days ("The Lone Ranger," "The New Adventures of Superman"). Travesties of real animation, they were inferior to the creakiest efforts of Terrytoons, the low end of cartooning until Saturday mornings came along. ABC, NBC, and CBS, convinced that domestic animation was still too expensive, imported shoddier products from Japan, and these in turn blighted the American output. At one point, adventure programs were so ubiquitous that Friz Freleng stated, "You could animate a Super series on toilet paper and the networks would buy it." What he failed to add was that he had become part of the problem. When the major studios pulled away from animation, Freleng agreed to make some shorts for the conservative Sloane Foundation. In the best one, "By Word of Mouse," a German rodent visits his American cousin. Willie lives in a department store. Setting paw inside, Hans professes astonishment at the profusion of goods and services. With the help of a mouse professor at Putnell University (P.U.), Hans learns the significance of mass production, mass consumption, and the benefits of rising corporate profits. In addition to the easily assimilated message, the cartoon has a subliminal one. The activity of shoppers takes place in an orderly fashion as the busy mice move from cube to cube, from elevator to the selling floors. Outside, vehicular traffic proceeds on a grid, crowded but methodically moving forward. The old cartoon anarchy, with all its looney tunes and merry melodies, is gone. Historian Norman M. Klein is acute on this issue: "The controlled setting is not unlike Disneyland . . . the animated space adjusts from movie allusion to consumer allusion, a very noticeable difference—not simply about flat or deep focus." Freleng's work is "more about the changing role of cartoons, from film toward more obviously consumer-driven television."

Bill Scott found children's television a little bit worse every time he looked at it. The old Bullwinkle hand saw that "all the networks really wanted was 'x' number of yards per film." Norm Prescott, an owner of the Filmation studio, a leading producer of animation in the sixties, conceded that "kidvid" was "a garbage pile. There were no executives directly assigned to it; nobody wanted to be in charge of it. Saturday was considered worse than the mailroom job." In part, the situation was due to economics: Under increasingly tight budget restraints, production houses cut every corner, further reduced the number of cels per second, and made the stories as flat as their assembly-line draftsmanship. In part, it was triggered by the changing domestic and foreign climate. Tooling up for defense had created more than a million jobs in the United States, and the early war protesters were overshadowed by good economic news, as well as reassurances from the White House that the fighting in Southeast Asia would be over soon—perhaps by Christmas. In the meantime, the old xenophobia, dormant since World War II, reawakened. In his searching history of television, Columbia University professor Eric Barnouw speculates that "A visitor from another planet watching United States television for a week during the Vietnam escalation period might have concluded that viewers were being brainwashed by a cunning conspiracy determined to harness the nation—with special attention to its young—for war." Actually, as he acknowledges, no conspiracy was required. Without any grand scheme except the willingness to do anything for profit, manufacturers, advertising agencies, producers, and broadcasters enthusiastically tapped the growing market for military vehicles and figures. By avoiding whatever seemed to undermine current policy, they gravitated, willy-nilly, toward its support. The fallout of conflict—dread of other governments, fear of local subversion—forced its way into the Saturday morning lineup. Gigantor's deadly enemy, Mr. Ugablob, planned to conquer the world through a freeze ray. On "Superman," an American physicist's pet parakeet, which had been taught to repeat a secret formula, was stolen by a foreign agent. The animated Lone Ranger fought a mad scientist aiming to control the world's weather. Naturally, these enemies had to be annihilated. When the country was young, President John Quincy Adams observed that the United States "goes not abroad in search of monsters". Now the young audience was being told again and again that its destiny was indeed to search out monsters, and destroy them.

These programs might have been tempered with a modicum of discretion, if only to keep children from being frightened by world conditions they could not understand, and which could not be cured by a mesomorph in a cape. But the networks had no intention of interfering with a source of revenue, no matter what the attendant damages. Surveys announced that some 16 million minors started their weekends by turning on the television set. Not unreasonably, advertisers concluded that commercials, shrewdly produced for children's uncritical eyes, might convert them into miniature consumers. It was worth a try, anyway, a try vigorously encouraged by the networks. Under the National Association of Broadcasters Code, prime-time programs could not carry more than 9.5 commercial minutes per hour. Children's programming had no such restraints; it allowed 16 minutes per hour. In fact, the disproportion was greater than that, since the main characters frequently acted as pitchmen in the ads, making the commercials and the entertainment indistinguishable. So for the rest of the decade and beyond, every fourth minute on Saturday morning was devoted to peddling sugar-coated cereal, candied vitamins, and expensive toys—some retailing for as much as $50. Those toys, like the shows they sponsored, expressed the spirit of the age. GI Joe's arsenal included a "ten-inch bazooka that really works" and gas masks "to add real dimension to your play battles." Mattel's Fighting Men had their own machine guns and tanks: "everything that fighting men use." Girls were expected to assume the customary role of homemaker with Kenner's automatic knitting machine—"a fast, fun way to knit," Cheerful Tearful dolls who cried "real tears," and other mock babies intended to remove imagination from childhood (in one commercial, a girl chortled as she cuddled her new doll, "Oh, Mommy, I don't have to pretend anymore!").

As the antiwar sentiment cohered, occasional truces were called in the battle for children's minds and dollars. A few well-meaning stations responded to the call for better programming with "Reading Room," "Exploring," and "One, Two, Three = Go." The programs did not survive for long. As advertising executive Cy Schneider noted in his candid study of children's television, the sponsors "eventually lost heart and were not willing to pay high rates for poorly rated shows. They preferred to concentrate their money on the cartoon shows where the audience was." Passive during the hours of viewing, that audience made potent statements at the checkout counters. Not only did children obediently consume the products advertised on television, they clamored for toys based on the shows' leading characters—one reason why animation houses accepted low fees for their cartoons. If they had learned one lesson from Disney, it was that millions could be made in the "after market" of figurines, stuffed dolls, and clothing. In 1967, when Hanna-Barbera was purchased by the Taft Corporation for $12 million, the licensing agreements for the Flintstones, the Jetsons, and all the rest promised more income than the programs on which they were based (in one year, the Pebbles doll earned close to $20 million).

With so much at stake, commercials would be researched, appetites created, brand names stressed as never before. One marketing analyst prophesied greater sales with each succeeding year, now that the trend was "for children to get more decision making authority and exercise that authority at a younger and younger age." Unsurprisingly, the networks and producers took no chances. On their nightly news programs, the antiwar sentiment grew in decibel strength and political intensity. The images of body bags sent home from Vietnam, of Buddhist monks immolating themselves, of four student protesters killed by the national guard at Kent State could not be erased from the national mind. Some four hundred campuses went on strike, and a sense of outrage built in the middle class, the old, the formerly uninvolved. Yet the ghetto of Saturday morning TV might have been sealed in a bell jar. War toys continued to pass in review, and the surrounding entertainment went on as banal as before. Developers knew that the more original a show appeared to be, the less likely it was to reach the screen—or to succeed if it got there. Sponsors wanted a sure thing: cartoon versions of highly rated live shows, including "The Addams Family," "The New Adventures of Gilligan," and "The Oddball Couple." Produced by various entities, these programs nonetheless sounded and looked alike, as though they had all come from a single conveyor belt of entertainment. "Making money had never been so easy," a former network executive reminisced. "It didn't take ideas, good production values, or witty scripts. We just put up a cartoon in color and no matter how stiff the characters were, it ran and ran, and the sponsors spent and spent. We weren't dumb enough to think it would never end, but we kind of wondered where the trouble would come from. We kept looking south, to Washington. Wrong place."

When it came, in 1968, the trouble originated from the unlikely city of Newton, Massachusetts. There, some young mothers, appalled at what their children were watching, organized a committee called ACT—Action for Children's Television. The spark plug of the group, Peggy Charren, did not believe in euphemisms. To her, Saturday mornings constituted, plainly and simply, "the nadir of broadcasting, a haven for poorly animated monster cartoons and candy commercials," and she was determined to do something about it. In a sense, ACT had pushed on an open door. Close-ups and documentaries of military horrors, coupled with the assassinations of Martin Luther King, Malcolm X, and Robert Kennedy, had brought a new awareness of American disorder. Maybe violence was, as one black leader famously insisted, as American as apple pie. Then again, so was the ability to change what could not be accepted, and ACT called for an end to the unrestricted use of guns and physical force as a staple of children's programming. Taking advantage of the new consumerism, it also condemned ads pushing "expensive toys and cereals that were sometimes 50% sugar." Charren agreed with Sherlock Holmes: "The Press is valuable, if you know how to use it," and she knew how to use it. ACT ran conferences on children's programming at Yale, at Harvard, at the Kennedy Center in Washington. Its president testified before government committees, and what she had to say was indisputable: The problem is "not only how we sell to children, but what we sell. Danger and hazard are a question of degree, not kind. Although explosives are safe when used by demolition experts, even matches are dangerous in the hands of children. An occasional candy bar after a meal can be a pleasant treat, but excessive use of candy in place of nutritious foods is a hazard to physical and mental health. A single vitamin pill can be a supplement to a deficient diet, but ingestion of a whole bottle of chocolate vitamins leads to children hospitalized for coma and shock."

Other than the energy of its leader, ACT's most effective weapon became the petition. In the early seventies, the organization asked the FCC to bar sponsorship of television commercials, to ban performers from plugging products and services, and to require that each station devote a minimum of fourteen program hours per week for children. The demands that no one else had dared to make were covered by almost every major newspaper, and brought national attention to Charren and her associates. Dean Burch, the Commission chairman, responded in a speech before the American Advertising Federation, making it clear that he had listened closely to ACT. Children, he told the executives, are a special, vulnerable audience, and not to be trifled with. It was "intolerable to seek to bilk the innocent with shoddy advertising appeals." Such conduct could be considered "akin to statutory rape." The result was everything a children's advocate could have hoped for: the Commission received baskets of mail from concerned parents and teachers, Burch created a permanent children's unit within the FCC, three drug companies voluntarily withdrew their child-centered ads, and subsequently the National Association of Broadcasters reduced the number of commercials per hour on children's TV from sixteen minutes to twelve. "It was little enough," Charren remembered, "and it would be a long time before animation got better, but other things improved, and people—especially children—learned that they didn't have to be victims, passively watching whatever the networks decided to put before them."

During this time, a handful of animators felt as disgusted as the audience, and they attempted some new directions for their art. Up to the late 1960s, educational television programs were earnest and resolutely drab, the medium's "sensible shoes"—everyone praised them, but no one wanted to be seen in them. Then came "Sesame Street."

Joan Ganz Cooney, a television producer hired by the Carnegie Corporation, developed the idea in hope of promoting "the intellectual and cultural growth of preschoolers, particularly disadvantaged preschoolers." Cooney later wrote, "We knew that young children watched a great deal of television in the years before they went to school. We knew also that they liked cartoons, game shows, situation comedies . . . and above all, they were attracted by fast-paced, highly visual, oft-repeated commercials." Since children were already buying products, why not sell them something more wholesome? Instead of G.I. Joes and Pop-Tarts, how about peddling the alphabet and the multiplication table?

To that end, animated "commercials" appeared between segments with live people and Jim Henson's inventive Muppets. Carried on the nonprofit Public Broadcasting System, the program swept the country; magazine covers celebrated Big Bird, there were repeated newspaper articles, hosannas from the critics. The problem, undetected at the start, was that Sesame Street used precisely the same strategies as the network advertisers—encouraging short attention spans, pushing toys and tapes, organizing promotional tours, hiring publicists to burnish the image of the parent organization, Children's Television Workshop. These promoters were familiar with the Disney operation, and they had learned their lessons well. For years, executives at rival studios could always get a laugh by citing the Mickey Mouse watches and the Donald Duck toilet seats. The gag and the response were poor disguises for envy: As all producers knew, the trinkets brought in more revenue than the films. There ought to be a way for *us* to cash in, the studio thinkers used to muse, but none of them ever cashed in as well as Walt—until Sesame Street and its spinoffs came along. In time, the Children's Television Workshop produced so many products and so much income (little of which went to PBS) that CTW was rumored to stand for Channel To Wealth. In the end, the Workshop, with its well-known disdain for network programming, came to remind more astute viewers of the final scene in George Orwell's *Animal Farm:* "The creatures outside looked from pig to man, and from man to pig, and from pig to man again; but already it was impossible to tell which was which."

The third route for animators opened up in the counterculture. A loose confederation of students, civil rights activists, war protesters, street politicians, drug users and bemused dropouts had found the dominant culture to be untenable, and expressed themselves in ways that outsiders—particularly those of middle age and beyond—found incomprehensible or threatening. Animation would seem to have no place here. A full-length cartoon required funds, discipline, and a mainstream distributor, all the symbols of the dreaded Establishment. Nevertheless, two very different cartoon features were destined to veer from tradition, and to find a large and youthful following.

The Beatles had become the most widely discussed rock group of the age, their recording personae translated to cinema by director Richard Lester in two larkish movies, *A Hard Day's Night* and *Help!* Then, with the aid of Al Brodax, a Yale professor of classics, his colleague Erich Segal (later to become more celebrated as the author of *Love Story*), scenarist Lee Minoff, and too many others, the Beatles starred in an animated film. The director, George Dunning, was a Canadian who had spent some time at UPA in the fifties. With an eye somewhat more acute than his story sense, he enlisted Heinz Edelmann, an innovative German designer who had influenced European graphics but who had no experience with animation. It showed. *Yellow Submarine* leaps from song to song, moving the quartet with color and dazzle, but with little of its unique Liverpudlian charm. The impression it conveys is of a Peter Max poster in constant motion. The wobbly plot concerns a group of totalitarians, the Blue Meanies, who invade Pepperland robbing it of color and joie de vivre. Boarding the title vehicle, the Beatles enter the fray, ultimately neutralizing the villains with songs of love and peace.

No one mistook *Yellow Submarine* for a mainstream feature; it ranged as far from Disney and Warner Bros. and Hanna-Barbera as it was possible to go in the late sixties and early seventies. Yet the public attended in swarms, more enchanted by the cascade of Pop Art and wild visions than by its pacifistic message. It was the time for "head" films, celebrating the visual and aural experience of a mind under the influence of hallucinogens. The Disney studio took advantage of the moment to rerelease *Fantasia,* and it enjoyed a popularity unknown during its 1940 debut. Disney's veteran animators were amused and appalled when students, newly bedazzled by all the old effects, asked if they had been on drugs in the old days. Yes, the animators told them, Bromo-Seltzer and Ex-Lax. In the end, *Fantasia* held up better than its junior. For all of *Submarine*'s radical appearance, the feature was actu-

ally a testament to big-time marketing, a shrewdly packaged film that aged more rapidly than the bell-bottom blue jeans of its stars. Looking back, Dunning confessed that his cartoon was more of a trip than an authentic feature. Audiences, he believed, "want this 'sensation' or 'experience.' Since the film was made of drawings and paintings, we decided to bring in all the images familiar to the popular mind that we could." He concluded, "the artistic validity of long animated films is often a question of their relative vulgarity. Distributors give backing to vulgar films." Just so.

In 1972, another quirky filmmaker tried his hand at full-length cartooning. In 1956, at the age of eighteen, Ralph Bakshi had joined Terrytoons; four years later, he rose to supervising director. Fred Silverman, then CBS programming president, took a look at the network's Saturday morning schedule and told his staff, "Look, we don't have to buy cartoons off the shelf. We can get involved with the storyboards right from the beginning and have them tailor made." One of his new tailors was Bakshi. Under Silverman, the wunderkind developed Mighty Heroes, a team consisting of Diaper Man and Cuckoo Man and other parodic types. The scripts had the customary story problems, and Bakshi's well-designed characters were too far out in front of young viewers. Few were surprised when, after twenty-six episodes, Bakshi moved on, this time to assume the directorship of Paramount's cartoon studio. His fervent, halting attempts to make social commentaries were cut short when the department shut down. Thus far, he had very little to show for his efforts. But like many others, Bakshi noticed that an underground style was beginning to find acceptability in the popular arts. *Easy Rider,* a low-budget picaresque that was originally dismissed by the major studios, made millions. Its cool, doomed protagonists, biking across America in a kind of pot-scented haze, seemed to speak a new language, best understood by those under thirty. The same group made a cult figure of Robert Crumb, an artist whose grungy, sex-obsessed figures displayed their wares in countless posters and comic books. One of Crumb's favorite characters, Fritz the Cat, looked to be the ideal subject for an adult animated feature, and Bakshi bought the rights. He felt an immediate affinity with Fritz's creator. The two were in their early thirties. Crumb had suffered through an afflicted and lower-middle-class childhood. His dysfunctional family moved from Philadelphia to Iowa to California to Delaware and then back to Philadelphia, where Robert landed his first job as an artist and designer of mainstream greeting cards. Bakshi's Russian Jewish family had migrated from Palestine to Brownsville, New York, where the troubled boy was directed to art school by a social worker. Given these similarities, the two men should have become fast friends and inseparable collaborators. They were just the opposite. Crumb wanted nothing to do with the movie, and when he saw it he sued—and won— the right to have his name removed from the credits. Others claimed to be just as indignant, though for very different reasons. The film review board, for example, found Fritz too explicit for minors and made it the first cartoon to receive an "X" rating. That was just the boost Bakshi needed; he parlayed notoriety into fame ("Fritz Lives!" blared the ads. "He's X rated and animated!"), and an $850,000 project into a $25 million hit.

What ticket holders saw—and a lot of them attended the film two or three times—was more daring in subject and execution than any animated film in history. Of course, there had been sexually explicit cartoons before this; until the early nineties, film buffs and lascivious viewers could buy a tape called "Sextoons," which contained samples of roughly made blue cartoons ranging back to the silent era, among them "The Adventures of Super Screw," "Little Genitalia," "Boobs A

Lot," and "Buried Treasure" starring Eveready Harton. Fritz was nothing like these. Unsubtle sex and foul language were what amateurs gossiped about; professionals could recognize that the film had been made by a serious director and first-class animators. Bakshi claimed that it took quite a long time to assemble the right staff. Those who entered with a smirk, "wanting to be very dirty and draw filthy pictures" did not stay very long, and neither did those with a low threshold of vulgarity. One cartoonist refused to draw a black crow shooting a pig policeman. Two women quit—one because she could not bring herself to tell her children what she was did for a living, the other because she refused to draw exposed breasts. Those who stayed received no comforting rationales from their employer. Asked whether the sex scenes were in good taste, Bakshi replied with a question: "Would you call a cat who chases a crow into a junk yard to fuck her in good taste?"

Nevertheless, in its strange way, *Fritz the Cat* could claim to be an art film. It had brilliant fantasy scenes; a well-drawn, wittily animated cast; good voices and music and a truly original point of view. The title feline has multiple lives, most of them spent away from his yammering wife. In the company of street people and revolutionaries, he wanders the streets of New York and San Francisco, deeply covetous of the crows, who represent the irrepressible spirits of black folk, and curious about radical animals and humanoids who doom their revolution by celebrating violence for its own sake. To Bakshi, no one and nothing is off limits; Fritz contains caricatures of politicians and statesmen and thugs (they are often the same), minorities and establishment figures, druggies and straight folks, yentas and flirts. Sympathy underlies the detailed urban comedy, and the sex is offensive mainly to bluenoses looking for dirt with white gloves.

Cinema and social critics found Bakshi's next films a good deal more objectionable, and with better reasons. Up until 1973, animation had no place for a Portrait of the Artist. Attempts at autobiography tended to be oblique and metaphorical: life as an endless pursuit of the inept after the uncatchable, libido masked as a dog, a cat, or a skunk. Then *Heavy Traffic* entered the picture. Without benefit of Aesop, Bakshi told the story of Michael, a very human young animator, green in every sense of the word, rising from the slums of New York and ultimately transforming his experience into art. Along the way, Michael wanders through worlds of violence and sexuality. Prostitutes, con artists, mafiosi, blacks—whom Bakshi now regards with an unstable mix of envy and fear—all pass in review, along with a vibrant mix of photographs and paintings. The result is a bright and disturbing film, uncompromising in its harsh vision of life on the street and in its scabrous dialogue.

The language was enough to earn another "X" rating and that, coupled with vigorous marketing, garnered more millions. With the exception of Walt Disney, no other American animator had produced consecutive hits. Radiating confidence, Bakshi gave interviews predicting a new direction for animation; it was no longer cute or even beautiful. It was candid, challenging, unlimited in its power. A fresh generation of cartoonists could put anything on the screen—*War and Peace,* if it wanted to. With the world open to him, Bakshi then proceeded to wreck his career. *Harlem Nights,* as it was first called, crystallized the director's view of black life in the big city. With a mocking leer at Disney's *Song of the South,* he updated the Uncle Remus stories, shuttling seamlessly from live footage to animation. Br'ers Rabbit, Fox, and Bear travel from the rural South to New York, where they run into a succession of comic and disreputable characters. A lively music track, and fine black actors, among them Scatman Crothers and John Phillip Thomas, gave the comedy a raw ebullience and style that seemed more like a concert of ad-lib comedians than a plotted cartoon. For reasons he could never fully explain, Bakshi retitled the picture *Coonskin* even before it was completed—and immediately ran into trouble. The Congress of Racial Equality interrupted a showing at the Museum of Modern Art and let it be known that there would be more vigorous protests when the movie went on national release. They never had a chance to demonstrate. An apprehensive Paramount changed its plans to distribute Bakshi's work, and once that decision was announced, no major distributor would touch it. A small company eventually agreed to represent *Coonskin;* for all practical purposes, though, the film was dead and its director an untouchable. He had not only failed to read the handwriting, he had failed to see the wall—a fate the networks were determined to avoid.

ABC, CBS, and NBC had already miscalculated the moral climate, and they had no intention of compounding their error. Once the antiviolence movement took hold, they issued public criticisms of their own programs for children. Pretty soon, everyone else was chiming in with an opinion. Charles Bronson, who starred in some of the most gratuitously bloody films of the 1970s, told the world that cartoons were "frightening," particularly those in which the Coyote was beaned by a rock. It "flattened him, but he popped right up again. That's really shocking to me because when a child grows up with that sort of thing, he feels he can go around hitting people on the head with a hammer and they'll be all right." Questioned about the grinding action in his own films, he replied, "The difference between someone seeing *Death Wish* and my child seeing a violent cartoon is the age. My movies are rated and the people who see them are not children. *Death Wish* wasn't that extreme. It was clean violence. When I shot a man he was shot, and that was the end of it." Other less hypocritical protests came in from the American Society of Pediatrics, teachers' unions, and religious organizations. Hoping to present a new image of themselves as family-centered, caring corporations, all three networks cut their losses, abandoned their immensely profitable adventure series, and encouraged shows of bland fantasy and inoffensive humor. But that was not enough. Terrified of federal censorship and private agitation, they gave sweeping authority to their own Standards and Practices departments. At these offices, no postcard of protest went unnoticed, and editors took it upon themselves to slice out every questionable piece of animation, no matter how revered by aficionados. Violence, rather than sex, became their bête noire. Clampett's "There's No Such Thing as a Sea Serpent" contained a song about a dinosaur: "All triceratops who try Sarah say she's tops." The line stayed. So did Jay Ward's Fractured Fairy Tale in which the prince admits that he is a "hog flogger," a reference to masturbation. But let there be the slightest collision of characters and objects and the censors appeared with scissors in hand. Out went the vitality of the Roadrunner and Daffy Duck cartoons. Now children saw Wile E. Coyote igniting sticks of dynamite but not the comic backfire; they watched Daffy's bill spinning around his head but not Elmer's shotgun blast that caused it—the rough equivalent of a comedian saying, "Ladies and gentlemen: mother-in-law" and leaving out the intervening joke. One broadcaster asked Bob Clampett to excise a character from Beany and Cecil because he resembled Walt Disney. "Where's Walt Disney in there?" Clampett demanded. "The character with the hook nose and mustache is my longtime villain, Dishonest John. Everyone knows that." Everyone except the people running the cartoons on television. In another cartoon, Honest John put the moon in little packages and sold them as cheese. "I had the word *Krafty* on the package," said Clampett, "and ABC was afraid Kraft Cheese would sue them. It was those kind of things they censored." In the late seventies, the watchdogs became more ferocious. A script for one of Hanna-Barbera's tamest shows, "Josie and the Pussycats," described a kitten running from an enemy and hiding in a plate of pasta. CBS excised the scene because "Kids'll put cats in the spaghetti." Another scene offered a little homily about the dangers of dictators, showing the images of Caesar, Napoleon, and Hitler. Der Fuhrer had to go because his image might cause offense to an unspecified group in the television audience. When the Smurfs made the transition from Belgian comic books to the American screen, they were swifly reined in. Said their creator, Peyo Culliford: "I had to do away with a trademark of most stories: the bespectacled Smurf who hits the moralizing Smurf on the head with a mallet as soon as the moralizing begins. Even some peace-loving people have their squabbles. That couldn't be shown on TV, I was told, because the little spectator could very go well go into his father's garage, take a hammer and hit his sister over the head with it." Filmation's internal memo showed how much power the censors had assumed: "Program Practices at CBS has ruled that a character that has been hit or in a fight Can not have: (1) eyes at halfmast (2) eyes twirling (3) tongue hanging out (4) dazed or hurt look (5) closed eyes (6) circle of stars around head. No Expression Of Pain Or Dazed Expression! The characters Can react with frustration or anger at having been foiled again. Camera: Do not shoot scenes you find with the no-no's in them." Occasionally, the New Sensitivity had a positive effect. Loud and egregiously violent adventures were toned down or banished. The old Tom and Jerry cartoons were reanimated in order to lose Mammy Two Shoes, the outlandish black domestic. Yet even here, stereotypes prevailed. The maid's legs were whitened, and her voice changed to that of an Irish washerwoman, still afraid of mice, still witless and hysterical, and now voiced by June Foray with a brogue.

In time, the guardians went wild. Fringe groups affected to see cartoon shows as satanic enticements. The insipid My Little Pony and Care Bears series could easily have been attacked for their relentless commercialism and their utter lack of wit. The religious censors had other objections in mind. To them, Pony's friend the unicorn was nothing less than a symbol of the one-horned Antichrist, and Papa Bear's homilies were carriers of unwelcome Eastern philosophy. Overseas, an African nation joined the cavilers, barring a line of dialogue in Disney's *The Rescuers* because a child uttered the blasphemous "Holy smoke." Finland chimed in: Donald Duck cartoons would not be allowed in the country because he spanked his nephews Hughie, Dewey, and Louie and appeared to have a common-law marriage to Daisy Duck. Standards and Practices had won the day—and the term *political correctness* had yet to be coined.

Small wonder that animators learned not to ask Friz Freleng about the old days. He tended to sound like a veteran ballplayer lamenting the time before free agency, when an pitcher stayed with a team from his rookie year to retirement. The trouble with the cartoon business nowadays, he would grumble, was not only the restrictions, it was the artists themselves. "People are not dedicated . . . anymore. Some of the people we've got working here next year will be working for Hanna-Barbera or Filmation, or Warner Brothers. We had a team, and we were trying to beat Disney. Today nobody cares." Unfortunately, that criticism could have applied to the new studio Friz co-owned with David DePatie, a producer he had met at Warner Bros. Using the established Warner troupe, they produced a series of inexcusable travesties. Roadrunner cartoons made without Chuck Jones, who had opened a smaller studio on his own, featured jagged outlines, maladroit animation, and tinny music. Daffy turned from a comic fall-guy into a one-dimensional maniac, usually in pursuit of a Mexican mouse named Speedy Gonzales. Speedy and the villagers snoring under their sombreros comprised the most derogatory caricatures since Disney's tours of Latin America. Like sexual double entrendres, these went through the censors unscathed. DePatie's best realized character, the Pink Panther, got his start in the titles for Blake Edwards's comedy of the same name (although there the panther in question referred to a jewel, not a character). The pink elongated cat moved silently with light abandon, the most promising personality in animated shorts since the fifties. It was his fate to become a celebrity in movie theaters, and then on television, without ever fulfilling his early potential. With each succeeding short, the plot and comedy slackened. In a strange role reversal, the *live*

Pink Panther films began to resemble cartoons. All of the features concerned the inept Parisian, Inspector Clouseau, in a Homeric struggle with the outraged head of the Sûreté, a smaller skirmish with his valet, Kato, and an unending war with a gaggle of thieves. What began as grand farce degenerated into loud unconvincing scenes of exploding props and unnatural disasters. Inexplicably, the inspector was always left undamaged. Even Peter Sellers's star turns failed to save these films. After his sudden death in 1980, there was a halfhearted attempt to revive Clouseau with other actors in the part, but the character and the cartoons had run out of ideas. From then on, they dwelt in the fabled land of reruns.

Movie producers had no room for negative thinking. Let the television people nickel-and-dime themselves to death; now that the Master was gone there were plenty of opportunities to make big money with animated features. Charles Schulz's minimalist comic strip was viewed as a natural for limited animation; Bill Melendez, a UPA veteran, had already shown how to make much of little in his Charlie Brown TV specials, using barely discernible movements, the voices of real children, and the agreeable jazz of Vince Guaraldi. A seminarian had written a book entitled *The Gospel According to Peanuts,* and four full-length films carefully preserved Schulz's Christianity Lite. In their own way, they paid homage to Walt, carrying on the notion of a suburban America, where the condition of the sandlot ballpark was the biggest worry, and small children never created major disruptions because they never reached adolescence.

Hanna-Barbera took a step up from Yogi Bear and Flintstone features. These amounted to extended television shows, cynically packaged and fobbed off on movie-going children. But the adaptation of E. B. White's lapidary novelette, *Charlotte's Web,* reached for distinction. It was not to be. Too many years had been spent on lucrative hackwork, and excellence was beyond the studio's capacity. The original tale, rich with the everyday humor and tragedies of farm life, was lost in styleless animation and a wash of saccharine numbers by Richard and Robert Sherman (onetime favorites of Walt, who had used them with profit on *Mary Poppins* and some lesser projects). Predictably, critics remarked on the wide gap between the book and the film, but even on its own terms *Charlotte* failed to charm or inform.

The most telling comment came from E. B. White himself. The old *New Yorker* writer was too mannerly to go public with his commentary. But when Chuck Jones asked for permission to bring *The Trumpet of the Swan* to the screen, White refused. Jones's Warner Bros. cartoons were his favorites, he said, but his heart had been broken by Hanna-Barbera's adaptation. White never again allowed his work to become the basis of an animated movie.

Jones's own effort at a full-length cartoon fell short of financial success, probably because he refused to compromise his standards. With a heady mix of mathematics and literature, Norton Juster's book *The Phantom Tollbooth* was called the logical successor to *Alice in Wonderland,* and Jones produced it with Carroll's work in mind. As might be expected, he had more luck with the cartoon portions than with the live ones, particularly an animated "Mathemagician" who gives life and form to the abstractions of arithmetic, and some hilarious Lethargians. They were not strong enough to carry the film. Too intellectual for children, and too basic for a purely adult crowd, *Tollbooth* enjoyed indulgent reviews yet never found its audience. Jones, who had proved his mastery of the short form, did better with three adaptations of Kipling short stories, "The White Seal," "Rikki Tikki Tavi," and, as if to show how far Disney had strayed from the source, a "Jungle Book" that strictly adhered to the originals.

Under Jones's supervision, the most gifted animator of the seventies, Richard Williams, directed an outstanding adaptation of *A Christmas Carol,* neatly evoking the Dickensian atmosphere and the sense of despair and renewal. Encouraged, Williams tried his hand at the long form with the full-length *Raggedy Ann and Andy—A Musical Adventure.* Here he came acropper, as did so many others who spent more time with the technique than with the story itself. "Get to know the characters before they get involved with the plot" had been Walt's watchwords to his staff, and when the writers and artists strayed from the ideal, he had invariably brought them back. An entry-level insight, one would think, and yet director after director lost track of it. *Raggedy Ann* faithfully reproduced the figures in John Gruelle's popular tales, just as Max Fleischer had done back in 1940. Williams and his large, capable staff made Ann and Andy dance and sing and display the hearts beneath their colorful outfits. What they failed to deliver was a compelling narrative and an appealing score. Joe Raposo's music, a main ingredient of Sesame Street, here seemed to be marking time rather than enhancing it. The Disney aces, Art Babbit and Grim Natwick, did little to modernize the antique notion of toys coming to life once their owner goes out of sight. And so another attempt at the animated feature failed to please filmgoers.

There were others. Bakshi decided not to make a sequel to *Fritz the Cat* after all; a new producer, with his eyes firmly on the cash register, offered *The Nine Lives of Fritz the Cat.* All the lives were badly drawn and voiced, and the film quickly expired. Meanwhile, Bakshi directed *The Lord of the Rings,* based on J. R. R. Tolkien's cult classic. After mocking Disney all these years, he made the same aesthetic mistake Walt did, and with far less pleasing results: He went for total realism. Tolkien's mythic figures moved precisely like humans because they *were* humans—the images had been Rotoscoped, frame by frame, from live-action footage. In essence, the artists were tracing rather than drawing, an inappropriate technique for a supernatural theme. Critics could hardly be blamed for asking why animation had been necessary in the first place.

John Hubley planned an ambitious version of Richard Adams's best-seller about the fate of a rabbit colony, *Watership Down.* No Bugs Bunny or Oswald types here. The animals were supposed to vary greatly in their personalities, and to display a rich emotional range just as they did in the book. Early on, Hubley clashed with his producer, and new and relatively unknown animators took over. They did a creditable job even though the cast tended to look alike, as rabbits will. Some of the voices helped to give them individuality—particularly those of Zero Mostel and Ralph Richardson—but they were not enough. Once again, an animated film fell between two groups: its explorations of life and death were rather mature for children, and not deep enough for their parents. The people who paid to watch *Watership Down* were like those who attended *The Lord of the Rings.* They came to see the movie because they had read the book, not because they were fans of animation.

Quite a few other cartoon features also fell by the wayside in the seventies and early eighties: *Shinbone Alley* failed to bring Don Marquis's poetic cat and cockroach, Archy and Mehitabel, to life. *Heavy Metal,* based on the magazine for adolescents with an equal interest in science fiction, sex, and cartoons, had little coherence and few real enthusiasts. Warner Bros. shamelessly ransacked their warehouses, splicing together the cartoons they had practically disowned a few years before, furnishing them with some new footage to provide the illusion of continuity, and slapping on titles like *The Looney, Looney, Looney Bugs Bunny Movie* and *Daffy Duck's Movie: Fantastic Island.* These amounted to exercises in nostalgia, not real features, and neither the critics nor the public were deceived. For a moment, animation enthusiasts took heart in the announcement that Don Bluth, a Disney studio director in the early 1970s, had gone out on his own. Better still, he had found enough investors to produce a full-length, fully animated film based on an award-winning children's book, *Mrs. Frisby and the Rats of Nimh.* The adventure of high-IQ experimental rats at the National Institute of Mental Health seemed right for the eighties, and Bluth appeared to be the new leader everyone had awaited. When *The Secret of NIMH* appeared in 1982, the letdown was palpable. The director and his staff had sedulously aped the thirties and forties style, complete with images refracted in water, sinuous tails of smoke, and a twinkling atmosphere. Sadly, predictably, the missing ingredient was Walt's story sense and timing. Placed in an ultramodern laboratory, the rats were incongruously outfitted with seventeenth-century costumes and proceeded from scene to scene without any sense of urgency. Bluth, who had left his last job because he and his colleagues "felt like we were animating the same picture over and over again with just the faces changed a little," had been unable to shake the Disney dust from his work. If it was to survive, animation required new faces in every sense of the words—fresh talent, different icons—and there was not a rescuer in view.

CHAPTER TEN

THE ANIMATED MIRROR

In the eighties, American cinema's new wunderkinder consolidated their fortunes. Leaning heavily on Jung and special effects, George Lucas made *Star Wars,* a series of glib and brilliantly manufactured pop epics. For his part, from *Raiders of the Lost Ark* to *Back to the Future,* Steven Spielberg showed the canniest use of sentiment and terror since Walt Disney himself. Both Lucas and Spielberg made much of their youths, a time when they invested their attention on comic books, movie serials, and cartoons. Both men lived off the interest of that capital in picture after picture. Individual films kept setting new box-office records; together the impresarios seemed to have an infallible commercial instinct. Yet when it came to animation, the art form they professed to love immoderately, both seemed to lose their way.

Lucasfilms was responsible for *Twice Upon a Time,* a full-length, oddly charmless film that mixed torn pieces of paper with traditional cel work. It received limited distribution and small interest; several historians correctly pointed out that such "silhouette" animation had been done in Europe more than sixty years before. Spielberg made no aesthetic distinctions in his appraisals of cartoon directors: In his introduction to Chuck Jones's autobiography, he wrote, "If Walt Disney was the first animator who taught me how to fly in my dreams, Chuck Jones was the first animator who made me laugh at them." Then he turned around and praised Hanna and Barbera for "the lasting and laughing impressions in a whole series of groundbreaking animated sitcoms." Still, Spielberg fared better than his colleague when he produced *An American Tail.* Don Bluth directed this story of immigrant mice journeying in steerage from the Old World to the New, where the streets are supposed to be paved with cheese. The problem was not at the box office, it was on the screen. Bluth had not merely paid homage to Disney, he had practically photocopied him.

The rodents of *American Tail,* clearly intended to be the counterparts of Jewish refugees, speak with foreign intonations but have no ethnic presence. The notion of pogroms is safely couched in vague terms about a past filled with feline cossacks. Wholly unequipped to handle unpleasantness, Bluth seems to reverse the unwritten dictum for Broadway comedy: "Write it Jewish and cast it goyish." The animals move fluently, and the ocean waves carry the same authority as the ones in *Pinocchio.* The vital missing ingredient, once more, is Walt's story sense. Swamped by cuteness, the drama never coheres. Although the central character gets separated from his family, little Fievel Mouskewitz seems to exist solely so that he can pipe the film's hit number, "Somewhere Out There." (Charles Solomon called cats chasing mice "an inappropriate metaphor for religious persecution." So it seemed at the time; yet that very metaphor surfaced in literary form several years later when Art Spiegelman's scarifying comic book *Maus* pictured the furry little animals in concentration camps run by jackbooted Nazi cats, and won the Pulitzer Prize.)

When *American Tail* turned out to be a sleeper—it grossed some $45 million, outperforming even the best of Disney's films—word went out once more that animation was alive and well and living in America. It did not live there for long. Seeking lower costs and a more favorable tax climate, Bluth joined with financier Morris Sullivan and relocated in Dublin. There, under the auspices of Lucas and Spielberg, Sullivan-Bluth Studios Ireland made *The Land Before Time,* a Neolithic *Bambi,* complete with creatures of the wild and a dinosaur mother killed before her child is ready to go out on his own. This was not a time when moviegoers were in the mood for negative presentations: President Ronald Reagan had recently assured them that America was standing tall. The threat of inflation and the memory of U.S. hostages in the Middle East had faded from the news. Deregulation had become something of a buzzword, and the edgy, competitive air was reflected on screen as in real life. Animated films could hardly be expected to show any signs of maturity or experiment during this period, especially from a studio that had never shown the slightest

inclination to experiment. So once again, Bluth offered a cloying atmosphere—in this case, one that turned big lizards to marzipan. Once again the script wandered around without landing anywhere, the animals sweet and pleasant to each other but lacking any resonance or edge. And once again, the profits were immense; *Land* did as well as *American Tail,* and—a source of great satisfaction to Bluth and his backers—better than *Oliver & Company,* a Disney film produced and released at the same time.

The events leading up to *Oliver* told a story more convoluted than the film's Dickensian plot. The Disney corporation was vast but vulnerable in the early eighties. Its theme parks had not increased their business, and the film division had suffered some expensive failures like the bloodless special effects movie *Tron,* the well-meaning coming-of-age drama *Tex,* and the cold adaptation of Ray Bradbury's haunting *Something Wicked This Way Comes.* Uncertain about its future and bereft of any creative, or for that matter managerial, vision of its future, Disney was ripe for a takeover. Late in 1984, after much backstage movement of furniture, threats from outsiders, frantic stock manipulations and biddings, Walt's son-in-law, Ron Miller, was forced out. Roy E. Disney, Walt's nephew, helped ease him to the door. It was an ugly business, well covered by financial reporters who speculated endlessly about the empty throne at the kingdom of the Mouse. Lucas and Spielberg knew who ought to be sitting there: Michael Eisner, formerly of CBS and ABC, where he had worked his own wonders. He was of their generation (all three were born in the 1940s), he was known for giving creative people a long leash, and when he believed in a project, he was reputed to be about as negotiable as an anvil. They got their wish. By early 1985, Eisner was in place as CEO of Walt Disney Productions. He had brought along one of his closest associates from network days, Jeffrey Katzenberg. Frank Wells, formerly of Warner, took over as president. The outsiders were in; the insiders were out.

Before Eisner and his cadre came to Disney, the studio's young animators had been hard at work on a full-length feature called *The Black Cauldron*. This was to be a sign of their emergence, blowing the last of the Disney dust to Ireland where Don Bluth could do whatever he wanted with it. Left to their own devices, they would then take cartooning to another level. Yet what emerged from two years of labor could hardly be called revolutionary—or even very fresh. The story concerns the good and valorous Taran, the wicked Horned King, and their battle for control of the Black Cauldron, font of supernatural power. The supporting cast includes the beautiful princess Eilonwy, a psychic pig, another creature of no known DNA, and a chorus of mini-fairies. Critics admired the film's techniques: shot in 70mm, it featured unusual angles and extraordinary detail. In all, some 2.5 million drawings went into the production. But the same critics placed *Black Cauldron* in the category of "sword-and-sorcery" and found it no more daring than any other Arthurian adventure. As Maltin points out, the film "made $21 million, but a reissue of *One Hundred and One Dalmations* later that year made $33 million, which seemed to say it all."

In 1985, *The Great Mouse Detective* created a very small splash by offering a slight, mildly amusing pastiche of Sherlock Holmes based on the popular children's book *Basil of Baker St.* What set the film apart from previous Disney features was the use, albeit sparingly, of computer animation. A key scene takes place inside Big Ben, where gigantic clockworks mesh before and behind the main characters. The mechanical pieces look disturbingly different from the animals, but a discerning viewer can catch glimpses of the future in those gears and axles. *Oliver & Company,* another uneasy collaboration between the standard and the new, followed in 1988. Eleven of the movie's seventy-two minutes were computerized. The best of them portrayed the tunnels of a subway, and an Erector set span of the Brooklyn Bridge. The voices of two celebrated recording artists, Bette Midler and Billy Joel, helped propel *Oliver;* it grossed $53 million, more than *Cauldron* and *Mouse Detective* combined. Various people claimed credit: the computer operators, director George Scribner, the stars, Katzenberg, who had persuaded Midler and Joel to come aboard. No one could be blamed for overlooking the most important ingredient. After all, the score contained songs by fifteen very different musicians and lyricists, including the superstars Rubén Blades and Barry Manilow. In the long list of credits, few movie people recognized the name of Howard Ashman. Along with lyricist Alan Mencken, who made no contribution to *Oliver,* he had written the score for the off-Broadway musical *Little Shop of Horrors.*

Signed for Disney's next animated feature, *The Little Mermaid,* Mencken and Ashman involved themselves with nearly every phase of the filmmaking—so much so that Mencken took on the additional title of co-producer. It was their idea to give the subaqueous co-star, Sebastian the Crab, a Jamaican accent; according to Ashman, this added a contemporary "energy and spice" to the score. And it was their idea to let the title character sit down and define herself in a song, just as the central figures had done in *Little Shop.* Comic numbers and state-of-

the-art animation gave *Mermaid* style; timing brought it fortune. The Broadway musical had become as moribund by the end of the mid-eighties. Theater after theater exhumed hit shows from the fifties and before: Cole Porters's *Anything Goes* was typical of the successful revivals. The old formula of sympathetic personnae, a strong plot and subplot, and a melodic score that sent the ticket holder away humming had become another of New York's homeless. Disney offered it shelter, and *Mermaid* went on to earn $84 million in domestic sales and millions more in licensing fees.

Katzenberg had left no doubt in anyone's mind that he now wanted Disney to produce pictures at sensible cost and maximum profits. There was to be no waste, no excess. Then came the live film *Dick Tracy*. For decades, the studio had refined the technique of promoting tie-in merchandise at the same time it produced a feature, aggressively distributing dolls and board games and lunch boxes to stores just as the movie was opening across the country. With the adaptation of Chester Gould's comic strip (a Disney natural, went the conventional wisdom), everything abruptly went into reverse. Not only was the movie an expensive failure, but the commodities—the yellow raincoats, the toy guns, and games—failed to move off the shelves. The CEO issued a memo to the staff, and it quickly leaked to the press. "We should now look long and hard at our blockbuster business," said the message, "and get out of it." Among many other things, *Dick Tracy* was "about losing control of our own destiny, and that's a high price to pay for a movie."

The highly publicized memo, as British historian Alan Bryman records, "seemed to bring a frisson of schadenfreude to many Hollywood watchers," and there were suddenly many "revelations about the dark side of the new Disney." In an interview, actor Bill Murray said that the company's reputation for "being difficult to work with and tough with a buck" was true. The agent for Nick Nolte and Richard Dreyfuss complained that "There was no way to overestimate Disney's stinginess." Film critic Michael Medved observed that "Everyone wants Disney to have a big black eye." For the first time since the postwar period, the establishment was turning against one of the most revered names in Hollywood—indeed, in America—and something had to be done. That something was animation—mixed with human performances.

Spielberg's company, Amblin, had collaborated with Disney's Touchstone division to produce *Who Framed Roger Rabbit?* A free adaptation of Gary Wolf's novel *Who Censored Roger Rabbit?*, it was to offer a pastiche of hard-boiled detection and farce set in the late 1940s. The prime components were a low-rent detective, a steamy ingenue, and a group of famous cartoon characters called Toons, dwelling in a community outside the view of "real" people. There they are allowed to caper and skirmish all they please—provided that their misconduct takes place within their own borders. The book leaves little doubt that the situation of the Toons is a metaphor for blacks and other minorities confined to ghettos. Raymond Chandler fans could see faint parallels with *Farewell, My Lovely* and its policemen uninterested in the murder of a black in Los Angeles because the incident was "just another shine killing."

Richard Williams, who now derived most of his income from commercials, would be responsible for the animation. Director Robert Zemeckis was to oversee the whole production, with emphasis on the live portions. The mere mixing of humans and cartoons required no special effort of imagination; what would make this mix unique was its style. From the days of the Fleischer brothers, right through MGM's dance of Jerry Mouse and Gene Kelly and Walt Disney's *Fantasia* and Ralph Bakshi's *Coonskin,* certain unwritten laws were obeyed as if they had been issued by the Supreme Court. The live-action camera always remained rooted to a single spot; and because of the expense and the labor involved, interaction between animated creatures and human beings was as formalized as a crossword puzzle. Zemeckis and Williams were having none of that; they wanted the camera to move as freely as the individuals it photographed. In addition, Williams recalled, "We thought the cartoon characters should be always affect-

ing their environment or getting tangled up with the live actors." That meant a totally mobile camera, and it implied the use of at least three cel layers for every frame in order to give the Toons a three-dimensional look (the creatures were required to handle real objects and to throw convincing shadows). By 1988, computers could have handled some of the action, but a decision was made to go with traditional hand-drawn methods, one reason for the extraordinary cost of *Roger Rabbit*—upwards of $45 million.

As it turned out, drawings and live action combined seamlessly, though the tempo soon becomes unrelievedly frantic and the hero deeply unattractive. His pneumatic girlfriend, Jessica, is a Playboy caricature gone two steps too far. Most of the supporting Toons appear to have been spilled from the wastebasket of a cartoonist on amphetamines. Aside from the unprecedented meeting of major cartoon stars (Daffy from Warner's and Donald from Disney collide, each duck accusing the other of having speech defects), what holds the film together is the performance of a very real actor. Bob Hoskins plays Eddie Valiant, the sleuth called in to clear Roger in the murder of a studio executive. Hoskins's reactions—given to empty chairs and blank spaces during the actual filming—are convincing and subtle, in direct contrast to the animals and humanoids who were put in afterward. But 1988 was a sparse season, and feature cartooning had become a synonym for uninspired children's fare. Whatever the film's flaws, it was an authentic original, unwilling to talk down to an underage audience. Naturally, the theme of life in the ghetto had a galvanizing effect on inner-city viewers, but it was the middle-class adults and their children who flocked to *Roger Rabbit*—often for two or three showings. The box-office phenomenon eventually grossed $145 million in the United States and an equal amount overseas.

The combination of these two movies did everything that Katzenberg & Co. had hoped for—and more. The clamor for toys based on the animated figures was so great that factories could not keep up with them. Figurines of the mermaid and her friends decorated children's rooms, while Jessica sat on the desks of executives, an acceptable sex symbol precisely because she was so exaggerated—and because she had originated from the Spielberg foundry and Disney's Touchstone, two places with a well-publicized regard for family values. Only later did some salacious rumors begin to circulate. A free-lance animator claimed to have drawn Jessica's genitalia in a few frames. This was adamantly denied by the producers, and frame-by-frame examination showed nothing but a suggestive shadow around the area in question. Probably both sides were right: The animator had his little joke and then covered it up; the producers knew nothing about the prank. Yet in some ways this little incident was the beginning of yet another attack on Disney, even though Touchstone actually had very little to do with the film.

A general enthusiasm greeted the next animated feature, *Beauty and the Beast,* based, in the best Disney tradition, on a classic legend. Here the tradition of the musical theater was fully co-opted—even to the use of Angela Lansbury and Jerry Orbach as character voices. Both were experienced Broadway performers and singers who knew how to make audiences hanker for an encore. Viewers were astonished by the computerized three-dimensional effect in a ballroom scene, and went out humming tunes from the flashy Mencken-Ashman score. There was not to be another from this team. Ashman had contracted AIDS; the Academy Award for best song came posthumously. "As grievous a loss as Howard's death was," recalled a Disney veteran, "nothing could stop us. We could see now that instead of the theater flowing to the movies, the process could be reversed. We could bring *Beauty and the Beast* from two dimensions to three dimensions, taking it east and reaping some very big rewards. It made us very pleased with ourselves."

And there were bigger rewards in the offing. When the accountants were finished adding up the columns, *The Lion King* appeared to be the most profitable film ever made. The jungle fantasy reflected some social concerns about the discredited male in society; it had a strong paternal figure, voiced in a rich bass by James Earl Jones, an Iago figure given the purr of motiveless malignity by Jeremy Irons, and a wide-eyed young lion who must one day replace his murdered father, played by Matthew Broderick. It also contained a group of goose-stepping hyenas, portrayed in a strange pastiche of Leni Riefenstahl's Nazi film *Triumph of the Will.* Probably less than 5 percent of the audience had any understanding of the reference, but no matter. Disney was convinced that it could do anything, including a politically incorrrect movie, and make it pay. This one paid in excess of $740 million worldwide, and as much as $1 billion in retail merchandising sales. Figures did not include the sale of some 20 million videocassettes.

Actually, long before *Lion King,* the company's arrogance had grown thick enough to cut. Taking *Beauty* to Broadway was accomplished with such ease that Disney planned film-to-stage transfers on a regular basis. (Eventually, the New Amsterdam theater on 42nd Street was acquired for that purpose.) And then there was the triumph of *Aladdin.* This new version of the *Arabian Nights* starred Robin Williams ad-libbing the voice of the genie with manic invention. Borrowing liberally from many sources, including the visuals of Alexander Korda's 1940 film *The Thief of Baghdad* and the sinuous line of Al Hirschfeld, the *New York Times* theatrical caricaturist, the film burst on the scene in 1993, became a megahit—and proceeded to run into trouble. First, a columnist in the *Los Angeles Times* took offense at a couplet sung by the Genie about Arabia, a place "where they cut off your hand if they don't like your face . . . it's barbaric but hey—it's home." Shortly afterward, an author of several books about Disney animation sent a fax to Katzenberg. He pointed out that way back in the 1930s, "Walt had changed the Big Bad Wolf's Yiddish intonations after he received objections." Surely, the writer went on, "you would not want to cause unintentional pain to innocent people . . . causing a child of Arabian descent to slink out of the theater because he saw something demeaning in a Disney film. . . . Your heart is big enough to include Arab-Americans."

Evidently, it was not; Katzenberg refused to change a line. He had not reckoned with steady pressure from the American-Arab Anti-Discrimination Committee. Eventually, the members and their sympathizers wore down his resistance, and by the time the film went to videotape, Arabia had been altered to a locale "where it's flat and immense and the heat is intense." This was a very small fissure in the Disney facade, reinforced by the film's huge financial profits—$217 million at home and abroad, plus the revenue that came in when 24 million copies of the videotape were sold. But insiders knew that all was not well at the corporation. Katzenberg, given great credit by the press for Disney's resurgence, had begun to grate on Eisner, and insiders predicted that the collaboration would not endure. The death of Disney president Frank Wells in a 1992 helicopter accident broke the chain of command and disoriented the commanders. Late in the year, the long-awaited divorce occurred. Infuriated when Eisner failed to name him as the new president, Katzenberg walked out. This backstairs conflict caused huge reverberations in the Disney stock price, particularly when Katzenberg co-founded a new company, Dream-Works SKG, with Steven Spielberg and the music producer David Geffen. The trio announced that one of their first projects would be *Prince of Egypt,* a full-length animated retelling of the story of Moses. DreamWorks's troika never openly expressed its aim; that was left to Rupert Murdoch, In his offices at 20th Century-Fox, the press and film mogul appraised the company. "DreamWorks, I mean they are driven," he said with a faint smile. "I mean, they are about the destruction of Disney." It would not be an easy assignment.

"Lots of talk and promises surrounded DreamWorks from day one," recalled an animation producer. "They were going to be the biggest animation house, with global impact. They had the music, the money, the brains to make the world forget Walt and all who took his place. But the fact remains that DreamWorks is playing chess with one piece—a queen, maybe, but still only a single player. Whereas Disney has all sixteen of their pieces—nights, bishops, castles, pawns, everything.

"When an independently produced animated film, *The Swan Princess,* came along in the early nineties, Disney simply rereleased *The Lion King* at hundreds of theaters and swamped it. Now, bear in mind that Disney has several dozen full-length classic animated features in the bank. They can trot them out any time they want against any*one* they want. Plus the new ones in the pipeline: *Hercules, The Legend of Mulan,* about a Chinese peasant girl turned warrior, and *Tarzan.* DreamWorks has nothing to offer except the names—admittedly, big—of the founders, plus one film."

There was also the problem of personnel. In order to hire proven talent, Katzenberg planned to raid the Disney ranks. Here he was frustrated by—Katzenberg. The *New York Times* noted the irony in its report: "When he was the studio chief, he had forced some of his top animators to sign three- and seven-year contracts to guard against poaching, never dreaming the long-term contracts might someday work against his own interests."

Hiring young, untried animators was, of course, another matter. Here, Dreamworks SKG counted on a widespread and well-known disenchantment with its main competitor. It had begun in the late eighties, when one honors graduate from the school Walt had founded, California Institute of the Arts, spoke out against the Disney studio. He and many of his classmates had taken to calling the institution "a silk-lined dead end." Another, who had succumbed to Disney's blandishments and then quit, recalled "their place in Florida where people could watch you animate. You felt like a gerbil in a Habitrail. Meanwhile, back in Burbank you drew Disney-style, or else. No real experimenting, no breaking the mold, no off-the-wall approaches. No thank-you." Cal Arts found that many of its graduates now preferred the challenge of independent filmmaking—or even television. On the home screen, one of the top-rated shows was not only animated, it offered comments on animation. "The Simpsons" had begun quietly as a regular five-minute episode on the Tracy Ullman comedy series. Based on characters created by underground comic strip cartoonist Matt Groening ("Life Is Hell"), the family members looked more like omelettes than people. The mother and father had a querulous, moronic air about them, and their three children provided a constant source of trouble. But the show was shrewdly produced by James L. Brooks, who had created the "Mary Tyler Moore Show" and directed the hit film *Terms of Endearment*.

Brooks had unerring commercial instincts. Under his supervision, the Simpsons established themselves as comic archetypes of the dysfunctional family. Yet he never allowed blue material or physical punishment. (Most of young Bart's penalties consisted of writing sentences over and over on the blackboard, such as "Goldfish don't bounce" and "I will not yell 'She's dead' during roll call.") Indeed, when the most egregious violence occurred it took place on the family's TV screen where two cartoon animals, Itchy and Scratchy—sharp parody of Saturday morning fare—went at the world with hammer and tongs.

For those who knew how to read it, however, the subtext of the show was not so agreeable. The late 1980s had seen a measurable decline in the family—nearly 50 percent of marriages ended in divorce—and even in intact households children were not so well off. Academic achievement had slipped to shockingly low levels; according to the National Assessment of Educational Progress, by the late eighties only 6 percent of graduating high school seniors could solve a two-step arithmetic problem. Asked to identify the nation south of the U.S. border, 25 percent of Dallas students shrugged their shoulders; in

Boston, 38 percent of the students could not identify the six New England states; in Kansas City, 40 percent failed to name any three South American countries. Distressed by what he had seen and read, Senator Bill Bradley of New Jersey found that the news about education was "not only shocking; it is frightening. When 95% of college students cannot locate Vietnam on a world map, we must sound the alarm. We cannot expect to be a world leader if your populace doesn't even know where the rest of the world is."

As the standards of education deteriorated, so did morale. Between the sixties and the eighties, the rate of teenage suicide tripled. Eating disorders became endemic among the young, and an administrator at the University of California traced them directly to "Mother's increasing presence in the workplace, father's failure to pick up the residual fifty percent of parenting . . . and marital instability." Under these conditions, children seemed unlikely "to receive . . . support and effective limit-setting." The results were there for all to see: each year, drug and alcohol abuse climbed; so did violent juvenile crime, adolescent pregnancy, and all the diseases associated with early and ignorant sexual experience escalating from herpes to AIDS. While doctors and social workers attempted to cope with these mounting catastrophes, the entertainment industry regarded them as the subject for comedy. Programs ranging from the long-running sitcom "Married, with Children" to the film *Dumb and Dumber* affected to find ignorance hilarious. Animation kept pace with them.

In addition to "The Simpsons," which at least displayed some affection between parent and child, there was "Beavis and Butt-head," which allowed no room for benignity. The title characters were two fourteen-year-olds, drawn with a crudity to match their manners. Their creator, Mike Judge, was a Texas-based print cartoonist who ventured into animation with the short film "Frog Baseball," starring a couple of boys squashing scores of amphibians with baseball bats, grunting, sniveling, and giggling in brief, imitable "huh-huhs" as they killed. MTV bought the film to show on its late-evening mélange of experimental works, Liquid TV, then commissioned Judge to create a series based on Beavis and his equally limited friend Butt-head. Without the help of the censorious, the show might easily have failed. Given an impetus by teachers and parents who labeled them "insensitive" and "inane," Beavis and Butt-head caught on and grew more popular with each succeeding episode. Young audiences watched, happy to mimic the trademark sniffles and giggles, and to confine their opinions to "Cool!" and "Sucks!" in homage to their favorite "retards." The highlight of the show was always the same; at some point, the boys viewed a video and rendered an opinion. Watching the twin sons of the fifties teen idol Ricky Nelson, for example, Butt-head snorted: "These chicks look like guys." Beavis: "I heard that these chicks' grandpa was Ozzy Osbourne." Butt-head: "No way. They're Elvis's kids." Licensees quickly produced T-shirts, hats, and other paraphernalia, as well as a *Beavis & Butt-head Ensucklopedia* in which the youths pontificate on various topics. Under "J is for Jobs": "Doctor—this guy operates on you and gives you shots and stuff. But it's not as much fun as it sounds, 'cause like you have to go to school extra for it. On the other hand, you also get to see chicks naked, which is as much fun as it sounds, huh-huh."

"Beavis and Butt-head" kept on its mindless way until October 1993. Late that month, a five-year-old boy set fire to his home in Ohio, killing his two-year-old sister. The mother blamed a pyromaniacal incident on "Beavis and Butt-head," the child's favorite TV program. The show's defenders, including Judge himself, contended that the press had distorted the story, and failed to comment on the sort of parent who would allowed her child to play, unsupervised, with a cigarette lighter. "You have to order cable," the cartoonist pointed out. "You have to say, 'I'm paying thirty bucks a month for these fifty-one extra channels. If you complain, it's like going out and buying *Hustler* and leaving it on your coffee table and complaining to the publisher that your kid is seeing pictures of nasty stuff. Raising kids isn't easy, but it's easy to lock cable TV out of your house." Perhaps, but MTV wanted no part of the controversy. Quietly, the programming department canceled "Beavis and Butt-head"'s early evening airing, and confined it to late night. (As a measure of the distance between network and cable animation, "The Simpsons" were credited with saving the life of an eight-year-old Texas boy. He and his ten-year-old brother were at home alone when the younger child started to choke on some food. The older one managed to dislodge the object. He had learned the technique from an episode in which Homer Simpson chokes on a doughnut as his co-workers stand around looking at a poster describing the Heimlich maneuver.)

Between these terminals was another kind of animated program, neither as cannily scripted as "The Simpsons," nor as aggressively imbecilic as "Beavis and Butt-head"—although it came close. Trained in Canada, animator John Kricfalusi made no secret of his admiration for the Three Stooges's eye-gauging comedy, as well as the raunchy and satiric attitudes of Ralph Bakshi, with whom he had worked on Mighty Mouse. Kricfalusi's team starred a scurvy chihuahua (Ren) who sounded very much like Peter Lorre, and an naïve, overstuffed alleycat (Stimpy). Together they ventured into fantasy lands, accompanied by canned classical music—Kricfalusi's private homage to Warner Bros. cartoons like "What's Opera, Doc?" and "Corny Concerto." "Ren and Stimpy" used a deliberately retro style reminiscent of the Golden Age, all bright hues and jaunty drawings, but beneath the surface things were quite different. Kricfalusi had the temperament of an anarchist, and he delighted in subversive messages. A fairy-tale version of Gulliver, with a giant Stimpy stomping around a village of tiny humans, contained the sounds—though not the sight—of crunched bones and gurgled screams. The show regularly skewered kidvid commercials with Log, an expensive toy that was nothing more than a piece of tree trunk. As an up-tempo tune played, boys rolled Log down the cellar stairs, while girls dolled Log up in a blond wig and makeup à la Barbie. A regular feature, "Ask Dr. Stupid" was an echo of Bullwinkle's "Mr. Know-It-All." Asked why children had to attend class, he explained that parents "are really aliens, and while you're at school they shed their human skins and breathe dryer lint." There was a brief moment when "Ren and Stimpy" seemed poised to fill the vacancy left when Jay Ward quit the scene; instead, Kricfalusi capitalized on the infinitely prolonged adolescence of its viewers. "Ren and Stimpy"'s jokes, known in the trade as "cocky-doody material," frequently centered on bodily functions: references to mucous and flatulence occurred frequently and "Don't pee on the third rail" served as a typical warning. Nickelodeon aired the show at 12:30 and 8:30 P.M., which ensured a large young audience. But it could not guarantee the stability of the staff. Kricfalusi argued with the network executives as well as with some staffers and abruptly quit "Ren and Stimpy" in the fall of 1992. The departure was made with maximum acrimony, particularly when the director's longtime assistant, Bob Camp, took over. "One thing John would never admit," Camp said later, "is that he didn't do everything on the show and that he needed people. I'm not afraid to admit I need the people around here." After viewing the new "Ren and Stimpy"s, Kricfalusi retorted, "The shows are later, they cost more money, and they're not as good." In a sense, he's right. The new animation seemed smoother, and the characters were basically the same, but something had vanished. If the vulgarity was still lamentably present, the energy seemed forced and arbitrary. The audience continued its unending search for fresh faces and a brand-new look.

These were to appear on the big screen in the winter of 1995. The *Toy Story* story had begun a quarter of century before, when the film's producer, Edwin Catmull, devised a method of digitizing a three-dimensional model of his hand and showing it on a TV monitor. George Lucas learned about the experiment and wasted no time in signing up the young computer scientist. Catmull became a maestro of special effects for Lukas's new company, Pixar, and with a group of like-minded innovators developed a galaxy of illusions for *Star Trek II* and *Return of the Jedi*. The trouble was, Lukas continually cast Pixar in a supporting role, and the artificers wanted to be stars. It was a familiar situation; one of Pixar's animators, John Lasseter, had recently come from Disney. There, he reported, "they were interested in computers only to save costs, not to explore the artistic edges of the medium."

In 1986, Lukas sold the company to Stephen Jobs, a founder of Apple computers, for $10 million. The unique hardware and personnel were relocated from Marin County to Point Richmond, a picturesque little town overlooking San Francisco Bay. Having spent millions, Jobs was required to spent almost five times as much to keep pace with technological improvements. "If I had known how much it cost to keep Pixar going," he admitted in 1995, "I doubt if I would have bought the company." Pixar first turned a profit in the early nineties, when it produced commercials for Life Savers, featuring a lively conga line of candies with holes in the middle. Then came short cartoons, among them Lasseter's "Tin Drummer," an Oscar recipient in 1988. Studio executives, originally hostile to the idea of computers, warmed to technology in 1991 when they saw the impressive scenes in *Terminator 2* as well as the ballroom sequence of *Beauty and the Beast*. That was the year the animator made his pitch to the big studio. Eisner and Katzenberg, then still on speaking terms, found the idea of a computerized feature appealing but insisted on doing it in-house. Lasseter offered an alternative: "I said to them, 'Why can't I do a film for you up here? We have this brilliant technology; it's a great setup.' That July we started on *Toy Story* as part of a three-picture deal."

Lasseter had in mind a "buddy movie" with a difference. In his machine-made animated film, the leading men would be playthings. "Toys are a natural," he noted. "The computer likes to make objects look plastic and perfect and manufactured." Lasseter conjured up a space ranger action figure and an old-fashioned cowpoke. As he saw it, Buzz Lightyear and Woody would begin as enemies: wary, jealous, hostile. Then, thrust into an incongruous life-and-death situation—Roy Rogers meets Buck Rogers—each would learn the meaning of friendship. En route, they would be surrounded by new toys and old favorites like Slinky and Etch-A-Sketch, as well as by a cast of computer-generated humans. The impresario and at least half a dozen scenarists labored over the script, a normal number for any Hollywood project. They had less trouble with the voice-overs: Tom Hanks and Tim Allen effortlessly gave personalities to Buzz and Woody, abetted by the insult comedian Don Rickles as a short-tempered Mr. Potato Head. The real challenges came when the staff had to engineer the personae to perform with fluency and wit. No cels would be used. Once they appeared on a monitor, the characters were out of reach. They existed only in cyberspace, and that was where they had to be tinted and manipulated.

Pete Docter, the film's supervising animator, traced the laborious process from storyboard to finished product. "We made models of everyone in the movie. Touching the figures in every conceivable place with a kind of magnet, we scanned them into the computer. That gave us a three-dimensional image. On that we added details, flesh, color, clothing and all the rest." Once the data was scanned in, animators and designers and artists blocked out the action, carefully defining lip synchronizations and the smallest facial and finger movements. Color was added in a process analogous to inking and painting. Lighting and shading demanded even more subtlety. There were no simple objects or easy sequences. The model of Woody had more than 1,000 animation control points, and some 400 other characters were almost as complex. Nearly 10,000 hairs grew on the head of a "human" boy; trees in the exterior scenes displayed more than a million leaves. And that was the simple part. Endowing toys with the ability to run and climb, argue and laugh was a labor-intensive operation involving 110 people, including 28 full-time animators, for almost four years. The unforeseen became a part of daily routine—and sometimes the best part. A regiment of soldiers, for example, moved with a gait that seemed too jaunty for toys. Animators were at a loss until Docter nailed an old pair of sneakers to a chunk of plywood. "I put them on," he said, "to see how it would feel to go on maneuvers with this base attached to my feet, the way toy soldiers do when kids move them around on their bedspreads." The awkward, poignant result became the film's defining moment.

The faces of *Toy Story*'s actors never equaled the range of sensations expressed by Wile E. Coyote doing a double take just before a locomotive runs him down. It took a resourceful use of body language and facial

characteristics—eyebrows, lower lids, cheeks—just to provide the toys with presence and credibility. Computerized colors aided the illusion, though putting them in place often drove the staff to distraction. "You can take your hottest red," art director Ralph Eggleston pointed out, "and then you put it on rubber, glass, metal, velvet, smoke—the exact same color on these different textures under the exact same light will cause them to look different. It was a very frustrating experience." But ultimately rewarding; the vigorous interplay of illumination and action outshone almost all of the live productions in 1995.

Pixar company went public at $17 a share. Before the end of the day, the price had reached the high forties. Jobs, who owned 82.2 percent of the company, had a paper fortune of over $1 billion. *Toy Story* went on to receive an Academy Award nomination, and to gross some $150 million in the United States alone. More millions came in from overseas, from toys and games licensed by the filmmakers—and from yet another method of running features at home, the CD-ROM version released in time for the Christmas holidays.

Jobs and his employees took to calling their location Silliwood. The portmanteau word, a combination of Silicon Valley and Hollywood, announced to the world that from here on technocrats would be on an equal footing with the cel makers. This was something more than braggadocio. *Toy Story* was surely the beginning of an epic—the animated soul of the new machine. And yet radical techniques did not render the old styles obsolete. For no matter how extravagant the futurists' predictions, or what jargon they used for their boasts, in order to develop their ideas they still had to use the basic imagery of the animated cartoon. Musing about graphics on the World Wide Web, the inventor of America Online called it "One Big Thunderlizard." Before the week was out, hundreds of animators were bent over their desks, drawing pen-and-ink versions of the reptile whose footprints would lead them into the next century.

Of America's three most original art forms—jazz, the Broadway musical, and the animated film—only the last has been able to widen its audience as it experimented and grew. Often, as we have seen, it survived by ruthlessly co-opting the other two. Because some features have been so immensely profitable and because television has so many hours to fill, animation has never been so omnipresent and animators have never been so employable. Professor John Canemaker, who has been teaching animation at the New York University film school since 1980, observes that "From Cal Arts to NYU, animation majors seem to find employment before they've taken off their caps and gowns. And no wonder. This is a visual age; it has a ravenous appetite for people who know how to create winning characters on paper as well as on the computer monitor, how to use color, how to direct, how to make drawings come alive."

Events bear him out. Take, for example, the outsized profits from recent Disney films. Women tended to give the nod to *Pocahontas*, a film best known for its beauty of place and its headlong political correctness. This comic-book history made Disney richer by more than $150 million, a number that was scratched on the pads of studio executives everywhere. The equally successful *Hunchback of Notre Dame* was preferred by most male viewers—but not all. In the *Weekly Standard*, film critic James Bowman found "the anti-Christian tendency" of the New Disney "more obvious in this film than ever before. The only prominently believing Christian in the cartoon, set in and around a church, is the evil Claude Frollo. In the novel, and even in Charles Laughton's version, which was largely devoted to an attack on 'superstition,' Frollo was a good man and a sincere believer tormented by a pride and a passion with which he could never come to terms. In the Disney version he is nothing but a villain and a hypocrite:

> Judge Claude Frollo wished to
>   Purge the world of sin
> And he saw corruption every
>   where—except within."

On the other side of the political spectrum, the *New York Times* critic Paul Goldberger was every bit as withering in his consideration of *Hunchback*. "Even a six-year-old could love it," he wrote. "Perhaps *only* a six-year-old could love it." He went on to deride the title character, Quasimodo, who "not only looks cute, but sings and dances too . . . accompanied by gargoyles. These have names. One is Victor, one is Hugo, and the third is named Laverne." This, he wrote, "is not animation turning its techniques on a great work of literature; it is grotesque, vulgar parody."

What next? Goldberger demanded. "Disney's *Job?* He could sing 'I've got a Pack o' Troubles.' Disney's *Moby Dick,* looking like an animated version of *Free Willy?* Maybe a Disney *Hamlet,* freed from anguish and indecision. He could smile sweetly while Ophelia, borrowing from another Disney classic, sang 'Some Day My Prince Will Come.'"

Studio officials refrained from a formal reply. They knew only too well that this was not a case of the New Disney squandering its precious heritage. The sainted Walt had received vituperative comments in much the same spirit, and sometimes worse. The *New Republic* sneering at *Bambi:* "Mickey wouldn't be caught dead in this"; the *New Yorker* labeling *Alice* "a dreadful mockery"; the *Herald Tribune* dismissing *Fantasia* as "a brutalization of sensibility"—the clip files were full of such objections, dating back to the days before *Pinocchio.* These critiques occurred with dependable regularity almost every time Disney attempted a breakthrough or adapted a book, even if—as in the case of *Hunchback*—the book had languished on library shelves for years. Actually, the case against Disney was weakest here. Hyperion, its publishing division, put out an edition of the Victor Hugo novel and enjoyed brisk sales; viewers of the film had actually been inspired to go back to the book. Not that it mattered; cartoons had always provided a large and tempting target; they always would. They could be portrayed as too dark and frightening for the young, or as too superficial and prettified to be taken seriously. Either way, the reviewers could enjoy a field day, and congratulate themselves on their role as moral and aesthetic guardians of the audience. The trouble was, the audience rarely hewed to the critical line. It voted with its tickets, and in the case of Disney films, sometimes voted for the same film three or four times. These were statistics no major studio could afford to ignore. By the close of the nineties, well aware that profits were often in inverse proportion to negative reviews, almost every producer had a full-length animated feature in development.

The parameters of a golden age have always been difficult to determine; historically, very few have recognized the era when they were in it. But it seems a fair assumption that this is the beginning of a long and fecund period for animation. For at the same time that computers were working their wonders and Disney was reestablishing its preeminence, the overpowering atmosphere of the Arabian Nights was captured in Richard Williams's *The Thief and the Cobbler* (later retitled *Arabian Night*), a traditional cel film that took some twenty years to complete. Meanwhile, Ted Turner's Cartoon Channel was operating twenty-four hours a day, recycling the classics and adding new programs. Cable TV welcomed experimental cartoons, among them "The Critic," the sharply written adventures of a film reviewer, and "Dr. Katz," the eccentric, intimate conversations of a psychiatrist and his comedian clients. Every subject seemed to be fair game, from the gritty black-and-white version of Slick Rick's rap record "Behind Bars," to the computerized urban fantasy "The Maxx," to the capers of a mainstream teenager Doug.

Steven Spielberg continued to produce the highly profitable TV shows, "Tiny Toons," "Animaniacs," and "Freakazoid." Mark Mothersbaugh, a former member of the rock group Devo, composed the scores for "Rugrats" and "Santo Bugito." "All of us are discovering a life after Rock 'n' Roll," he said, "where we can deal with concepts and ideas." Clive Barker, British master of horror fiction and self-described "fan boy" of animation, adapted his novel *The Thief of Always* for an animated film. Bruce Willis, not content with starring in adventure movies, developed a cartoon series entitled "B.R.U.N.O. the Kid," about a ten-year-old computer genius. William Bennett oversaw the transfer of his best-seller *The Book of Virtues* to a cartoon series, "Adventures from the Book of Virtues," produced by the Public Broadcasting System. And even the Bard became a cartoon star on the HBO series "Shakespeare: The Animated Tales." *Animato!,* best of the many magazines devoted to the art, barely has space to include the manifold activities and personalities in its thick quarterly issues.

As all this has transpired, viewers have become acutely aware of the grammar of film. Sophisticated about technique if not subject matter, ticket buyers—even young ones—will no longer sit still for the ungainly images and poorly prepared stories of the past. Second-rate animation rarely gets into first-run theaters anymore. Relegated to tape, the films sit on shelves at video stores until naïve adults rent them for their children's entertainment. They are rarely taken out a second time by the same person.

Beyond all considerations, there remains the sheer popularity of the art form and the increasing skills of its practitioners. Animation has always had its adherents; from the days of the chalk talk through the rise of Mickey Mouse, the first important features, the impudent hilarities of Termite Terrace, the coming of television, the various redefinitions of Disney to the new age of computer imagery. But never have there been so many enthusiasts of the cartoon in all its manifestations. Those searching for their lost youth can recover it any time merely by strolling through animation galleries, where the icons of childhood caper on colored cels. The process began in the 1970s when Chuck Jones began to offer redrawn and painted cels bearing his signature for about $60 each. "I hoped that a handful of fans might remember Bugs and Daffy and the Roadrunner, and perhaps buy a hundred or so drawings a year. I had no idea of how much to charge, really, or whether what I did might increase in value." Today, a signed Jones original costs upwards of $1,200. Not many stocks could boast a growth rate of 2,000 percent over the same period, and production cels from Disney's early films have appreciated even more.

Those who would rather peer through the windshield than into the rearview mirror can attend touring projects like Spike and Mike's Festival of Animation. These shows select the best work of unknown and experimental artists. The work is invariably promising and often brilliant, suggesting that these young men and women will be what Winsor McCay called the Michael J. Angelos of the twenty-first century. As for the vast majority of fans who simply enjoy watching sketches come to life, home screens and theaters provide a museum of just about every cartoon ever made. Every day new audiences trace the winding journey from "Gertie" to *Toy Story* only to find that it is not nearly as long as they thought.

There are more similarities than differences between the shy dinosaur and the confident heroes of cyberspace. After all, both of them began as all works of art do, in any epoch, under all conditions: with a blank surface and an instrument, and an artist drawing flat and seeing round. And both had two tales to tell: the one on screen and the one that reflected their times. We laugh at them because they seem so different from what we know. But as we have seen, this is deceptive. To watch these funny pictures—and all the animations that came between—is actually to peer into a distorted looking glass that catches the light and gives back pictures of ourselves.

NOTES

CHAPTER ONE:
"IT'S ALL IN DREAMLAND, YOU KNOW"

(N.B.: The major portion of *Serious Business* was written with the aid of interviews, personal sources, and countless hours of viewing animated films and short subjects. Even so, certain books were indispensable and they are listed below. Where the page numbers are not given, the entire text bears on the subject discussed.)

17 *black boy juggling with his own head et seq.:* Ralph Stephenson, *Animation in the Cinema* (Tantivy Press, 1967).

19 *"iridescent polychromous effulgence":* Stefan Kanfer, "Yellow Journalism," *Civilization,* May 1995.

20 *"he remembered Arthur" and McCay biographical details:* John Canemaker, *Winsor McCay* (Katonah Museum, 1988).

25 *"he was such a rapid worker" et seq.:* Charles Solomon, *Enchanted Drawings* (Knopf, 1981), 16.

27 *"a young man turns":* Claude Bragdon, *More Lives Than One* (Knopf, 1938), 49; Canemaker, *Winsor McCay,* 133.

28 *"There are skeletons":* Canemaker, *Winsor McCay,* 137; see also Leslie Cabarga, *The Fleischer Story* (Nostalgia Press, 1976).

32 *"three strikes against him":* author interview.

CHAPTER TWO:
WHAT WE CALL "PERSONALITY"

33 *"Sabotage the adjective":* Peter Vansittart, *Voices 1870–1914* (Avon Books, 1986), 205.

35 Rastus in Zululand: Donald Bogle, *Toms, Coons, Mulattos, Mammies and Bucks* (Continuum, 1989).

37 *"If a lion was chasin' him" and Sullivan, Messmer biographical details:* John Canemaker, *Felix* (Pantheon, 1991).

39 *"The big gag":* Donald Crafton, *Before Mickey* (MIT Press, 1984), 305.

40 *"The majority of Negroes in Washington":* Geoffrey Perrett, *America in the Twenties* (Simon & Schuster, 1982).

42   *"always explicitly states a moral truth"*: Bruno Bettelheim, *The Uses of Enchantment* (Knopf, 1986), 43.

46   *"The little inkwell clown" and Fleischer biographical details*: Leslie Carbaga, *The Fleischer Story* (Nostalgia Press, 1976).

48   *"Heeza Liar"*: Crafton.

50   *"celebrated excitement"*: Ann Douglas, *Terrible Honesty* (Knopf, 1996).

CHAPTER THREE:
FIGHTING THE MOUSE

55   *"When I sat down to play"*: Marshall Stearns: *The Story of Jazz* (Mentor, 1958), 118.

55   *"I am such a bug"*: Benny Goodman, *The Kingdom of Swing* (Stackpole Sons, 1939).

56   *"There was never a script"*: Donald Crafton, *Before Mickey* (MIT Press, 1984), 313.

56   *"What the cinema can do" et seq.*: Charles Solomon, *Enchanted Drawings* (Knopf, 1981), 34.

56   *"God only knows"*: Crafton, 214–15; see also John Canemaker, *Felix* (Pantheon, 1991), 124.

57   *"There were supposed to be"*: Seamus Culhane, *Talking Animals and Other People* (St. Martin's, 1986), 56.

58   *"Walt would have an idea" and early Disney details*: Russell Merritt and J. B. Kaufman, *Walt In Wonderland* (Johns Hopkins Press, 1992).

60   *"Everybody was conspiring"*: Crafton, 208.

64   *"Old Man Opportunity"*: Marc Eliot, *Walt Disney: Hollywood's Dark Prince* (HarperCollins, 1994).

65   *"Mickey is made"*: John Canemaker, *Disney Animation Art* (Abrams, 1982), 15.

65   *"a scandalous element"*: E. M. Forster, "Mickey and Minnie," *Abinger Harvest* (Edward Arnold & Co., 1945), 50.

66   *"He begged"*: Crafton, 319.

68   *"Pat was an alcoholic"*: Canemaker, *Felix*, 134.

71   *"gathered for a weekly bout"*: Culhane, 3.

73   *"Hollywood was beating Manhattan"*: Ann Douglas, *Terrible Honesty* (Knopf, 1996).

74   *"Spring styles say CURVES!"*: Frederick Lewis Allen, *Since Yesterday* (Bantam, 1965), 115.

75   *"It was, and still is"*: Culhane.

CHAPTER FOUR:
THE WILDER SHORES OF COMEDY

77   *"I'm the guy"*: Katherine Barrett and Richard Greene, *Walt Disney: The Man Behind the Magic* (Viking Penguin, 1991).

78   *"Really, Walt"*: Leonard Mosley, *Disneys's World* (Stein and Day, 1985), 122.

78   *"felt overlooked"*: Marc Eliot, *Walt Disney: Hollywood's Dark Prince* (Harper Paperbacks, 1994), 59.

80   *"Ubbe kept trying"*: author interview.

81   *"You could just say"*: Joe Adamson, *Tex Avery: King of Cartoons* (Da Capo, 1975).

82 *"Walt had made"*: author interview.

82 *"many critics preferred"*: Leonard Maltin, *Of Mice and Magic* (Plume, 1987), 41.

83 *"more of Hoover"*: Richard Schickel, *The Disney Version* (Touchstone, 1985), 154.

83 *"I couldn't sleep"*: Mosley, 132.

86 *"What do you do"*: Jack Kinney, *Walt Disney and Assorted Other Characters* (Hamony Books, 1988), 26; see also Eliot, 92, 93.

86 *"I had sympathetic dwarves"*: Barrett and Greene, 80.

86 *"just a character"*: Charles Solomon, *Enchanted Drawings* (Knopf, 1981), 100.

88 *"the characters are cute"*: Jerry Beck and Will Friedwald, *Looney Tunes and Merrie Melodies* (Holt, 1989), 7.

90 *"When I was a kid"*: Steve Schneider, *That's All Folks* (Holt, 1990), 140–42.

91 *"a serious handicap"* et seq.: Adamson.

93 *"anyone who marvels"*: Mel Blanc and Philip Bashe, *That's Not All, Folks* (Warner Books, 1988), 83.

93 *"We used to kid him"*: Adamson, 164–65.

94 *"In order to save ourselves"* et seq.: Chuck Jones, *Chuck Amuck* (Farrar, Straus and Giroux, 1990), 90–91, and author interview.

95 *"What Makes Betty Boop?"*: Norman M. Klein, *Seven Minutes* (Verso, 1993), 81.

97 *"I'd have him walk"*: Maltin, 103–104; see also Leslie Carbaga, *The Fleischer Story* (Nostalgia Press, 1976).

CHAPTER FIVE:
MORE HELLS THAN SWENDENBORG

101 *"proceeded to intrigue us"*: Richard Hollis and Brian Sibley, *Walt Disney's Snow White and the Seven Dwarfs: The Making of the Classic Film* (Hyperion, 1994), 7.

103 *"thought of as living underground" and historical and literary references to dwarfs*: Leslie Fiedler, *Freaks* (Simon & Schuster, 1978), 39–69.

105 *"what was unique"*: Stanley Green, *The World of Musical Comedy* (Grosset & Dunlap, 1962), 245.

106 *"a hatful of money"*: Various versions of this anecdote appear in Bob Thomas, *Walt Disney* (Simon & Schuster, 1976); Marc Eliot, *Walt Disney: Hollywood's Dark Prince* (Harper Paperbacks, 1994); Leonard Mosley, *Disney's World* (Stein and Day, 1985); and others.

108 *"I met a guy"*: Hollis and Sibley, 35.

109 *ample and well-kept grounds*: Seamus Culhane, *Talking Animals and Other People* (St. Martin's, 1986), 203–204.

110 *"shows the smallness"*: Leslie Carbaga, *The Fleischer Story* (Nostalgia Press, 1976), 112–13.

113 *Who were Zeus, Athena*: Culhane, 214.

120 *"Mountains have gotta look"*. Mosley, 178.

121 *"mistaken for an American"*: Leonard Maltin, *The Disney Films* (Popular Library, 1989).

122 *"I say nothing" and comments on* Fantasia: Thomas, 50.

CHAPTER SIX:
LAUGHING AT THE ENEMY

126 *"even though he was prone"*: Leonard Mosley, *Disney's World* (Stein and Day, 1985), 188.

126 *"A more unwise choice"*: Seamus Culhane, *Talking Animals and Other People* (St. Martin's, 1986).

127 *Disney strike*: author interviews; see also Mosley, "Rebellion in Burbank" chapter 15; Marc Eliot, *Walt Disney: Hollywood's Dark Prince* (Harper Paperbacks, 1994), chapter 10, "Strike!"; Richard Schickel, *The Disney Version* (Touchstone, 1985), chapter 26.

129 *"disillusion and discouragement"*: Mosley, 196.

130 *"voices and appearances"*: John Grant, *Encyclopedia of Walt Disney's Animated Characters* (Hyperion, 1989).

131 *"more camera angles than Citizen Kane"*: Mosley, 112.

131 *"Gunny doesn't know"*: Mosley, 203.

131 *"OK, Davy boy"*: Eliot, 173.

131 *"The army is moving in"*: Bob Thomas, *Walt Disney* (Simon & Schuster, 1976), 99.

132 *"so-called phony war"*: Michael S. Shull and David E. Witt, *Doing Their Bit: Wartime Animated Films, 1939–1945* (McFarland, 1987).

133 *"To get myself a Jap"*: Studs Terkel, *The Good War* (Knopf, 1985), 5.

133 *"this underground haven"*: Otto Friedrich, *City of Nets* (Harper & Row, 1986), 103.

136 *"Mr. Mayer"*: Friedrich, 48, 49.

137 *"The government had a real dilemma"*: author interview.

137 *"They irreverently called"*: Culhane.

138 *Geisel furnished Snafu*: Judith and Neil Morgan, *Dr. Seuss and Mr. Geisel* (Random House, 1995), 110.

139 *"I'm happy to think"*: Culhane, 270.

140 *"It is a coward"*: ibid.

141 *"The British thought"*: Leonard Maltin, *The Disney Films* (Popular Library, 1989), 140.

142 *"In an attempt"*: Charles Solomon, *Enchanted Drawings* (Knopf, 1981), 129.

142 *"self-interested"*: Schickel, 272.

143 *"Goofy Gaucho"*: Eric Smoodin, *Animating Culture* (Rutgers University Press, 1993), 141, 142.

CHAPTER SEVEN:
WHO'S DIRECTING THIS PICTURE?

149 *"New Deal melodrama"*: Norman M. Klein, *Seven Minutes* (Verso, 1993), 135.

150 *"the most startling advancement"*: Leonard Maltin, *The Disney Films* (Popular Library, 1989), 143–48.

150 *"Latin American beauty"*: Eric Smoodin, *Animating Culture* (Rutgers University Press, 1993), 102.

152 *"Tattered ol' Uncle Remus"*: *Time,* October 27, 1941; see also Smoodin, 106, 107.

153 *ruefully watching*: Murray Kempton, *Part of Our Time* (Simon & Schuster, 1955), 194.

153 *"Totally disinterested"*: Richard Schickel, *The Disney Version* (Touchstone, 1988), 282.

154 *"constant anonymous threats"*: Marc Eliot, *Walt Disney: Hollywood's Dark Prince* (Harper Paperbacks, 1994), 199, 200.

156 *A young husband*: James Baughman, *The Republic of Mass Culture* (Johns Hopkins University Press, 1992), 36–41.

158 *"I found out" et seq.*: Joe Adamson, *Tex Avery: King of Cartoons* (Da Capo, 1975).

161 *"Theresomethingnewtakeitout"*: Chuck Jones, *Chuck Amuck* (Farrar, Straus and Giroux, 1990) and author interview; see also Hugh Kenner, *Chuck Jones: A Flurry of Drawings* (University of California Press, 1994).

161 *"Just what the hell"*: Steve Schneider, *That's All Folks* (Holt, 1990), 106, 107.

163 *"long, slim, sick and sorry-looking"*: Jones.

165 *Benchley's ineptitude*: Nathaniel Benchley, *Robert Benchley* (McGraw-Hill, 1955), chapter 14.

169 *"All the cartoons"*: Judith and Neil Morgan, *Dr. Seuss and Mr. Geisel* (Random House, 1995).

CHAPTER EIGHT:
WE COULD GET AWAY WITH LESS

173 *"At the time"*: Joe Barbera, *My Life in 'toons* (Turner, 1994), 3.

174 Finian's Rainbow: John Canemaker, "Lost Rainbow," *Print,* March–April 1993.

178 *"Is it because"*: *Saturday Review,* June 3, 1950.

179 *"I kept telling you"*: Leonard Mosley, *Disney's World* (Stein and Day, 1985), 214.

180 *"What better way"*: Donald Crafton, "Walt Disney's Peter Pan," *Storytelling in Animation,* vol. 2 (American Film Institute, 1988).

181 *"must have surely ranked"*: Leonard Maltin, *Of Mice and Magic* (Plume, 1987), 148.

182 *"I wish you would come up"*: Eric Barnouw, *Tube of Plenty* (Oxford, 1990), 264–65.

183 *"We wanted to get"*: Charles Solomon, *Enchanted Drawings* (Knopf, 1981), 230.

183 *"The Frostbite Falls Review"*: John Cawley and Jim Korkis, *Cartoon Superstars* (Pioneer, 1990), 166–67.

186 *"We took the film"*: Barbera.

191 *"naïve young man"*: Barnouw, 300–301.

CHAPTER NINE:
AKIN TO STATUTORY RAPE

195 *"a garbage pile"*: Gary H. Grossman, *Saturday Morning* (Dell, 1981), 352.

196 *"goes not abroad"*: Eric Barnouw, *Tube of Plenty* (Oxford, 1990), 377.

196 *sugar-coated cereal*: Les Brown, *New York Times Encyclopedia of Television* (Times Books, 1977), 82, 83.

197 *"eventually lost heart"*: Stephen Klein, *Out of the Garden* (Verso, 1993), 169.

198 *"It didn't take ideas"*: author interview.

198 *ACT*: author interview.

199 *"Sesame Street"*: Martin Mayer, *About Television* (Harper & Row, 1972), chapter 6, and author interviews.

202 " 'sensation' or 'experience' ": Giannalberto Bendazzi, *Cartoons* (Indiana University Press, 1995), 281.

202 "*we don't have to buy*": Grossman, 271.

204 "*wanting to be very dirty*": Jim Korkis and John Cawler, *Cartoon Confidential* (Malibu Graphics, 1991), 35, and author interviews.

208 "*People are not dedicated*": Leonard Maltin, *Of Mice and Magic* (Plume, 1987), 346.

212 "*animating the same picture*": Maltin, *Of Mice and Magic,* 78.

CHAPTER TEN:
THE ANIMATED MIRROR

214 "*an inappropriate metaphor*": Charles Solomon, *Enchanted Drawings* (Knopf, 1981).

216 "*made $21 million*": Leonard Maltin, *The Disney Films* (Popular Library, 1989).

221 "*As grievous a loss*": author interview.

222 "*you would not want*": author interview.

223 "*Lots of talk*": author interview.

223 "*When he was the studio chief*": *New York Times,* April 9, 1996.

224 "*silk-lined dead end*" *et seq.*: author interview.

224 *Asked to identify:* Sylvia Anne Hewlett, *When the Bough Breaks* (Basic Books, 1991), 68.

225 "*not only shocking*": *Washington Post,* April 2, 1987.

226 *Watching the twin sons et seq.*: *Los Angeles Times,* November 22, 1994.

229 "*We made models*": author interview.

232 "*From Cal Arts*": author interview.

234 "*All of us*": *America Online Animation Report,* April 1996.

ACKNOWLEDGMENTS

The term *labor of love* has become so worn that I hesitate to use it. But no other seems appropriate. I have been in love with animated cartoons since I first saw them as a child, and although that love was never blind, and was occasionally sidetracked by other affections, it never disappeared. Then, when I became a film critic, it was renewed with great force as I stepped, in effect, backstage to watch drawings rise from sketch pads to pencil tests to fully animated sequences with voices and music.

In time, I introduced my children to animation and animators. Chief among these talents was the most brilliant and innovative popular artist of our time, Charles M. "Chuck" Jones. When my son met him, at the age of four, he decided then and there to make his living as an animator. Unlike his father, he never swerved off course, was graduated from California Institute of the Arts, and became the object of his desires. Watching him learn and work, I began to study animation as an unselfconscious art form—and as an often unwitting social commentary. Numerous experts and artists aided my education. Understandably, Nate Kanfer was the most provocative. The most anecdotal and insightful was Chuck Jones, who never hesitated to share his time, his talent for creative work, and his gift for friendship. Even when my questions must have seemed irksome or trivial, he never lost his sense of humor—the nearest thing we have now to Mark Twain's. Chuck's anecdotes have filled two autobiographies, and from what I have seen and heard he could easily compose another. This book could not have been conceived, much less written, without him.

Scholars are often unwilling to share their hard-earned insights with others. In contrast, John Canemaker was the personification of generosity, relating incidents, indicating the places where troves of information could be found, and allowing me to ransack his fine collection of early animation. As long as he continues to head the animation department of New York University's film school, the cartoon in all its manifestations will be in the right hands, and students will receive some of the most detailed and discerning instruction in the country.

Marianne Macy took time from her own book to help on this one, indefatigably negotiating with studios and tracking down many of the illustrations that illuminate the text. That text was shaped by Scott Moyers, whose all-seeing eye and unfailing cheer made tasks seem easier than they actually were.

The institutions that offered the most aid were, once again, the Sterling Library at Yale, where John Bennett provided numerous obscure works; the libraries of New York University and Lincoln Center; and Cal. Arts, where the staff and faculty gave invaluable assistance. The bookstore, riverrun, in Hastings-on-Hudson, New York, tracked down various out-of-print volumes and magazines. Peggy Charren recalled the TV wars with clarity and wit. Heidi Leigh and Nick Leone, owners of one of the greatest collections of cels and sketches in the world, Animazing Gallery at Soho, Manhattan, lent museum-quality material for illustration as well as continual encouragement. Their assistant, Sandi Gaglio, was unfailingly courteous and helpful. Some animators, artists, writers, and producers preferred to go off the record with their experiences; among those whom I can acknowledge, and whose anecdotes are both revealing and diverting, are Ralph Bakshi, Ray Bradbury, Linda Clough, Cornelius Cole, John Culhane, Stan Freberg, Josh Greenfeld, Erich Hobbing, Ollie Johnson, Steve Leiva, Paul Maslansky, Phil Roman, John Bartholomew Tucker, Jack and Mark Zander.

Like a float in a parade, the family rolls by at the end, cheering. Thanks encore to May and Nate and Sari and Lili and Andy and the dedicatees, Lea and Aly.

Action for Children's Television (ACT), 198–99
Adams, John Quincy, 196
Adams, Richard, 211
Adamson, Joe, 91, 116
advertising agencies, television censorship and, 182
Aesop's Fables:
    Bray studio animation of, 49
    Terry cartoons of, 42–44, 63
Agee, James, 142–43
Aladdin, 222
Aladdin and His Wonderful Lamp, 113
Alice in Wonderland, 178–79, 233
"Alice's Wonderland," 57–59
All About Eve, 156
"Alvin Show, The," 185–86
Amblin, 218
American, 29
    comic strips of, 19, 28–29, 48
American-Arab Anti-Discrimination Committee, 222
American Broadcasting Company (ABC), cartoons on, 182, 187
American Tail, An, 213–14, 215
Amos 'n' Andy, 88, 130
Anderson, Ken, 101
Andy Panda, 113
Animal Farm (Orwell), 200
Animated Cartoons: How They Are Made, Their Origin and Development (Lutz), 52
animated shorts, *see* animation, animators; cartoons
animation, animators, 15
    audiences for, 234
    computers and, 228–31
    counterculture, 201–5, 224
demand for, 231–32
experimental, 235
IFS contributions to, 48
in infancy of film, 17–32
unions and, 98–99, 125–28, 131
    see also cartoons; *individual animators, studios and titles*
Arabian Nights (*The Thief and the Cobbler*), 233–34
Armstrong, Louis, 74
Ashman, Howard, 217, 221
Avery, Fred "Tex," 81, 90–95, 97, 117
    cartoon creations of, 159, 162, 163–64
    partial blindness of, 90–91
    screwball comedy and, 158–59
    tall tales of Southwest by, 91

Babbit, Art, 127, 131, 154, 175, 211
Backus, Jim, as voice of Quincy Magoo, 169
Bagdasarian, Ross, 185–86
Bakshi, Ralph, 202–5, 211, 219
Bambi, 123, 141–42, 233
    critical reactions to, 142
Barbera, Joseph, 160–61, 173, 186, 188
Barker, Clive, 234
Barnouw, Eric, 195
Barre, Raoul, 41
Beatles, The, 201
Beauty and the Beast, 221, 228
"Beavis and Butt-head," 225–26
Beavis & Butt-head Ensucklopedia, 226
Beck, Jerry, 87–88
Before Mickey (Crafton), 16, 39, 49
Benaderet, Bea, 188
Benchley, Nathaniel, 165–66
Benchley, Robert, 123, 165–66
Bendazzi, Giannalberto, 16

Bennett, William, 234
Berle, Milton, 157
Berlin, Irving, 83
Bettelheim, Bruno, 42
  on Disney's *Snow White,* 107–8
  Betty Boop, 70–75
  appeal of, 95
  character of, 71, 73
  Code of Production and sexual content of, 74–75
  Mae West and, 73–75
  New York vs. Hollywood in cartoons of, 73
Bimbo, as Fleischer studio's Mickey Mouse, 69–70, 71
"Bimbo's Initiation," 71
Black Cauldron, The, 216, 217
blacks:
  "Boogie Woogie Boy of Company B" as portrayal of, 133
  cartoon stereotypes of, 36–37, 39, 40, 87–88, 130, 151–52, 160
  comic strip stereotypes of, 35
  film stereotypes of, 35
  as portrayed in "Coal Black and De Sebben Dwarfs," 134–35
Blackton, James Stuart, 18, 25
Blake, William, 21
Blanc, Mel, 93, 94, 116, 169, 188
Bluth, Don, 212, 213–15, 216
Bluto, 96, 97
"Boogie Woogie Boy of Company B," 133
Boop, Betty, *see* Betty Boop
Bosch, Hieronymus, 21, 23
"Bosko, the Talk-Ink Kid," 86–88, 89, 181
Bosustow, Stephen, 168–69, 177
bouncing ball shorts, *see* Car-Tunes
Bowman, John, 232
Bradley, Bill, 225
Brandon, Claud, 27
Bray, John Randolph, 42, 45
Bray Studio, 51
  Colonel Heeza Liar series of, 48, 49
  Fleischer brothers and, 45–46
  Lantz at, 48–51
  Terry and, 41–42
Br'er Rabbit, 117, 205
Breughel, Peter, 21, 23
Brewer, Roy, 175
Britain, "Felix Fever" in, 41
Bronson, Charles, 206
Brooks, James L., 224

"Brother Can You Spare a Dime?" (song), 12
Brown, John Mason, 177–78
Brown, Treg, 93
Bryman, Alan, 218
Buddy, 89
Bugs Bunny, 116-18, 163, 167
  anti-Axis cartoons with, 145
  "Eh, what's up Doc?" trademark of, 117–18
  Mel Blanc as voice of, 116
  origins of, 116–17
  as World War II GI mascot, 118
"Bugs Bunny Show, The," 183
Burch, Dean, 199
Burdette, R. J., 23–24

California Institute of the Arts, 223–24
Calloway, Cab, 74, 109
  as Ko-Ko in "Snow White," 72
Campos, Florencio Molina, 143
Canemaker, John, 20–21, 232
Cannon, Robert, 170
Capra, Frank, 83, 137
Carbaga, Leslie, 69
Carmichael, Hoagy, 149
Carroll, Lewis, 178
cartoon noir, 71–72
cartoons:
  as army training films, 137–39
  budgets of, 95
  as cinema, 93–94
  color in, 98, 104, 170, 231
  as easy targets for criticism, 233
  ethnic stereotypes in, 40, 79, 82, 88, 134–35, 143, 145, 150, 208, 222
  Golden Age of, 115–23, 168–72
  merchandising and, 41, 96, 197, 220, 221, 231
  music in, 63, 74, 78, 82, 89, 92, 104–5, 110, 111–12, 122, 135, 209, 216–17, 221
  popularity of, 234–35
  as reflection of societal attitudes, 15, 39, 40, 41–42, 88, 189–90, 214–15
  screwball comedy and, 158–59
  sexual content of, 74–75, 158-59, 203–4
  sound effects in, 93
  sound tracks of, *see* sound tracks
  on television, 177, 181–90, 194, 195, 196, 198, 206–8, 224, 225–28, 234
  television network censorship of, 206–8

three-dimensional illusion in, 104
in World War II, 132–34, 135–45
see also animation, animators; *individual characters and titles*
Cartoons (Bendazzi), 16
Car-Tunes, 57, 69
Catmull, Edwin, 228
cels, 30, 48, 220
as art investment, 235
Chaplin, Charles Spencer, 38, 42, 51, 67, 75, 116
cartoon based on "Tramp" of, 37
Charlie Brown TV specials, 209
Charlotte's Web, 209
Charlotte's Web (White), 209
Charren, Peggy, 198, 199
Chesterton, G. K., 49, 111
Chicago Examiner, 33
children's television:
commercials on, 196–97, 198, 199
network self-censorship of, 206–8
"Sesame Street" and, 199–200
Children's Television Workshop (CTW), 200
Christmas Carol, A, 210
Chuang-tzu, 21
Churchill, Frank, 82, 104, 113, 129
Churchill, Winston, 141
Cinderella, 177–78
Clampett, Robert, 89, 90, 91, 93, 162
Beany and Cecil cartoons of, 183, 206–7
"Coal Black and De Sebben Dwarfs" cartoon of, 134–35
Daffy Duck and, 116
Claude Frollo, 232
Clokey, Art, 183
Clurman, Harold, 15
"Coal Black and De Sebben Dwarfs," 134–35
Cobean, Sam, 128
Code of Production, *see* Hollywood Production Code
Cohl, Emile, 18, 25, 34
Cohn, Harry, 83, 131, 186
Cohn, Jack, 34
Cold War, 167
Collodi, Carlo, 118
"Colonel Heeza Liar and the Forbidden Fruit," 49
Colonel Heeza Liar series, 48–49
color, in cartoons, 98, 104, 170, 231
Color Classics, 98

Columbia Broadcasting System (CBS), cartoons on, 181
Columbia Pictures, 83, 131, 168–69
Columbia University, 195
Colvig, Pinto, 82
comic strips, 19–24
American life influenced by, 23
animated, characters of, 33–34, 75, 96, 97
black stereotypes in, 35
Felix the Cat as basis for, 66
McCay and fantasy in, 20–23
see also individual titles
Commercial Artists and Designers Union (CADU), 98–99
commercials, children's television and, 196–97, 198, 199
computers, animation and, 228–31
Congress of Racial Equality (CORE), 205
Cooney, Joan Ganz, 200
Coonskin, 205, 219
Coppola, Francis Ford, 176
Crafton, Donald, 16, 39, 49
on *Peter Pan,* 179–80
"Critic, The," 234
Crosby, Harry Lillis "Bing," 81
Crothers, Scatman, 205
Crowther, Bosley, 153, 179
Crumb, Robert, 203
Crusader Rabbit, 183
Culhane, Seamus, 71, 75, 79, 109, 111, 126, 137, 154
Culliford, Peyo, 207

Daffy Duck, 94, 115–16, 163, 166–68, 206
Daily News, 40
Darwin's Theory of Evolution, 57
Davy Crockett, 180
DCA, *Finian's Rainbow* project and, 175, 176
Death Wish, 206
De Forest, Lee, 62
Deitch, Gene, 181
DePatie, David, 208
Depression, Great, 68–69, 108
"Oswald" cartoon about, 81
"Who's Afraid of the Big Bad Wolf?" as anthem of, 83
de Seversky, Alexander, 141
Dickens, Charles, 103
Dick Tracy, 218
"Dinnertime," as first Aesop's fable sound cartoon, 63

Disney Animation: The Illusion of Life
    (Thomas and Johnson), 128
Disney, Lillian, 59–60, 61, 78, 83, 123
Disney, Roy, 51, 53, 57, 63–64, 77, 83,
    105, 106, 126, 179
Disney, Roy E. (Disney's nephew),
    215–16
Disney, Walter Elias, 51-53, 55, 83–86,
    213
  as analytical leader, 84–85
  anti-Semitism of, 82, 131, 132, 140
  death of, 193
  Hughes and, 154–55
  Iwerks and, 52, 57, 59, 60, 61, 64,
    77–78, 83, 125, 127, 150
  Messmer offered job by, 66
  Mickey Mouse created by, 61
  Old World tales used by, 118, 121
  paternalism of, 125–26, 128
  personal biases of, 52
  right-wing politics of, 152–53
  and scenario of *Snow White,* 101
  Snow White as personal triumph for,
    108
  structured working style of, 56–57
  testimony before HUAC by, 174
Disneyland, 180
Disney Productions, *see* Walt Disney
    Productions
Disney studios:
  "Alice's Wonderland" series from,
    57–59
  budgets of, 95
  commercial work of, 179
  ethnic and racial stereotyping in car-
    toons of, 82, 88, 130, 143, 151–52,
    222
  financial problems at, 122–23, 126,
    154–55
  Hollywood Production Code and, 74
  Latin America as portrayed by,
    142–43, 150–51
  live action movies of, 180, 194, 218
  military "occupation" of, 131–32
  1950s cartoons of, 177–80
  1980s cartoons of, 215–22
  Oswald the rabbit created by, 59
  Powers and, 63, 65, 77, 78–79
  practical jokes at, 120
  rural backdrop in cartoons of, 58
  Silly Symphonies of, 78, 88
  "Steamboat Willie" as first sound car-
    toon of, 63–64

  strike at, 127–28, 131
  "Three Little Pigs" of, 12, 82–83
  UPA style vs. style of, 171
  war policy influenced by, 141
  World War II cartoons of, 139–41
Disney Version, The (Schickel), 83
Docter, Pete, 229–30
Donald Duck, 142, 150–51, 208
  in World War II cartoons, 139–40
Donaldson, Walter, 42
Douglas, Ann, 51, 73
Douglas Paul, 133
Dragonette, Jessica, 111
"Dreams of the Rarebit Fiend," 19–21, 57
Dreamworks SKG, as Disney competi-
    tor, 223
"Dr. Katz," 234
"Duck Amuck," 167–68
"Duck Dodgers in the 24½th Century,"
    167
Dukas, Paul, 121
Dumbo, 129–31
  black stereotypes in, 130
  critical acclaim for, 130–31
  as Disney "pastiche," 129
Dunning, George, 201, 202
dwarfs, in *Snow White and the Seven
    Dwarfs,* 103

Eastman, Philip, 169
Easy Rider, 203
Edelmann, Heinz, 201
Edison, Thomas Alva, 17, 19, 118
Educational Films Corporation, 67
Edwards, Cliff, 121, 140
Eggleston, Ralph, 231
"Eh, What's Up Doc?," 117
Einstein, Albert, 56–57
Eisner, Michael, 216, 222, 228
Elmer Fudd, 118, 166
Enchanted Drawings (Solomon), 16
*Encyclopedia of Walt Disney's Animated
    Characters* (Grant), 130
Episcopal Commission on Motion Pic-
    tures, 74
Esquire, 106

fables, fairy tales vs., 42–43
Famous Studios, 149
Fantasia, 121–22, 128, 129
  as box-office flop, 122
  critical reception of, 122, 233
  live and animated footage in, 122

rerelease of, 201
"Sorcerer's Apprentice" episode of, 122
Stokowski conducting in, 122
Farmer Al Falfa, 41–42, 181
"Farmer Al Falfa's Cat-Astrophe," 41
Federal Communications Commission, 190
children's unit of, 199
"Feline Follies," 38
"Felix at the Circus," 56
"Felix in Love," 40
"Felix Kept on Walking" (song), 41
Felix the Cat, 58
as black stereotype, 39
comic strip based on, 66
creation of, 38–40
Mickey Mouse as rival of, 65, 67, 68
personality of, 39
sound and, 67
as world-renowned character, 41, 56, 66
"Felix the Cat Woos Whoopee," 67–68
"Felix Trifles with Time," imaginative use of numbers in, 66
"Felix Turns the Tide," 39–40
Fiedler, Leslie, 103
Fields, W. C., 115
film:
animation in infancy of, 17–32
black stereotypes in, 35
Loner as portrayed in, 170–71
pre-World War II, 115
television as threat to, 155–57
Film Daily, 41, 67
Finian's Rainbow (Lane and Harburg), 174–76
Fisher, Bud, 34, 41
Fitzsimmons, John, 25
Flaubert, Gustav, 12
Fleischer, Dave, 44–47, 112–13
as director of Ko-ko the Clown cartoons, 46
war cartoons of, 132, 143–44
Fleischer, Louis, 69, 109
Fleischer, Max, 44–47
creative philosophy of, 75
improvisational working style of, 56
paternalism of, 98, 109
physics film by, 56–57
as producer of Ko-ko the Clown, 46–47
Fleischer, William, 44–45

Fleischer brothers, 44, 45
Fleischer Story, The (Carbaga), 69
Fleischer studio, 58
"Betty Boop" cartoons of, 70–75
"Bimbo" as Mickey Mouse of, 69–70, 71
"cartoon noir" style of, 71–72
Car-Tunes series of, 57
Color Classics produced by, 98
decline of, 149
in Depression, 69
early sound cartoons of, 62–63
German Expressionism and cartoons of, 71
Gulliver's Travels produced by, 109–12
Miami relocation of, 109
New York vs. Hollywood in cartoons of, 73
Popeye and, 75, 96–98
sound tracks of cartoons of, 70–71
strike against, 99
Talkartoons series from, 69
urban backdrop of cartoons from, 58, 73
"Flintstones, The," 187–88, 197
anachronisms of, 188
"Flip the Frog" cartoons, 79–80
stereotypes in, 79
Ford, Henry, 118
Forster, E. M., 65
Four Poster, The, 171–72
Freaks (Fiedler), 103
Freleng, Isidore "Friz," 52, 60, 89, 90, 116, 161, 162, 163, 173, 194–95, 208
Freud, Sigmund, 21
Friedwald, Will, 87–88
Fritz the Cat, 203–4
as art film, 204
Frollo, Claude, 232
Fudd, Elmer, 118, 166
Fuseli, Henry, 21

Garity, William, 104
Geffen, David, 223
Geisel, Theodor (Dr. Seuss), 138
as creator of Gerald McBoing-Boing, 169–70
George V, King of Britain, 29
Gerald McBoing-Boing, 169–70, 171
use of color in, 170
"Gerald McBoing-Boing Show, The," 176–77

"Gertie the Dinosaur," 28, 33, 45, 47, 235
Goldberger, Paul, 232–33
Golden Age, of cartoons, 115–23, 168–72
Goldwyn, Samuel, 156
Goodman, Benny, 55
Good War, The (Terkel), 133
Goofy, 142
Gould, Chester, 218
Graham, Don, 84
Grant, John, 130
Great Depression, *see* Depression, Great
"Great Guns," 59
Great Mouse Detective, The, 216–17
Green, Stanley, 105
Griffith, D. W., 24
Groening, Matt, 224
Gruelle, John, 210
Guaraldi, Vince, 209
Gulliver's Travels, 109–12, 149
    box-office grosses of, 112
    characters of, 110
    quality of, 111
    reviews of, 112
Gumby, 183

"Ha-ha-ha-HA-ha! Ha-ha-ha-HA-ha!" laugh of Woody Woodpecker, 114
Hal Roach Studio, 137–39
Hanna, William, 160–61, 173, 186, 188
Hanna-Barbera, 197, 207, 213
    Charlotte's Web cartoon by, 209–10
    derivative cartoons of, 187–90
    quality of cartoons of, 187, 188, 189
"Hannah and the Barbarians," as code-word for shoddy animation, 188
Harburg, E. Y., 174
Hardaway, Ben "Bugs," 89, 116
Hardin, Lil, 55
Harline, Leigh, 121
Harman, Hugh, 52, 86, 89
Harman-Ising Co., 86–88, 104
Harris, Joel Chandler, 117, 152
Hays office, 51, 182
    cartoons cut by, 158–59
    Hearst, William Randolph, 19, 28, 31, 41
    International Film Service (IFS) of, 48
    as isolationist, 29, 30
Heavy Metal, 211
Heavy Traffic, 204–5

"Hell Bent for Election," 146, 168
Henson, Jim, 200
Herald Tribune, 122
Herbert, Victor, 24
Hilberman, David, 168, 174
Hindemith, Paul, 56
Hitler, Adolf, caricatured in cartoons, 136, 138, 145
Hollywood Production Code, 74
    Mae West and, 74–75
    sexual content in Betty Boop cartoons and, 75
Hollywood Quarterly, 153
Hollywood Reporter, 182
homosexuals, cartoon stereotypes of, 40, 79, 88
"Honeymooners, The," "Flintstones" as derivative of, 187–88
Hopper, Hedda, 153
Horne, Hal, 104
Horner, W. G., 17
Hoskins, Bob, 220
House Un-American Activities Committee (HUAC), 153, 157
    Disney's testimony before, 174
    Hubley and, 174–76
Howe, Irving, 44
Hubley, Faith, 174, 175
Hubley, John, 137–38, 168, 171
    as creator of Quincy Magoo, 169
    and HUAC, 174–76
    Watership Down and, 211
Hughes, Howard, 154–55
Humorous Phases of a Funny Face, 18
Hunchback of Notre Dame, 232–33
Hurtz, William, 138–39, 170, 174
Huxley, Aldous, 56, 177, 178

Industrial Films and Poster Service, *see* United Productions of America
International Alliance of Theatrical Stage Employees, 175
International Film Service (IFS), 48
Ising, Rudy, 52, 57–58, 86, 89
Iwerks, Dave, 78
Iwerks, Ubbe, 52, 57, 59, 60, 83, 92, 125, 127, 150
    as defector from Disney studios, 77–78
    as designer of Mickey Mouse, 61, 64, 78
    "Flip the Frog" character of, 79–80
    Willie Whopper designed by, 80

Jackson, Wilfred, 63
James, Henry, 118
Japanese, World War II film stereotypes
  of, 133–35, 145
Jazz Singer, The, 62, 63, 67, 86
"Jetsons, The," 189–90, 197
Jews, cartoon stereotypes of, 40, 82,
  88
Jobs, Stephen, Pixar and, 228, 231
Johnny Tremain, 180
Johnsin, Sammy, 36, 37, 39
Johnson, Ollie, 119, 128
Jolson, Al, 67
Jones, Chuck, 80, 82, 91, 93, 95, 118,
  132, 137, 138, 147, 159, 161,
  173–74, 187, 208, 210, 213, 235
  as director in 1950s, 166–68
  F.D.R. reelection cartoon and, 146
  literature as influence on cartoons
    of, 162–63
  Phantom Tollbooth and, 210
  "Wile E. Coyote" as reflection of
    ineptitude of, 164–65
Jose Carioca, 142, 150
Judge, Mike, 225, 226
Julian, Paul, 171
Jungle Book (Disney film), 193
"Jungle Book" (Jones film), 210
Jungle Book (Kipling), 193, 210
Juster, Norton, 210

Kane, Helen, 71
Katz, Ray, 94
Katzenberg, Jeffrey, 216–18, 220,
  222–23, 228
Kaufman, J. B., 58
Kazan, Elia, 157
Keaton, Buster, 42, 51, 64, 67, 116
Kelly, Walt, 120, 128
Kempton, Murray, 153
Kennedy, John F., 190
Kimball, Ward, 119, 125, 126, 127
King Features, 75
King Kong, 73
King of Jazz, 81
Kipling, Rudyard, 193, 210
Klein, I., 32
Klein, Norman M., 95, 190, 195
"Knock Knock," 114
"Ko-ko Gets EggCited," 47
Ko-ko the Clown, 46–47
Kricfalusi, John, 227–28
La Fontaine, Jean de, 43

Land Before Time, The, 214–15
Lane, Burton, 174
Langdon, Harry, 67
Lantz, Walter, 47–51
  Aladdin and His Wonderful Lamp
    scrapped by, 113
  cartoons produced for Bray by, 49
  as director of "Oswald the rabbit"
    series, 81
  Woody Woodpecker created by,
    113–14
  on "Woody Woodpecker Show,"
    182
Lasseter, John, 228–31
Latin America, as portrayed by Disney
  Studios, 142–43, 150–51
Laugh-O-Gram Films Inc., 52, 53
Lerner, Sammy, 97
Lessing, Gunther, 125, 126, 131
Lewis, Jerry, 157
Life, 178–79
Lion King, The, 221–22, 223
Little Black Sambo, 35
Little Herman, 41
Little Mermaid, The, 217–18
  Ashman and Mencken's involvement
    with, 217
"Little Nemo in Slumberland," 21–24
  animated film of, 24–27
  as operetta, 24
  Queen Crystalette episode of, 23
"Little Sammy Sneeze," 19
Little Shop of Horrors (Ashman and
  Mencken), 217
Lloyd, Harold, 67
Loesser, Frank, 149
Loew, Arthur, Sr., 173
Lonely Crowd, The (Reisman), 170
Loner, as portrayed in film and cartoons,
  170–71
Looney Tunes, 89
Lord of the Rings, The, 211
Lorenzini, Paolo, 121
Lucasfilms, 213
Lucas, George, 213, 216, 228
Lumière, Louis and Auguste, 17
Lusitania, 29–30
Lutz, Edwin G., 52

McBoing-Boing, Gerald, 169–70, 171
  use of color in, 170
McCay, Winsor, 18–32, 33, 235
  cartoons of, 24–31

McCay, Winsor, (cont.)
  comic strips of, 19–24
  fantasy in comic strips of, 20–23
  first use of "cels" by, 30
  as influence on younger cartoonists,
    45, 47
  on vaudeville circuit, 24, 25–27, 28
McKimpson, Bob, 173
McLemore, Henry, 133
McManus, George, 34
Magoo, Quincy (Mr. Magoo), 169, 171
  in 1001 Nights, 177
Make Mine Music, 151
Maltese, Mike, 161, 166, 167–68
Maltin, Leonard, 16, 72, 216
Mankiewicz, Joseph, 136
Marriner, William F., 35
Marx Brothers, 44, 115
Maus (Spiegelman), 214
Mayer, Hy, 34, 45
Mayer, Louis B., 104, 136
Medved, Michael, 218
Melendez, Bill, 209
Mencken, Alan, 217, 221
Mencken, H. L., 23
Mercer, Jack, 96
merchandising, cartoons and, 41, 96,
    197, 220, 221, 231
Merrie Melodies, 89
Merritt, Russell, 58
Messmer, Otto, 34, 45, 46, 68
  as animator in Sullivan's studio,
    36–37
  as creator of Felix, 38–40
  as director of Sullivan's studios, 66
  Disney job offered to, 66
  improvised working methods of, 56
  World War I influence on, 38, 40
Metro-Goldwyn-Mayer, 80, 89, 143,
    158, 160
  animation studio closed at, 173
Miami Art School, 111
Mickey Mouse, 173
  appeal of, 65
  creation of, 61
  difficulty in marketing of, 61–62
  Felix the Cat as rival of, 65, 67, 68
  sadism of, in "Steamboat Willie," 64
  in "Sorcerer's Apprentice" segment
    of Fantasia, 121–22
"Mickey Mouse Club," 182
Miller, Ron, 215
Minnow, Newton, 190–91

Mintz, Charles, 58–59, 60, 65, 77
Modern Times, 75
Moore, Bob, 120
Moore, Marianne, 9
Moore, Phil, 171
Moreau, Gustave, 21
Morey, Larry, 104
Morgenthau, Henry, 139
Morison, Samuel Eliot, 189–90
Mothersbaugh, Mark, 234
Motion Picture Alliance for the Preserva-
    tion of American Ideals (MPA),
    152–53, 175
Motion Picture Weekly, 49, 56
Motion Picture World, 59
"Motor Mat," 34
Moving Picture World, 46
Mr. Bug Goes to Town, 149
Mr. Magoo, see Magoo, Quincy
Mrs. Frisby and the Rats of Nimh, 212
MTV, 225, 226
"multiplane camera," three-dimensional
    illusion and, 104
Muppets, 200
Murdoch, Rupert, 223
music, in cartoons, 63, 74, 78, 82, 89, 92,
    104–5, 110, 111–12, 122, 135, 209,
    216–17, 221
"musical mews," 39
Mussolini, Benito, 115, 121, 136
"Mutt and Jeff," 23, 34, 41

Nast, Thomas, 19
National Association of Broadcasters,
    190, 199
  Code of, 196
National Broadcasting Company
    (NBC), 155, 185, 186
National Labor Relations Board, 154
National Legion of Decency, 74
Natwick, Grim, 70, 71, 211
Nazis, as portrayed in cartoons, 136
Neiburg, Al, 112
"Newlyweds, The," 34
New York, N.Y., in 1920s, 51
New Yorker, 151, 157–58, 165, 168, 178,
    210
New York Times, 40, 68
  on Ko-ko the clown, 46
New York University, 232
Nickelodeon, 227
nickelodeons, 24, 33
Noble, Maurice, 166, 167

Office of War Information, 134, 135
  softening of Hollywood propaganda
    by, 144–45
Of Mice and Magic (Maltin), 16
Old Curiosity Shop, The (Dickens), 103
Olive Oyl, 96, 97
Oliver & Company, 215, 217
1001 Nights, 177
Orwell, George, 200
Oswald the rabbit, cartoons of, 59–60
  directed by Lantz, 81
  villain in, 59
Outcault, Richard F., 35
Out of the Inkwell Productions, 46–47,
  51

Pangolin, The (Moore), 9
Paramount, 39, 42, 69, 74–75, 108, 143,
  203
Paramount Screen Magazine, 37, 45
Partch, Virgil, 128
Pathé, 45
Paul, William, 107
Pepe Le Pew, 161, 163
Peter Pan, 179–80
Phantom Tollbooth, 210
Phantom Tollbooth, The (Juster), 210
Pickford, Mary, 82
Pink Panther, 208–9
Pinocchio, 118–21, 128, 129, 214, 233
  artwork in, 120–21
  characters of, 120
  financial losses of, 121
  Jiminy Cricket in, 119, 121
  pressures on animators of, 119–20
  reviews of, 121
  story revised for, 119
Pinocchio (Collodi), 118
Pixar, 228, 231
"Plane Crazy," 61
Pocahontas, 232
Popeye, 75, 96–98
  in anti-Japan cartoons, 134
  as "respectable" cartoon, 96–97
Porky Pig, 89–90, 92–93, 132, 167
"Porky's Hare Hunt," 117
Potter, H. C., 141
Powers, Pat, 83, 125
  Disney Studios and, 63, 65, 77,
    78–79
  Iwerks and, 77, 78–79, 80
Praxinoscope ("action-look"), 17
Prescott, Norm, 195

Prince of Egypt, 223
Princeton University Press, 40
Private Snafu series, 138
Public Broadcasting System (PBS), 200,
  234

Questel, Mae, 70–71, 96, 109
Quimby, Fred, 136, 159, 160, 161
Quincy Magoo, *see* Magoo, Quincy

racism:
  in cartoons, 36–37, 39, 40, 87–88, 130,
    151–52
  in comic strips, 35
  in films, 35
*Raggedy Ann and Andy—A Musical Adven-
  ture,* 210–11
Rainger, Ralph, 110, 111–12
Raposo, Joe, 210–11
Red Hot, Hays office and, 158–59
Redon, Odilon, 21
Reisman, David, 170
Reluctant Dragon, The, 123
"Ren and Stimpy," 227–28
Reynaud, Émile, 17
RKO Pictures, 107, 154–55
Roadrunner cartoons, 164, 208
Robin, Leo, 110, 111–12
Rockefeller, Nelson, 128
"Rocky and His Friends," 184–85
Roosevelt, Franklin D., 81, 83, 121, 141,
  146, 168
Rosenberg, Joseph, 105–6
Ross, Lanny, 111
Rotoscope, 45, 46, 110, 113, 211
Roughing It (Twain), 163–64
"Ruff and Ready," 186–87

Saludos Amigos, 142–43
"Sambo and His Funny Noises," 35
Sammy Johnsin, 36, 37, 39
Sandburg, Carl, 91
Saperstein, Henry G., 177
Saturday Review, 177–78
"Scarlet Pumpernickel, The," 166
Schickel, Richard, 83
Schlesinger, Leon, 86, 88–89
  lisp of, as inspiration for Daffy Duck,
    94
Schlesinger studio, 89–90, 145
  profits earned by, 95
  see also Warner Bros.
Schneider, Cy, 197

Schull, Michael S., 132
Schulz, Charles, 209
Schwartz, Fred J., 175–76
Scott, Bill, 184, 195
Screen Cartoonists Guild, 127
Screen Gems, 186
screwball comedy, cartoons and, 158–59
Sears, Ted, 82
Segar, Elzie, 96, 97
Seldes, Gilbert, 106, 171
Sellers, Peter, 209
Seltzer, Edward, 161
Selznik, Lewis, 41
"Sesame Street," 199–200, 210
Sevareid, Eric, 193–94
Seven Minutes (Klein), 95
"Sextoons," 203
Sharples, Winston, 112
Sherman, Richard and Robert, 209
Shinbone Alley, 211
Shore, Michael, 175
"Silliwood," 231
Silly Symphonies, 78, 88
Silverman, Fred, 202
"Simpsons, The," 224–25, 226
"Sinking of the *Lusitania,* The," 29–31
"Snow White," as Fleischer studio's "cartoon noir," 72
Snow White and the Seven Dwarfs (Disney), 86, 101–8, 129
    budget of, 104, 105, 106
    characterization in, 102–3
    critical reactions to, 107–8
    dialogue in, 105
    as "Disney's Folly," 99, 104
    grosses of, 108
    RKO as distributor of, 107
    Rosenberg screening of, 105–6
    script of, 101–2
    songs delineating character in, 104–5
    three-dimensional illusion in, 104
Solomon, Charles, 16
Song of the South, 152
sound effects, 93
sound tracks:
    of early Disney cartoons, 63–64, 70
    of early Fleischer cartoons, 70–71
Spiegelman, Art, 214
Spielberg, Steven, 213, 216, 218, 223, 234
Spike and Mike's Festival of Animation, 235
Spike Jones and his City Slickers, 140

Stalin, Joseph, 145
Stalling, Carl, 63, 64, 78, 79, 92
Steamboat Bill, 64
"Steamboat Willie," 63–64
Steinberg, Saul, 66, 168
stereotypes, in cartoons, 40, 79, 82, 88, 134–35, 143, 144, 145, 150, 208, 222
Stokowski, Leopold, 121–22
stop-motion animation, 183
"Story of a Mosquito," 28
Stravinsky, Igor, 122
studios, unions and, 98–99, 125–28, 131
Study of American Intelligence, A (Princeton University Press), 40
Sullivan, Marjorie, 68
Sullivan, Morris, 214
Sullivan, Patrick, 34–37, 58
    cartoon studio of, 35–37, 66
    creation of Felix claimed by, 40–41
    deterioration and death of, 66–68
Sullivan-Bluth Studios Ireland, 214–15
Sunday Funnies, *see* comic strips
Sunset Boulevard, 156
Swan Princess, The, 223
Swift, David, 131
Swift, Jonathan, 109–10

Talkartoons, 69
Tashlin, Frank, 93–94, 105, 131
Technicolor, 82
television:
    cartoons on, 177, 181–90, 194, 195, 196, 198, 206–8, 224, 225–28, 234
    censorship of, 182
    children's programs on, 194, 195, 196, 197, 198, 199–200, 206–8
    "Gerald McBoing-Boing Show" on, 177
    1950s fare on, 180–81
    networks self-censorship of, 206–7
    as threat to movies, 155–57, 180
Terkel, Studs, 133
Termite Terrace, 91–92, 94, 115, 116, 120
Terrible Honesty (Douglas), 51, 73
Terry, Paul, 41–44, 51, 181
    Aesop's Fables animated by, 42–44, 63
    as creator of Farmer Al Falfa, 41–42
Terrytoons, 181, 194
Theater Arts, 151, 171
Thimble Theater, 75, 96
Thomas, Frank, 128
Thomas, John Phillip, 205

Thompson, Dorothy, 122
Three Caballeros, 150–51
"Three Little Pigs, The," 12, 82–83
   personality animation in, 82
Thurber, James, 157, 172
Timburg, Sammy, 112
Time, 131, 151–52, 171, 178
"Tin Drummer," 228
Tolkien, J. R. R., 103, 211
Tom 'n' Jerry, 143, 160–61, 173, 186,
   207
"Tom Terrific" series, 181
Toons, 218–19, 220
Touchstone division, of Walt Disney
   Productions, 218, 220, 221
Toy Story, The, 228–31, 235
"Travels of Teddy," 34, 45
"Trials of a Movie Cartoonist" (film), 46
Turner, Ted, 234
Twain, Mark, 12, 91, 163
Tweed, William Marcy "Boss," 19
Twice Upon a Time, 213
Tytla, Vladimir "Bill," 128, 130, 175

Uncle Remus, 117
unions, studios and, 98–99, 125–28, 131
United Artists, 82, 84, 107
United Productions of America (UPA),
   168–72
   animation by, in *The Four Poster,*
     171–72
   breakthrough cartoons of, 171–72
   cartoon characters of, 169–70, 171
   as critical rival of Disney, 171
   demise of, 177
   "Gerald McBoing-Boing Show" of,
     176–77
United States:
   1980s education standards in, 224–25
   pre-World War II atmosphere of,
     114–15
United States v. *Paramount, et al.,* 155
Universal, 34, 59, 60, 104, 108, 113
   Disney film distribution offer of,
     64–65
   as distributor of Oswald cartoons, 81
Uses of Enchantment, The (Bettelheim),
   42

Van Beuren, 68, 88, 98
Victory Through Air Power (de Seversky),
   141
Vitagraph, 25

Waldman, Myron, 97
Walker, Hal, 67, 68
Wallace, Oliver, 129, 140
Walt Disney Productions:
   corporate shakeup at, 215–16
   as public company, 126
   Touchstone division of, 218, 220,
     221
Ward, Jay, 183–85, 206, 227
Warner, Harry, 162, 173
Warner, Jack, 86, 136, 162, 173–74
Warner Bros., 50, 69, 81, 86, 89, 145,
   161, 212
   animators employed by, 88–95
   anti-Nazi cartoons and films of,
     136
   Blanc as cartoon voice for, 93, 94
   budgets of cartoon studio at, 95
   closing of animation of, 174
   see also Schlesinger, Leon;
     Schlesinger studio
Washington, Ned, 121
Watership Down, 211
Watership Down (Adams), 211
Wells, Frank, 216, 222
West, Mae, 73–75, 139
"What's Opera Doc?," 166
White, E. B., 209–10
Whiteman, Paul, 81
Who Censored Roger Rabbit? (Wolf),
   218
Who Framed Roger Rabbit?, 218–20
   live-action/animation interaction
     in, 219–20
"Who's Afraid of the Big Bad Wolf?"
   (song), 12, 82, 104
   as Depression-era anthem, 83
Wile E. Coyote, 164–65, 206, 230
Wilhelm II, Kaiser of Germany, 29, 31
Williams, Richard, 210, 219–20, 233
Willie Whopper, 80
Willis, Bruce, 234
Wilson, Edmund, 115
Wilt, David E., 132
Winkler, Margaret, 58
Wizard of Oz, The, 102, 115
Wolf, Gary, 218
women:
   cartoon stereotypes of, 40
   as portrayed in World War II
     cartoons, 144
Woody Woodpecker, 113–14
   laugh of, 114

World of Musical Comedy (Green), 105
World War I, 38, 40, 45, 51
World War II:
    Bugs Bunny as GI mascot in, 118
    cartoons and, 132–34, 135–45
Wyler, William, 136

"Yellow Kid," 23, 35
Yellow Submarine, 201–2

Zemeckis, Robert, 219
Zoetrope ("life-wheel"), 17
Zomo, 116–17